dancing with the dead

Asia-Pacific:
Culture, Politics, and Society

EDITORS:
Rey Chow, H. D. Harootunian,
and Masao Miyoshi

Duke University Press   Durham and London 2008

memory,
performance,
and everyday life
in postwar okinawa

dancing with the dead

CHRISTOPHER NELSON

© 2008 Duke University Press

All rights reserved

Printed in the United States of America on acid-free paper ∞

Designed by Katy Clove

Typeset in Quadraat by Keystone Typesetting, Inc.

Library of Congress Cataloging-in-Publication

data appear on the last printed page of this book.

contents

acknowledgments

For more than ten years, I have carried this book with me everywhere. Now that it is finished, I am delighted to be able to thank the people who have helped me in so many ways. I owe an immense debt of gratitude to my mentors at the University of Chicago. Terry Turner introduced me to the intellectual rigor and ethical responsibility of the discipline and opened my eyes to the possibilities of Marxist anthropology. John Kelly has been a tremendous source of intellectual inspiration and moral support during my years at Chicago, and I learned a great deal from him about what it means to be a teacher. Joe Masco joined my committee during my final months at Chicago, and I am grateful for his close readings and incisive comments. Finally, it has been my good fortune to work with Harry Harootunian. His example and his encouragement have made this project possible.

I am also deeply indebted to my friends and colleagues who read this manuscript at different stages. I would particularly like to thank Jeff Bennett, Kevin Caffrey, Sean Gilsdorf, Sharon Hayashi, Heather Hindman, Bill Marotti, Ochi Toshio, Rob Oppenheim, Paul Ryer, Amanda Seaman, Kimbra Smith, Umemori Naoyuki, and Hylton White. I can never fully repay their generosity nor adequately acknowledge their contributions. My thanks as well to Linda Angst, Jan Bardsley, Davinder Bhowmik, Mark Driscoll, Judith Farquhar, Gerald Figal, Larry Grossberg, Carie Little Hersh, Jim Hevia, Glenn Hook, David Howell, Igarashi Akio, Masamichi Inoue, John MacAloon, Ota Yoshinobu, James Roberson, Patricia Sawin, Rick Siddle, Robert J. Smith, Greg Smits, Robert Sukle, Tomiyama Ichirō, Mark and Kyoko Selden, Amanda Stinchecum, and Brad Weiss for their comments and encouragement over the years. My students and colleagues in the Department of Anthropology at the University of North Carolina have given me an intellectually stimulating and amazingly pleasant environment in which to teach and to write. I have been fortunate to work out my thoughts in discussions at the

"Cultures of Economies" and "Cultures of Memory" working groups at Carolina, and to present my ideas in seminars at Columbia, Duke, New York University, Sheffield, and the University of California, Los Angeles. During the fall of 2006, the fellows at Carolina's Institute for the Arts and Humanities kept me on track and helped me to put the final pieces in place. Reynolds Smith and Sharon Torian at Duke University Press steered me through the turbulent waters and rocky shoals of academic publishing. I am especially grateful to my readers, Anne Allison and Michael Molasky, for their critical readings and thoughtful suggestions. Anne in particular found something in that first, awkward draft and I am very glad that she encouraged me to bring it out. Finally, I want to thank Matt Hull and Margaret Wiener for the long hours that we've spent together reading and discussing our work. They were able to see this book in me, and helped me bring it to the page.

I must also thank the countless people in Okinawa who helped me over the years. Hiyane Teruo at the University of the Ryukyus was a constant source of support and I am grateful for his sponsorship. I am also indebted to Ishihara Masaie for his help in organizing my fieldwork in Okinawa City. Akamine Masanobu, Kumada Susumu, Tsuha Takashi, and all the members of the Okinawa Minzoku Gakkai welcomed me into their group and shared their extensive knowledge of Okinawan culture. Aoyama Yūji and the members of the Uchināguchikai in Okinawa City were also extremely kind and helpful. The staff of the Peace and Culture Promotion Section at the Okinawa City Hall were always willing to provide information and assistance, and to listen to my ideas. I am also grateful for the friendship and support of scholars such as Matt Allen, Tony Jenkins, Kawabata Miki, Nameki Ibuki, Satō Takehiro, John Whalen-Bridge, and Craig Willcox.

I owe a special thanks to Maetakenishi Kazuma and his family for their generosity and kindness. My thanks as well to the Higa and Miyazato families, the late Ōyama Chōjō, the late Ahagon Shōkō, Arasaki Moriteru, Arime Masao, Maeshiro Gentoku, Chibana Shōichi, Kina Shōkichi, Miyanaga Eiichi, Takara Ben, Takara Kurayosi, Gakiya Yoshimitsu, Sadoyama Yutaka, the late Teruya Rinsuke, and Teruya Rinken. Tamaki Mitsuru made the resources of the Shōchiku Kagekidan and Ashibinā available to me, and he and his family were always unstintingly generous. Fujiki Hayato was an endless source of ideas, humor, and advice. I would also like to thank Bise Katsu for sharing his encyclopedic knowledge of Okinawan performing arts.

The residents of Sonda welcomed my family and me into their community and allowed me to join their *seinenkai*. I will be forever thankful for their kindness. My thanks to the Sonda Jichikai, the Sonda Seinenkai and its "Old Boys," especially Iha Masakazu, Kuba Masayuki, Higa Eizō, Okuma Masakazu, Maeagura Ken, Miyazato Yōichi, and all those with whom I danced between 1997 and 1999. I am particularly grateful to the Kohama family for their friendship and consideration.

My initial fieldwork from 1996 to 1998 was made possible by a fellowship from the Fulbright Foundation. A grant from the Gakujutsu Furontiā project at Rikkyo University allowed me to return to the field during the summer of 1999. I received a dissertation writing fellowship at the University of Chicago from the Toyota Foundation, as well as additional support from the Center for East Asian Studies and Lichtstern Fund of the Department of Anthropology. My work at the University of North Carolina at Chapel Hill was supported by a junior faculty development grant, research and travel grants from the Carolina Asia Center and the Freeman Fund, and a prepublication grant from the University Research Council. I also received a faculty study and research leave and spent a wonderful semester at the Institute for Arts and Humanities.

Finally, my deepest gratitude goes to my families in both America and Japan. They have supported me in so many ways since I first announced a vague scheme to resign my commission in the Marines and look into graduate school. To my wonderful daughters, Fiona and Siobhan, whose love and laughter has been a daily inspiration. Most of all, to Atsuko, my partner in everything.

the battlefield of memory

So the same river swirls, snatches, sheds its veils, and runs by, under the spell of the sweetness of the stones, the shadows, and the grasses. The water, mad for its swirls like a real mane of fire. To glide like water into pure sparkle—for that we would have to have lost the notion of time. But what defense is there against it; who will teach us to decant the joy of memory?—ANDRÉ BRETON, Mad Love

THE STREETS OF KOZA

My first visit to Okinawa City—Koza, as the signs on the buses still read—was on a warm, late summer night in 1985. The years pass and I think of it often, but I can never seem to fit my memories into a coherent narrative. It seems that all I have are fragments, sensations. I remember standing on a sidewalk alongside Route 330. I was a twenty-three-year-old Marine lieutenant, an infantry officer. I had just stepped out of Apple, a bar crowded with GIs and young Okinawans. Although I'd like to describe the bar as it was when I was a Marine, what I remember is the way that it looked during my fieldwork. By then, it had closed—its façade peeling in the remorseless subtropical sun, its windows filthy, its sign missing. Ghostly, faded figures of the Beatles from the cover of *Sgt. Pepper's Lonely Hearts Club Band* staring blankly at traffic.

I do remember young Marines by the door, laughing, drinking beer from longneck bottles. I remember the feeling of my head, newly shaven, as I ran my hand over it. My shirt, pale green from a surf shop in southern California, was wet and cold against my back in the evening breeze. Music from inside the club pounding—Dead or Alive singing, "You spin me right round, baby." The smell of the street, asphalt and exhaust, frying oil, sewage. I can't be sure of much more than that. I find myself recalling the moment overlain with other memories formed a decade later, added to each time that I return to those streets.

Did a full moon hang over the city, competing with the neon signs to illuminate the rough concrete and glass storefronts, the oily asphalt pavement? Somehow it always seems to me that there's a full moon in the sky over Koza, but I suppose that's just the memory of other nights. In a soldier's rare moment of solitude, I looked across the street at the cars rushing by, the dingy stores, the parking lot, the pachinko parlor and the bars, the darkened alleys lined with Okinawan houses. A postwar neighborhood that already looked ancient.

On the corner opposite where I stood, an old man in working clothes paused for a moment, looking across at me. I watched him for a while as he turned and walked slowly down the street. Suddenly, I was seized by the thought, "He's old enough to have lived through the war." And I wondered, how do you live the rest of your life after experiencing something like that? How do you feel when you see the world of bars and bases that has been built here, when you see Marines like me on your streets? Uncomfortable with my thoughts, I turned and rejoined my friends in the club.

Since then, I've wondered what might have happened if I had crossed the street and spoken to him. If I had left my friends and walked back into the quiet, narrow streets of Sonda. Would I have been drawn by the sound of music and laughter to a field where young men and women danced? Would I have had a presentment that this neighborhood would be so familiar to me in another decade? Would I have begun to work through the questions that I uneasily put aside? Or would I have only felt alone in the strangeness of the darkened streets?

Although I allowed the moment to slip away, its memory blurred and fragmented, the questions that it inspired have remained with me. I have returned to them again and again as the years passed. As I studied Japanese, as I learned to be an anthropologist, as my fieldwork brought me again to the streets of Koza, as I wrote this book. How do Okinawans understand their past? How do they recall the horrors that they endured, the pleasures that they renounced, the sacrifices that they made? How do they reflect on the practices that they have maintained and abandoned? What do they do with their memories—those they struggle to recall, those they work to accept, those they allow to fade into oblivion?

In Okinawa, as perhaps anywhere else, the past exists uneasily alongside the present. It can pass unnoticed, occasionally rising for a moment of recognition, slipping away again under the weight of the routine tasks of daily life. Like the unexploded bombs that still lie close to the surface of the Okinawan landscape, it can erupt into the present with painful and unexpected consequences, casting its shadow over a future not yet experienced. Memories often return unbidden. A gesture or a position of the body recalls a dance practiced in childhood. A glimpse of a young girl in an indigo kimono evokes images of everyday life in a now-ruined mountain village. The slow melody of a folksong from a neighbor's radio stirs memories of *moashibi*, romantic parties in moonlit fields long since swallowed by urban expansion.

Tinged with pleasure and regret, accounts of memories such as these are deeply personal to the Okinawans who experienced them; and yet, their form is not unique to Okinawa itself. Similar narratives can be found in any struggle with modernization, in any account of an individual's passage through life in the modern world. However, there are other memories, stunning in their profound horror, that are perhaps only shared by those who bore the burden of Japanese and American colonialism. They lay a powerful claim to the present: memories of the brutality and relentless transformations of the Japanese colonial era, the genocide of the battle of Okinawa,[1] the callous indifference and exploitation of the American occupation. A fragment of a nearly forgotten school song jars memories of humiliations endured in colonial classrooms. Each spring, the flame-red blossoms of the *deigo* tree[2] summon images of a home destroyed in an artillery barrage, a family killed. A chance encounter with a Japanese-American child brings a painful reminder of an earlier life in a base town bar or brothel. The morning breeze carries the unexpected and terrifying stench of corpses. I've been told that little force is necessary to conjure these memories: the taste of Spam or mayonnaise, the sight of a Japanese flag or an American fighter overhead, the scent of burning fuel or of incense offered at a household altar. The past can even return without any apparent prompt, the result of some chthonic process, slipping through the deep rhythms of repression. It arrives unexpectedly, urgently, stirred by the silent call of an ancestral spirit or deity.

When we speak of memories such as this, we are far from the terrain of bittersweet nostalgia. These are remembrances that are wrenching and traumatic, tearing the fabric of daily life, plunging those who experience them into despair and even madness. They demand attention. How does one come to grips with the experience of a past that so insistently reaches into the present? Dominick LaCapra has argued forcefully that it is more than a matter of creating therapeutic strategies to work through individual loss.[3] Of course, it is necessary to decathect oneself from a lost object and to articulate conceptual and affective bonds once again with the world at hand. At the same time, loss must be addressed collectively, not simply at the level of individual experience. Moreover, actual, historical loss must be acknowledged and attended. The failure to do so, LaCapra argues, can lead to the conversion of the historical experience of loss into a structuring sense of absence, an ahistorical originary account that authorizes repetitions of violence and ideologies of subjugation. In this failure, subjects may find themselves in an impasse of endless melancholy and impossible mourning, trapped in naturalized, repetitive cycles that seem to be beyond their understanding and control.

It has not been an easy thing for Okinawans to work through their relationships with the past. For survivors to even undertake the project is to confront anew the reality of memories that might otherwise slip into welcome oblivion. With this encounter comes the realization that the comfortable patterns of daily life could once again be thrown into a nightmare of horror and abjection. I can only imagine how harrowing it must be to acknowledge that the past continues to work upon the present, that the forces and relationships that came together at earlier moments still extend into daily life. For those who did not experience these events themselves, there are other dangers. They risk shattering the security of the lives that they live in the present by taking up memories of a nightmarish past; they also risk unfairly appropriating the experiences of those who have suffered terribly.

The collective struggle of Okinawan survivors, secondary witnesses, and activists to critically reexamine the past unearths complex and overdetermined traces inscribed in memory and in graphic representation. For those traces are not simply—if such a thing could ever be simple—of terror and loss.[4] The Okinawan past is also a reservoir of possibility. For Japanese nativist artists, scholars, and politicians, as well as for Okinawans themselves, it has become a powerful archive of romantic imagery and practices. Traditional Okinawan villages are represented as sites where the Japanese people (for these discourses often appropriate Okinawans as something like living traces of the ancestral Japanese) could truly dwell, places of organic totality lost to life in the modern world. Life could be lived, from birth to death, in the same site; people, spirits, and deities living and working in harmony. Agrarian rituals, songs of thanksgiving, the ruses of traders, invocations of ancestral spirits and local deities await nothing more than recovery in the practices of the present.

Thus, the production and circulation of images of the rural Okinawan past as signs—small wooden houses with thatch or tile roofs and walled courtyards, stone tombs, rice paddies and cane fields, tree-ringed shrines, oxen-driven sugar presses—are characterized by the powerful and unsettling ambiguity of horror and possibility. Recollections of the colonial era, of wartime life, of the American occupation conjure intertwined and contradictory feelings of hope and loss, pleasure and horror, origin and apocalypse. It seems that however carefully the narrative is crafted to emphasize one aspect, its counterpart remains just at the edge of perception. I do not mean to suggest that this is a natural property of the sign; rather it is the outcome of the interwoven practices of progressive historiography, native ethnology, popular folksongs, imperial apologia, storytelling, conversations with the dead, political debate, and more. Perhaps it is because of the perceived power of these images of the past that Okinawans dare to return to them.

In the chapters that follow, I will consider this return: the way that practices, images, and sites associated with the past are taken up in Okinawan performances. In storytelling, song, and dance, individually and collectively, Okinawans work through the horror and explore the unfulfilled possibilities of the past. Searching for ways to make and remake themselves, they also struggle to transform their world.

IN THE HANGMAN'S HOUSE, ONE SHOULDN'T SPEAK OF THE NOOSE

As I have said, Okinawans are not the only ones who desire the Okinawan past; they are not alone in the attempt to craft performances that could mobilize its possibilities. On August 23, 1997, Prime Minister Hashimoto Ryūtarō addressed the Okinawa Regional Conference of Nihon Seinen Kaigisho—the Japanese Junior Chamber of Commerce, or the Jaycees. The day was almost unbelievably hot. Hoping to attract a large audience, the sponsors had reserved the spacious but simple Naha Municipal Gymnasium. The building was not air-conditioned, and, despite the huge fans placed to the front and sides of the room, the air was thick and still. Blocks of ice steamed in the aisles, providing at least the illusion of a respite from the heat. Volunteers passed out glasses of iced tea and cold towels. Security was tight. My friends and I passed through electronic screening devices as we entered, and hard-looking plainclothes police were posted at the doors and near the stage.

It was an important time for the prime minister. In April, after months of negotiations, litigation, and demonstrations, the Diet followed Hashimoto's lead and passed an amendment to the Special Law for Military Land Use.[5] A potential constitutional crisis was averted and American military bases would remain securely in place, regardless of any Okinawan popular opposition.[6] Now it was time to demonstrate that the state could be generous in victory. It was also a political opportunity for the ruling Liberal Democratic Party to shore up its faltering reputation and to build support for its policies and for local party figures.[7]

Opening remarks by local politicians and conference officials were already under way as my friend and I found our way to our seats. It was not long before Prime Minister Hashimoto was introduced. As the audience applauded, he stepped to the podium, dressed in a severe dark business suit, the pomade in his hair glistening, his appearance immaculate. After thanking the conference officials for his invitation, he urged everyone to get comfortable and relax; then he took off his jacket and continued his speech in his shirtsleeves.

Now this is something that I also talked about when I attended the meeting at the Okinawa Convention Center in Ginowan on September 17th of last year. One thing that made a strong impression on me was the wartime sinking by an American submarine of the ship Tsushima Maru in which schoolchildren had been embarked so that they could escape from the prefecture to Kyūshū—this became known as the Tsushima Maru incident. A delegation of families came to see my father with an introduction from Ōhama Nobumoto. It is from [my father's] mouth that I heard about the fourteen hundred souls that were lost on the Tsushima Maru. And it was at that time that I realized that there were still terrible tragedies in Okinawa. Happening as it did in my youth, this really kindled a spark in me. After that, I followed in my father's footsteps and became a representative to the Diet. Unfortunately, the *Tsushima Maru* incident was left just as it was, without any resolution. The families of the war victims did not receive any of the pensions due to families who had lost members during the war. Dealing with this inequity became one of the first objectives of my political career. In 1977, we were finally able to pass a special law awarding pensions to the surviving families.[8]

Hashimoto's speech worked to awaken a feeling of commonality in his Okinawan listeners, to bridge the gap between the mainland politician and the local audience. The implicit theme: Japanese everywhere suffered during the war. Like his father before him, Hashimoto has dedicated himself to giving voice to their claims, to honoring their sacrifices, and to alleviating their pain. These actions on Hashimoto's part were grounded in his membership in an institution committed to memoration. Throughout his career, he has been deeply involved in the activities of the Nihon Izokukai—the Japanese Bereaved Families Association, or JBFA—one of the most aggressive and reactionary of the various organizations committed to the remembrance and political representation of the soldiers who fought in the Pacific War and their survivors. In fact, it was only upon his election as prime minister that he resigned his presidency of the organization. Over the years, the JBFA has been committed to renewing government sponsorship of Yasukuni Shrine and has relentlessly pressured politicians to refuse to apologize or accept responsibility for Japanese actions in the Pacific War.[9] Moreover, their objective has been to create and sustain a collective subject made up of those who suffered. Hashimoto's startling anecdote is clearly an attempt to appropriate Okinawa, to draw it into this melancholy community in which loss can only be redeemed by the possibility of state memoration.[10]

Listening to his speech, I was stunned at its audacity. I wondered how he would deal with the unruly memories of Japanese colonization, genocide, and abandonment to American occupation that would be stirred by his invocation of wartime death. After all, the real occasion of his visit was the management of yet another rejection of Okinawan calls for justice and the reaffirmation of Okinawa's inescapable role as an island of American bases. However, Hashimoto did not hesitate to recall the past and to acknowledge Okinawa historical difference. He noted that in the days of the kingdom of Ryūkyū,[11] Ok   an expansive trading system that linked Japan and China. He praised Ryūkyū for its international orientation as well as the energy and vigor of its commercial networks. Then, having introduced the place of Ryūkyū in the Okinawan past, he rapidly moved beyond it. He did so with a confidence that suggested that no one should expect him to discuss more troubling memories: repression and exploitation by Satsuma with the consent of the Tokugawa Bakufu, the destruction of Ryūkyū, and the brutal colonization of Okinawa.[12]

Instead, he soon merged Ryūkyū and Japan in his narrative, the two unaccountably becoming one. Hashimoto returned to the subject of the Pacific War with the odd observation that Okinawa was the only part of the main islands (hondo) to be subjected to a ground war. To use hondo—literally the mainland or the home islands—in reference to Okinawa is marked, whether the speaking subject is mainland Japanese or Okinawan. From the perspective of the mainland Japanese, Okinawa occupies an ambiguous place that is part of the contemporary Japanese state, yet a late addition to the space that was originally constituted by just the home islands. Japan it may be, but it is that which lies beyond hondo. On the other hand, I have never heard Okinawans use hondo to speak of Okinawa. I have never heard it used to express anything other than the home islands of Honshū, Kyūshū, Shikoku, and Hokkaido. Like naichi (the internal territories) it represents the part of Japan to which Okinawa has been joined. It describes Yamato, the cultural zone that is not Okinawa or Uchinā,[13] regardless of the fact that both are subsumed under the Japanese state.

For Hashimoto to speak of Okinawa as hondo is to willfully recategorize it, to ignore routine geographic and historical differences, and to efface the distinctions that have contributed to the discrimination that Okinawans have endured—at the hands of other Japanese—for more than a century. It is to intentionally recover Okinawa to a unified national subject. What's more, it is a subject that Hashimoto has defined, not by ethnicity, common language, or contiguity, but by the sacrifices shared and losses endured in a war waged by the United States against Japan. At the same time, Hashimoto seems to have little interest in building antipathy toward the United States: he went on to describe America and Japan as partners in the contemporary project of Asian regional security. He was, however, attentive to the travails that Okinawa has endured since the end of the war: twenty-seven years of American occupation, economic disadvantages, and social hardship. For this, Hashimoto said, he was profoundly sorry.

> When I became prime minister, it was my chance to once again reconsider the problems that Okinawans had been   e to get
> people to think of the sadness and   :hin the
> peace and prosperity of modern Japa   r me—I
> want to say that I am deeply apologetic because our determination to try to understand what Okinawans were going through each day simply was not adequate.

An apology in the decade of strange apologies offered, recanted, and denied. Only four years earlier, former prime minister Hosokawa Morihiro had used the annual ceremonies that commemorate the end of the Pacific War as an opportunity to publicly apologize for the *senryaku sensō*, the war of aggression that Japan had waged in Asia.[14] Not surprisingly, it was Hashimoto as a member of the oppositional Liberal Democratic Party who attacked Hosokawa's statement, arguing that Japan's aggression could only be understood in the context of the aggression of the Western powers.[15] Although later prime ministers such as Murayama Tomiichi also spoke out against Japanese aggression, groups like the Japan Bereaved Families Association brought intense pressure to bear, and their loyal representatives in the Diet and cabinet ministries spoke out, many suggesting that stories of Japanese wartime atrocities were no more than fabrications.

Hashimoto's apology bears the mark of prohibition: although it is his own narrative that recalled this moment, there are things that he simply cannot say. He does not speak of the strategic decisions by Japanese civilians and military officials that made Okinawa into the final battlefield of the Pacific War. He does not refer to the Okinawan soldiers and civilians whose lives were squandered in meaningless attacks ordered by Japanese officers. He is silent about Okinawans who were compelled to commit suicide or murdered outright by the Japanese army. He does not comment on decisions made by the postwar government of Japan to allow the American occupation of Okinawa to continue for decades after that of hondo ended. He cannot speak of what Japan has done; neither can he fully address what Japan failed to do. He apologizes only for what he did not do enough: completely comprehend Okinawan suffering, encourage his countrymen to empathize with the experiences of Okinawan people.

For all that he was unable to speak of actions in the past, Hashimoto insisted that he would make up for what Okinawa had endured by acting in the present. He had come to Okinawa to announce a host of plans for economic improvement and aid packages for the prefecture. Still, his enthusiasm could not suppress the problem of the past that loomed over his presentation. A decade after the German defeat in the Second World War, Theodor Adorno wrote of strange attraction that drew the guilty back to the very past that they had tried to efface: " 'Coming to terms with the past' does not imply a serious working through of the past, the breaking of its spell through an act of clear consciousness. It suggests, rather, wishing to turn the page and, if possible, wiping it from memory. The attitude that it would be proper for everything to be forgiven and forgotten by those who were wronged is expressed by the party that committed the injustice."[16]

What most interests me in Adorno's savage critique is the way that he exposes the appropriation of the place of the victim by the aggressor. Simply getting away with an act of aggression is not enough; the aggressor also wants to settle accounts on his own terms, to eliminate the past as the basis of any claims that might arise in the future. Surely this is one of the objectives of Hashimoto's speech. Under the ruse of an apology, he attempts to replace the specificity of Okinawan historical experience with the content of a national narrative. His speech hails the victims, calling them to the place of those who committed the injustice.

In writing of the relationship between memory and forgiveness, Paul Ricoeur argues that, in order for the question of forgiveness to be considered, the event that gives rise to this situation must be open to reflection: "There can, in fact, be forgiveness only where we can accuse someone of something, presume him to be or declare him guilty. And one can indict only those acts that are imputable to an agent who holds himself to be their genuine author. In other words, imputability is that capacity, that aptitude, by virtue of which actions can be held to someone's account."[17]

Hashimoto came to Okinawa to offer his apologies—but for what? His remarks were astonishingly silent on more than a century of oppression endured by Okinawa. It may be that Hashimoto felt that, as prime minister of the Japanese government of the time, he could not reasonably be held accountable for actions that reach back into the imperial Japanese era. Given his evocation of the *Tsushima Maru*, it is also possible that Hashimoto was convinced that the United States bears the burden of guilt for war and occupation. However, in Okinawa, Hashimoto made no mention of any concerns that could mitigate the responsibility of the Japanese state. As for imputability, he carefully chose the act for which he offered his public apology: his failure to adequately understand Okinawan conditions despite his best efforts to do so. In this way, he has silenced all other acts, disregarding what Ricoeur has provocatively called the negative magnitude of fault, the depth that separates the subject who seeks forgiveness from the subject who is in a position to grant it. The depth that would characterize an apology that addressed the colonial era, war, or occupation is collapsed. A history of transgression becomes a trifling matter.

What could possibly encourage Okinawans to entertain this apology, to take up their positions in this spectacle, this theater of forgiveness? This question is sharpened if one considers Ricoeur's insight that pardon cannot be substituted for justice. Regardless of the decades that have passed since the Second World War, events such as the Okinawan genocide cannot be dismissed, cannot be consigned to the resolved past. Under international law, crimes could still be prosecuted and punished; an accounting is still due. But what if one knows that justice will never be done? What of the decades of Okinawan experience, renewed once again in the Japanese state's dismissal of their protestations against forced military occupation? Could they reasonably believe that they have any hope of seeking justice and restitution from these same institutions? Moreover, the inducements that Hashimoto offered to the prefecture cannot be discounted. To the poorest prefecture in Japan, a place where the memories of colonial and postwar privation are still raw, these gifts carry tremendous weight. The *omoiyari yosan* (the so-called sympathy budget that subsidizes the American military bases that dominate the Okinawan landscape) and its tremendous collateral public and private investments, drive the Okinawan economy. The uncertainty of a future in which the government may not be willing to provide these subsidies is a powerful inducement to accept an apology.

What is it that Hashimoto asks of Okinawans in return for the gifts that he has promised? The first, as I have suggested, is to simply play a part in this drama of apology and forgiveness, if only for the duration of the speech. It is a performance that provides a counterpoint to the antibase demonstrations and tense negotiations that had dominated the previous two years. Against this field, images of a conciliatory prime minister and a grateful and respectful Okinawan audience have a real currency. However, there is another gift that he asks of Okinawa—a small one, perhaps, but one with profoundly important implications. That is the gift of the Okinawan past. Okinawans are asked to offer up the differing and specific memories of the dead, the remembrance of wounds inflicted on those still living, and the recollections of particular moments of destruction, degradation, and sacrifice. They will, of course, receive something in return—is that not the promise of the allegory of the *Tsushima Maru*? If Okinawa surrenders these things to Japan, Hashimoto invites them to find a place in hondo, to share in the melancholy community of the nation. And, like those who received their pensions from the state, their sacrifices will be rewarded.

Hashimoto's performance is grounded in a narrative that has been crafted since the beginning of the modern era in Japan, a central narrative of national history to be substituted for the content of divergent local or individual remembrance. A powerful ideological complex that suggests a unified subjectivity, a shared origin, and a common destination. It has been mobilized in the past to demand the total commitment of the Japanese people, even the sacrifice of their lives.[18]

Again and again since the late nineteenth century—first as Ryūkyūans then as Okinawans—the inhabitants of the Ryūkyū archipelago have been offered this narrative. It has been proffered through educational institutions, military service, books and newspapers, films and public lectures, children's songs, and patriotic anthems. It has been inserted into the fabric of daily life through calendrical rituals and national holidays, memorative sites and practices, prescribed bodily positions, and gestures. And yet, rather than a share in progress of the national subject or the prosperity of the imperial or postwar Japanese state, Okinawans have received poverty and famine, forced labor and migration, military conscription and occupation, annihilation. Now, after nearly 150 years of shifting relationships with the Japanese state, the national narrative as experienced in Okinawa is shot through with heterogeneous and contradictory objects of memory, still powerful and yet open to challenge at every point. Despite the continued representation of this national narrative, Okinawans are well aware of the experience of unevenness, of the social and economic disparity of capitalist modernity in Japan. At the same time, they do not simply feel the sting of marginalization. They experience what Ernst Bloch has called subjective nonsynchronism—the sense that the future that ought to be available to them has been foreclosed. As young men and women, they may have anticipated and expected lives that they would one day lead. Now, these bright images of the future exist only as remembered dreams.[19]

That the prime minister turns again to these same narrative strategies speaks to anxiety over the continuing recession, fear of economic competition and isolation, and the fragmentation of conservative political hegemony as much as it does to the perduring nature of these practices and formulations. Perhaps he can secure Okinawan labor through the panoply of industrial, commercial, and financial projects offered by the state, to bind it with gratitude, obligation, and debt. Perhaps Okinawans can be conscripted for the work of memoration, routinizing, and incorporating their distinct and unruly memories through technologies resuscitated by the state. To subsume individual, household, and community practices in a network linked to the spatialized mourning of Yasukuni Shrine and the resuscitated tokens of imperial Japan such as the emperor and emblem of the Rising Sun.

Although some in the audience must have felt uneasy, Hashimoto's speech appeared to be well received. There was enthusiastic applause from the party loyalists to the front, and laughter and nods of agreement throughout the room. And yet it seemed to me that there was a troubling ambiguity to Hashimoto's remarks, an undercurrent of menace that belied his energetic affability. Having extended the embrace of Japan to Okinawa, he qualified it. Up until now, he said, Okinawa had been so closely identified with problems that he fears that the terms "Okinawa" and *mondai* (problem) have become synonymous for many Japanese—Okinawans and mainlanders as well. He wants to put the notion of "problem" aside for a time; instead, he would like to offer Okinawa's strength as an example to the nation.

Turning away from Okinawa's unresolved past allows Hashimoto to shift the discussion to culture. "It is not just that this place is beautiful"—and here he pauses for effect—"the people here are beautiful as well." He praises the traditional practices that he's seen. The depth of Okinawan culture has profoundly affected him, as has the gentleness of the people with their bright and kind personalities. Even under American occupation, these things have not just endured—they have prospered. This is good news for those who fear for the destruction of Okinawan culture, for the erosion of tradition by the relentless march of capitalist modernity. And yet, is there any impetus to alleviate social problems when we know that Okinawan culture, strong and enduring, lies beyond their reach?

Hashimoto tells his audience that, despite the injustice and oppression that they have experienced, the cultural beauty and profound spirituality that shine through in their daily lives will be a lesson to the rest of Japan. These are kind words, but the aspirations of the people can be policed through compliments and flattery as well as through discipline and repression. And the policing of Okinawa is surely one of the objectives of Hashimoto's visit: to once again fix in place the spatial division of labor that constitutes the Japanese nation state—an order in which, unfortunately, it falls to Okinawa to provide a home for 75 percent of the American military forces in Japan as well as the Japanese security forces that support their operations. Hashimoto acknowledges as much. He will work to alleviate the problems associated with the bases by negotiating so that they can be moved to a less populous area in Okinawa, he will even try to get America to reduce its overall troop strength. However, there is no offer of a more equitable distribution of the bases through the rest of Japan, no offer to allow any of the other eighty-two prefectures to share the experiences that have allowed Okinawan culture to shine so brightly.

In spite of Hashimoto's warmth and enthusiasm, the notion of a culturally diverse Japan should be regarded with some suspicion. As Marilyn Ivy has written: "The hybrid realities of Japan today—of multiple border crossings and transnational interchanges in the worlds of trade, aesthetics, science— are contained within dominant discourses on cultural purity and nondifference, and in nostalgic appeals to premodernity: what makes the Japanese so different from everyone else makes them identical to each other; what threatens that self-sameness is often marked temporally as the intrusively modern, spatially as the foreign."[20]

If this characterizes the relationship of Japan to what is perceived as external to it, what are the possibilities of diversity within Japan? Michael Molasky, Laura Hein, and Mark Selden have all commented on the ambivalent valorization of the distinctiveness of Okinawan culture against the backdrop of a Japan that is still defined by sameness.[21] In this context, to be praised is to be marked, to be set apart.

To understand the complicated truth of Hashimoto's argument is, as Jacques Rancière has said in another context, really a matter of dividing in two—a procedure in which the "division of shares leaves each in his place."[22] Okinawans are welcome—required, in fact—to contribute their labor to the production of the nation state of Japan. They may work in the factories and the construction sites of the mainland, they may struggle and sacrifice to sustain the bases built in the fields of Okinawa, they may offer up their efforts to the national project of memoration. At the same time, the words of praise that depict Okinawa as different, regardless of the value that they seem to attach to Okinawan culture or practices, serve to gently close the door on real inclusion. *Be Japanese, by all means, but never forget that you are Okinawan.* Which is to say, so long as you remain Okinawan, you will be, at best, ambiguously Japanese.

This is a problem that has haunted Okinawa since the early days of the colonial period. In it, one can see the articulation of the ideology of a unified nation-state and the actuality of Okinawan experience. Tomiyama Ichirō has written of Okinawan scholar Iha Fuyū's tortured struggle to develop a formulation that could account for a relationship between the Japanese and Okinawan—or Ryūkyūan—people that did not consign Okinawa to a subordinate position in the Japanese state. Efforts by Okinawan people to assimilate were both demanded and rebuffed by the Japanese state. This is not simply a matter of interest to scholars: it is an impulse that has been behind the suicide of patriotic Okinawans during the final days of the Pacific War; their execution as accused spies by imperial Japanese soldiers; their abandonment by the Japanese state during the American occupation; and their political struggle during the era of decolonization to return to Japan, their one-time colonial overlords, under the sign of the *hi no maru*—the Rising Sun.

It has taken years to begin a critical interrogation of memory in postwar Okinawa. To simply assemble oral histories and survivors' testimonies has been extraordinarily difficult and painful.[23] The struggle of scholars such as Ishihara Masaie to come to grips with the memories of the war in Okinawa have been nothing less than heroic. His tireless work has enabled many to give voice to their experiences, allowed many more to bear witness, and respected the silence of those who do not wish to speak.[24] Moreover, he has recognized the need, the right, and the ability of ordinary people to act on their own concerns with the past. He has not only compiled volume after volume of critical texts—oral histories of the Pacific War, the experiences of labor and performance under the American occupation, black marketeering, and the postwar malaria epidemics;[25] he has also trained generations of ethnographers who can conceive of and carry out these projects. A formidable number of oral histories that have been created in recent decades were made possible by the students in his undergraduate research seminars, by graduates who have become historians and activists in communities throughout Okinawa, and by people who were inspired by their efforts.

I believe that this is a critical point. Orthodox educational institutions and practices have prospered in postwar Okinawa. There is an extensive network of schools now integrated with the Japanese national education system, a growing number of private and public universities, public libraries sponsored by the prefectural and municipal governments, repositories for the acquisition and maintenance of archival material and museums for display and reflection, and research institutions sponsored by the prefecture and by local governments committed to the exploration of the Okinawan and Ryūkyūan past.

The work of Ishihara and others has both contributed to this growth and served to destabilize the institutional monopoly on the production and circulation of knowledge. Ordinary people, creative and intelligent, have also come to realize that they do not need to depend solely on the efforts of those who work in universities and research institutes to mediate their encounter with the past. They have learned that they have the right and perhaps the responsibility to undertake their own projects.[26]

The Okinawans whom I will consider in the following chapters also take up these questions. In contrast to the narration of personal experiences or acts of commemoration, these Okinawans have engaged their concerns in performance. Their work is a challenge to the notion of a proper place, to totalizing national narratives that account for everything in the embrace of the Japanese nation-state. These Okinawans are construction workers and welders, letter carriers and clerks, housepainters and students; they are also storytellers, comedians, musicians, dancers, and artists. They labor in service stations, hotels, small shops, fishing boats, and housing developments;

they do the work of historians, ethnographers, and critics. In the time normally set aside for rest or for recreation, they turn to different kinds of creative, productive activity. In doing do, they contest the very divisions of everyday life. In Jacques Rancière's words:

> The core of emancipation was an attempt to break away from the very partition of time sustaining social subjection: the obvious partition being that workers work during the day and sleep during the night. Therefore, the conquest of the night was the first step in social emancipation, the first material and symbolic basis for a reconfiguration of the given state of things. In order to state themselves as sharing in a common world, they had to reconfigure their "individual" life, to reconfigure the partition of day and night that, for all individuals, anticipated the partition between those who were or were not destined to care for the common. It was not a matter of "representations" as historians would claim. It was a matter of sensory experience, a form of partition of the perceptible.[27]

In very different ways, Okinawans take up the cultural practices that Hashimoto praised. However, they use them, not as a palliative for the burdens of the modern world, but as a resource to think through their past, their present, their future. They produce performances, struggling to find forms adequate to their concerns, bringing genres associated with the traditional performing arts—prewar comedic dialogs, dancing associated with the era of postwar American occupation, singing in the style of the kingdom of Ryūkyū—together with the forms and images of the present: the humorous monologues of television performers, the fieldwork of contemporary ethnographers, and the martial arts films of Tokyo and Hong Kong. By bringing these forms together in performance, they enlist the collaborative efforts of artist and audience, conjoining their labors to create a moment of creativity and expression.[28]

I am particularly concerned with the production of these moments, the appropriation and production of a space—a courtyard, a classroom, a street—in which the uneasy relationship of past and present can be brought before their audience. For, as Ernst Bloch understood, something of this relationship must be resolved in order to act in the moment: "Utopian consciousness wants to look far into the distance, but ultimately only in order to penetrate the darkness so near it of the just lived moment, in which everything that is both drives and is hidden from itself. In other words, we need the most powerful telescope, that of potential utopian consciousness, in order to penetrate precisely the nearest nearness."[29]

Separated—if only for the duration of the performance—from the spatio-temporality of the nation and the demands of labor, those present can grapple with the forms and the experiences of the past. It is not mechanical repetition of the familiar or the melancholy inability to escape the trauma of the past. Rather, it is a creative and reflexive engagement with it. For some, the moment veers close to the terrain of nativist thought. In the authenticity of voice and gesture, something of the past is brought forward into the now, recovered from loss, and used to reinvigorate the moment. For others, representations of the forms of the past and present are engaged, not to drag the indeterminate past into the present but to work though unresolved experiences of the past, moments that continue to resonate with the present. Finally, for others, this engagement represents something like Benjamin's constellation, linking the remembered and repeated forms of the past with an interruption of the present, the whole assemblage figuring the possibility of transformation toward the future.

YUNTAKU—CONVERSATIONS

This was not the project that brought me back to Okinawa, a decade after my first visit. Instead, I came to write an ethnography of land ownership, governance, and cultural transformation—something, I hoped, like "A Rule of Property for Okinawa." Arriving in Okinawa late in the summer of 1996, I followed up introductions to local scholars and activists, visited archives, attended seminars at the University of the Ryukyus, and explored the streets of Okinawa City. In those early weeks, I encountered obstacles similar to those that I suppose all anthropologists find in unfamiliar situations: the silence and hostility of some landowners, the superficial accessibility and routine narratives of others, the convoluted bureaucratic unresponsiveness of the Japanese and American officials responsible for base land management. At the same time, I found something else. Okinawa was alive with demonstrations, meetings, and marches. In the aftermath of the rape of an Okinawan schoolgirl by American soldiers, in the summer leading up to the referendum on the American bases, veteran activists and newcomers alike had taken to the streets. Everywhere I turned—in bars and classrooms, at cafes and festivals, in newspaper essays, television reports, and local radio broadcasts—people seemed to be struggling with the burden and the promise of the past. They spoke of an everyday world shattered by the imposition of Japanese customs and practices, and of autonomy crushed by the Japanese state.[30] They argued about promises too long deferred, justice denied, a future undreamed. I began to think that it would be a foolish thing to cling to a plan conceived in a snowbound apartment in Chicago, far from the commitment, the hope, and the passion that charged the moment. Finally, a day came when I knew I would have to change.

Shortly after the referendum, one of my friends took me to the village of Yomitan to meet the activist Chibana Shōichi.[31] As one of the oppositional leaders at the center of the base land crisis, Chibana had refused to renew the lease of a plot that he owned at the center of the Sobe Communication Facility in Yomitan.[32] Although he was extremely busy—reporters and activists were leaving his office as I arrived, faxes and letters were stacked everywhere—he took the time to show me around the community and discuss his feeling about the antibase movement. We spent the rest of the day driving down narrow country roads and walking the hills and the fields of Yomitan. We stood on the beach where the invading American forces came ashore. We visited caves where villagers sheltered against the horrors of the invasion, where they had committed mass suicide or were massacred by Japanese soldiers. We walked across an abandoned runway at a derelict American airbase. We stood on the ramparts of the ruins of Zakimi Castle. We gazed through the fence surrounding the massive array of antennas at Sobe—the Elephant's Cage as everyone called it—looking at Chibana's small parcel of land within. Finally, we sat down to talk at a small coffee shop managed by his sister-in-law.

An incredible manifold of the past—the American occupation, the war, the Japanese colonial rule, the kingdom of Ryūkyū—seemed so powerfully, so materially present. I wondered again, as I had so many times, how Okinawans lived their lives with this presence. I knew that Chibana had been interested in ethnography as a student, and I knew that he had been closely involved with an oral history project about the traumatic memories of his neighbors in Yomitan.[33] Who better to help me to rethink my research? I asked him about the kind of project that he thought could help me to understand these problems. Without hesitation, he replied that I should think about *eisā*—a dance performed for ancestral spirits during Obon, the festival of the dead. Eisā, he said, dealt with the past by creating something in the present. Looking up from her work at the counter, Chibana's sister-in-law added that I should also consider what eisā meant to the people who watched it. The performances were amazing—the dance so dynamic, the drumming so forceful, the young dancers so handsome and vital.

I had long since run out of tape to record the interview, so I had to pause to write everything in my notebook. During the lull in the conversation, Chibana's sister-in-law offered me another suggestion. She asked me if I knew anything about the work of Fujiki Hayato, the comedian and storyteller. His performance might give me a sense of Okinawan history and culture quite different from what they were talking about at the university. Pointing at the newspaper spread out on the counter in front of her, she said that he was performing that evening at a small theater at Paretto Kumoji—a department store in Naha. I should say then that I owe the performances that I explore in this book to Chibana and his sister-in-law. I went to Fujiki's *Hitori Yuntaku Shibai* that night, and to several others in the following weeks. I began to meet with Fujiki, engaging in long discussions as challenging and exciting as his performances. He introduced me to actors, artists, and musicians in Okinawa City. I was fortunate to become friends with Tamaki Mitsuru, a brilliant playwright, storyteller, and comedian. Fujiki and Tamaki were extraordinarily generous with their time and provocative with their comments; both of them taught me a tremendous amount about performing arts and about daily life in Okinawa.

Although I duly wrote Chibana's suggestion about eisā in my notebook, it was months before I would act on it. Instead, while learning about comedic performances from Fujiki and Tamaki, I became interested in communities that had once been located inside the American bases. After reviewing documents about these shattered villages at the prefectural and municipal archives, I joined the Okinawan sociologist Ishihara Masaie for a series of interviews with survivors living in Okinawa City. The project was fascinating —Ishihara was a masterful ethnographer, and the men and women that we interviewed had compelling stories to tell. Still, as interesting as their narratives were, I hoped to find some way to see how experiences of the past were reflexively worked through in contemporary practices. One night, I sat with

Fujiki at his bar, explaining my concerns. Without hesitation, he responded that I had the right idea—I was just working in the wrong place. He said that I needed to move a couple of blocks to Sonda. A tough, working-class neighborhood famous throughout Japan for its eisā, Sonda was organized around a nucleus of families, former Ryūkyūan nobles who had been driven from their farms in what is now Kadena Air Base. Fujiki said that the *seinenkai* (youth group) in Sonda had helped his friends enormously when they were forming the Rinken Band. In fact, when Fujiki and Takami left the band, they were both replaced by young men from the seinenkai. While I sat there at the bar, Fujiki called the community center in Sonda and told Iha Masakazu, the current head of the seinenkai, about my interests. Fujiki then passed me the phone. After exchanging courtesies, Iha said that I should stop by early the following morning and we could talk about my project.

I arrived at the Sonda Community Center at about eight o'clock the next day. Iha was there, along with five or six men in their thirties or early forties—all former dancers. One or two of them were sleeping on chairs pushed together inside; a couple more slept on the steps. A meeting the night before to plan the upcoming season seemed to have turned into a party—as I found out later, a not uncommon practice. I introduced myself to Iha and briefly told him about my research. I said that I had heard a lot about the Sonda eisā, and Fujiki had told me that he couldn't think of a better place for me to work. So, I said, I'd like to spend some time at the community center—observing their practices, interviewing members, talking with people in the audience. Iha thought for a moment, looked around at the other men who were slowly waking up. "No, I don't think that we can do that."

I was surprised and embarrassed. As I stammered a polite response, I tried to think of how to finish the conversation so that I could leave quickly. Iha interrupted me, continuing to talk as if I hadn't said anything. "You can't watch," he said. "But you can join." Zukeran Masahide, one of the older members, came in from outside, lit a cigarette, and sat down with us. "If you want to learn about what it is that we do, you have to do it too." I couldn't believe my good fortune—after all, this is the kind of entrée that anthropologists dream about. But Zukeran wasn't finished.

Don't think that we're doing you any favor. Yeah, you'll learn a lot about eisā, about all the things that interest you about Okinawa culture. But it has a cost.

introduction

You'll have to meet our standards—every dancer represents our neighborhood. That shouldn't be too hard—everyone here can do it so I can't see why you can't either. That's not really what I mean. From now on, every year as summer begins, you'll hear the drums. It doesn't matter where you are or what you're doing. It's like a ringing in your ears—when you go to sleep at night, when you wake up in the darkness. You'll be called. And you can't believe how it hurts when you can't come.

Night after night for two summers we practiced together. I danced one year, and became a drummer the next. I joined them for performances at local festivals and weddings, during the grueling nights of Obon, and at the island-wide Eisā Festival. More than that, we shared our daily lives. The community center was the focus of activity for the young men and women who danced the eisā, but also for the older members like Zukeran. In the evenings after practice, and on winter afternoons when the dance was still more than half a year away, we told jokes and stories, talked about history and politics, interpreted dreams, learned to play the *sanshin* (a three-stringed instrument resembling the Japanese *shamisen*), watched baseball games on television, and drank *awamori* (distilled rice liquor). I worked with them— construction jobs, moving, painting. I helped with campaigns for the city assembly. My family was drawn into the neighborhood—my wife and I became friends with local families; my younger daughter, Fiona, enrolled in the nursery school across the street in Moromizato; my older daughter, Siobhan, joined her friends in the children's eisā group. The members of the seinenkai became my teachers and my audience. They taught me about everything from Ryūkyūan verse to welding. They critiqued my ideas and suggested new directions for my research.

Following Chibana's suggestions gave me a tremendous opportunity to learn about the past and its memoration in Okinawa. More than that, it made me attentive to the ways in which ordinary people struggle with the categories that configure their daily lives. I was able to learn about the creative practices of contemporary Okinawans and to experience the ways in which they are able to go beyond the burdens of a traumatic past and the divisions of labor that structure their present, to challenge the world around them with courage and creativity. I was able to see that, as artists, they have found ways to say and to do things that could not otherwise be given form.

DRAWING A CIRCLE

My book begins with a discussion of a series of performances by the Okinawan actor and storyteller Fujiki Hayato, dramatic monologues that emerged from mid-1990s protests against American occupation and Japanese economic and political exploitation.[34] Fujiki's work synthesizes a variety of genres as diverse as Japanese popular theater, Okinawan storytelling and ritual, and scholarly investigations of war memory. In doing so, his work reevaluates the possibilities afforded by traditional forms of representation and practice. At the same time, his performances enact a critique of everyday life, urging his audience to confront the troubled legacy of the Okinawan past, to examine their personal and shared responsibilities, and to accept the obligation to act.

In the second chapter, I situate Fujiki's critical project in the context of a history of the Okinawan performative genres that inspired him. I am most interested in the creation of new forms of storytelling, comedic theater, and music in the aftermath of the Pacific War. Artists such as Teruya Rinsuke (Terurin) and Onaha Būten combined established Okinawan genres with techniques drawn from Japanese radio broadcasts, film narration, and Western popular music in order to create a new, more complex style of performance. They worked with a sense of urgency, driven by a conviction that these new forms would be necessary to revitalize their devastated towns and villages. It was at this time that Terurin also began his long and complicated engagement with Japanese colonial anthropology—a discipline that produced knowledge of a subjugated people while constructing a romantic notion of the hardy and mystical Okinawan folk and conflating the Okinawan and Japanese pasts. In time, Terurin's interest in popular performance and native ethnology came together, and he began to present himself as an ethnographer delivering public lectures about Okinawan culture and history. It was through these performances that he was able to combine the authority of the ethnographer with the competence of the native. In doing so, he emphasized the unique cunning of the Okinawan people in order to reclaim a powerful sense of subjectivity, of the possibility of meaningful activity. And yet, despite these transformations, his argument remains within the framework of a romantic critique of life in the modern world. Preoccupied with his concern for the value of Okinawan culture and the recovery or reconfiguration of native practices, it is difficult for Terurin to confront Okinawan responsibility for the traumatic history that they have experienced.

Chapter 3 explores the ways that Okinawans have received Fujiki's performances, focusing on a seminar on Okinawan history and culture that he organized the winter of 1997. Drawing on Terurin's synthesis of humor, storytelling, and ethnography, he structured the seminar around an unconventional mode of learning, emphasizing practical interaction and direct experience of the object rather than a rigidly academic approach. The seminar provided an opportunity for Fujiki to present his own notions of culture, ideology, and creative practice while giving students the space to evaluate and transform these ideas. Lectures and discussions were interwoven with individual and collaborative performances—both of Fujiki's own texts and of those constructed by the students themselves. Students were challenged to move beyond a passive concern with the questions posed in the course and to engage them at the level of physical embodiment, through active participation in recitations and short plays. From the very first session, the brutal experience of Okinawan history was discussed explicitly. Students struggled to make sense of Japanese colonialism and American occupation, stereotypes of Okinawan culture in Japanese discourse, Okinawan complicity in the project of assimilation to the Japanese state, and the development of a national culture. They also engaged Fujiki's revised notion of cunning, a concept based on experience and determined action rather than an attribute of Terurin's essentialized folk. Fujiki implicitly challenged the implications of authenticity in Terurin's work by demanding that students do more than simply uncover a putative native competency that they had always unknowingly possessed. This meant nothing, he argued, unless they mobilized their recovered capabilities to confront and transform the legacy of the past.

The fourth chapter is an interlude that deepens my discussion of the images and practices that organize the first three chapters and lays the groundwork for the fifth chapter. I explore the will to memory that brings Okinawans again and again to the image of the rural village. One of the foundational representations of native ethnography, it is a central trope in nostalgic reflections on an idyllic Okinawan past. Mobilized in popular performance and tourist discourse disseminated across Japan, these images draw visitors to Okinawa in search of an authentic experience of a lost Japan.

However, not all acts of memory resuscitate an idealized and idyllic past. The work of contemporary artists such as Takara Ben's *Yādui* (A Samurai Village) reveals the struggle to recall rural communities in their historical actuality, their particularity, in order to shatter unified romantic images.

Reflection on Takara's work leads me to consider the ways in which Okinawans have worked through the traumatic experiences of colonial oppression and wartime death. Conceptions of mourning and memorative practice must take into account the maintenance and reconfiguration of relationships with the dead when the boundary between life and death is seen as open and traversable, when the living and the dead have endless effects upon one another. Thinking through this relationship brings me to a close reading of the *kōkai shinri*, a series of public hearings conducted by Okinawa Prefecture in the spring of 1997 in order to evaluate the Japanese state's ongoing expropriation of Okinawan land for American military bases. In particular, I focus on the testimony of the *hansen jinushi*, or antiwar landlords, who suggest that acts of memory are more than melancholy encounters with objects lost from their daily lives. Instead, the dead themselves are materially reconstituted and relationships with the spirits of the dead are reconstructed to empower the struggle of Okinawans for social justice.

The final chapter builds on my analysis of Okinawan performance to consider the ways in which Okinawans have confronted the traumatic heritage of their times, and the projects that they have created in order to transform everyday life. I reflect on the creative practices of the young men and women who live and work, who dance and create in the streets of Sonda, the streets that I turned away from in my account of my first visit to Okinawa as a Marine. Sonda was settled in the aftermath of the Pacific War, a refuge for those whose communities were destroyed in battle or appropriated in the construction of the American bases that still dominate the island. It is home to those whose labor sustains the American occupation and the Japanese tourist economy; it is also a place of vibrant artistic production, a site that figures in the careers of performers such as Teruya Rinsuke and Fujiki Hayato. My analysis will focus on the performance of eisā—the traditional dance for the dead—during this period of intense political and economic turmoil. Resuscitated in the aftermath of the battle of Okinawa after having been forbidden by Japanese military authorities, eisā has become the largest public ritual memorializing the dead in contemporary Okinawa, as well as one of the most popular forms of Okinawan performing arts.

I provide close readings of a series of rehearsals and performances of the Sonda eisā, considering remembrance and aesthetic production as they come together in the dance. I also note that eisā is productive of a form of value known as karī: its distribution is necessary for the revitalization of the community and the health and happiness of its members. My analysis considers the complex interrelationship between the production of karī and the dancers' engagement with the trauma of Okinawan history. I discuss the creative and transformational ways in which recent history is cleared away, and a kind of indefinite time of everyday life once lived is drawn—if only for the duration of the performance—into this opening. In clearing away the traumatic wreckage of contemporary history, the dancers perform a moment that allows them to engage their own pasts, and to recreate themselves as artists and warriors as well as clerks and laborers.

fujiki hayato, the storyteller

Our campaign slogan must be: reform of consciousness, not through dogma, but through the analysis of that mystical consciousness which has not yet become clear to itself. It will then turn out that the world has long dreamt of that which it had only to form a clear idea of in order to really possess it. It will turn out that it is not a question of any conceptual rupture between past and future, but rather the completion of the thoughts of the past.—KARL MARX, *Letter to Ruge*

In chanpuru rhythm, we happily combine new lines of scientific inquiry, unscientific traditions passed on from older generations, as well as outright lies. I am convinced that when absolutely incompatible perspectives are brought together and the boundaries between this and that are weakened, a new truth, a new culture will be born.—TERUYA RINSUKE, *Terurin Jiden*

HISTORY AND THE EVERYDAY

It was the autumn of 1945. The battle of Okinawa had ended. Their villages destroyed and their farms confiscated, thousands of Okinawans remained confined in resettlement camps under the haphazard administration of American military authorities.[1] During the day, people gathered in the muddy streets between the ramshackle tents and shacks in which they were forced to live. Shocked, saddened, bored, they struggled to piece together the fragments of their daily lives. One day the dentist and comedian Onaha Būten joined them, laughing impishly.

> I know that things have been terrible, but you can't go on this way. Here's what I'm going to do. Everyone gather around—I'll tell some stories and maybe we can sing a few songs. Now I know that times are tough, but I need to survive too. So I'll just put my hat down in the middle here. Then, everyone can close their eyes and pitch in whatever they can afford. That way, someone without much money

won't be embarrassed. Once everyone has put their money in, I'll give a signal. You can open your eyes and I'll go on with the show.

They all agreed that this was a good idea. Būten put down his hat and told his audience to shut their eyes. Everyone dug into their pockets and threw money into the hat. After a few minutes, Būten shouted, "Open your eyes!"

When they looked around, Būten had taken the hat and gone. Laughing, he waved to them from his bike as he raced away down the street.

"Don't you ever learn?"[2]

In the spring of 1997, the Japanese Diet acted with extraordinary—almost unprecedented—dispatch, passing a special law enabling the central government to compel Okinawan landowners to continue to lease their land for use by the American military. With this decision, the exuberance and determination of the previous months came to an abrupt and shocking halt. Nearly two years before, in 1995, the prefecture had erupted in anger over the rape of an Okinawan child by American soldiers—the latest in a series of attacks visited upon young women by American servicemen.[3] Since that incident, there had been a prefectural referendum on the future of the bases, a series of public hearings on the renewal of leases, and several massive demonstrations.

A tremendous amount of critical effort had been directed at reconsidering the Okinawan past, and not merely the history of American military occupation. Essays in newspapers and journals, public discussions, and private conversations debated Okinawa's history of Japanese colonialism, wartime genocide, modernization, and incorporation into the Japanese nation-state. Questions of Okinawa's subjection to nativist analysis and cultural commodification were aired in the mass media. Angry commentators and politicians revisited Okinawa's history of discrimination at the hands of both the American and Japanese states. Calls were heard for greater regional autonomy, for recognition of Okinawa's unique status in the Japanese nation, even for independence. Commentators on both the right and the left urged Okinawans to seize this opportunity to determine their future; of course, the choices that these commentators enjoined their fellow Okinawans to make were radically different.[4] In the midst of all of this, complex negotiations with the Japanese national government and American authorities continued. When landowners were finally forced to renew the leases held by the Japanese government, when the Diet enacted special legislation making leases compulsory, Okinawans were amazed to once again find their claims so summarily dismissed.[5]

An editorial in the journal *Kēshi Kaji*[6] explored the deep emotions that swept through Okinawa following the Diet's stunning actions. The author, Miyazato Chisato, described how a feeling of *chirudai* came to pervade everyday life. In this case, *chirudai* can be understood to be a state in which the boundary between waking life and dreams has become blurred and charged with feelings of disappointment and loss. Politicians, activists, and critics would soon reorganize, particularly in the context of announcement of U.S. plans to build a new helicopter base in Nago.[7] However, in a series of performances throughout Okinawa—at the Terurinkan in Okinawa City, at Ryubo Hall in Naha, and at the Nakamurake in Kitanakagusuku—the humorist and essayist Fujiki Hayato had already organized a different sort of response to the state of despondency described in the *Kēshi Kaji* essay. Evoking the work of Teruya Rinsuke and the aforementioned Onaha Būten,[8] Fujiki attempted to both transform the sense of chirudai—of disappointment and loss—and provide a critique of everyday life in contemporary Okinawa.[9]

"One does not have to be a resentful reactionary to be horrified by the fact that the desire for the new represses duration."[10] Theodor Adorno wrote these words in a critique of modern art; however, at this historical conjuncture it would be impossible to separate the cultural from the economic, the aesthetic from the quotidian. The modern era has been characterized by a kind of ceaseless impulse toward change. In the case of Japan, postwar economic growth was driven by a relentless mobilization of resources directed toward domestic development:

> During the period of rapid GNP growth Japanese cities and industrial areas were virtual war zones. "Scrap and build" was the phrase the Japanese themselves used to describe the situation. The particular development strategy of government and business was reminiscent of the wartime strategy of resource mobilization. . . .

fujiki hayato, the storyteller

During the war the Japanese were made to work selflessly in the attempt to win. After the war similar sacrifices were evidently expected in the interest of GNP growth.[11]

Okinawan space is inscribed with the signs of these catastrophic transformations. In the name of parity with mainland Japan—hondonami—tremendous levels of capital have been committed and natural resources sacrificed to develop the Okinawan economy. Successive municipal governments and prefectural administrations routinely develop and deploy complex and ambitious plans for modernization and development: "international cities" and "free trade zones" are conceived and attempted, if never completed. Enormous construction projects—dams, highways, oil storage facilities, municipal buildings, conference centers—compete with the network of American bases for domination of the countryside.

This ceaseless orientation toward the future has also required Okinawans to defer the satisfaction of their desires until the constantly receding horizon of parity has been reached.[12] Although much of this remains within the discourses of postwar modernization theory,[13] it also resonates uncannily with the prewar Okinawan experiences of seikatsu kaizen, or lifestyle reform. In the aftermath of the colonial era, Okinawans were urged to renounce their backward culture and commit themselves to an ideology of shusse,[14] of self-improvement. In the pages to come, I will consider the disturbing parallels between these discourses. However, for now, I want to focus on the experience of living in a present, a "now," where the experience of duration is constrained by the relentless practical orientation toward the future. And yet, this orientation is constantly brought up against the unfulfilled promises of the past that continue to manifest themselves in Okinawan social space and the practices of everyday life.

THE *HITORI YUNTAKU SHIBAI*

Central Okinawa, dominated by the sprawl of Kadena Air Base, is haunted by this complex and unresolved dialectic between past and present.[15] The base itself is a massive network of runways, hangars, and magazines, hardened against nuclear attack. It is ringed by neighborhoods of suburban bungalows, apartment complexes, and shopping and entertainment centers, all

fujiki hayato, the storyteller

surrounded by miles of chain link fence and razor tape, pierced at intervals by guarded gates. And yet, fragmentary remains of other orders belie the monolithic permanence of the base: here, a monument to the Japanese troops who died during the defense of the Japanese air field that occupied the same space during the Pacific War; there, signs that mark the mouth of a cave where Okinawan civilians took refuge during the battle for Okinawa. Family tombs and village shrines continue to stand on the carefully groomed lawns of the base, the fresh offerings of incense and flowers linking them to communities that have been dispersed or destroyed. Aging farmers pass through the gates, undeterred by armed sentries, to tend gardens and cut fodder on the margins of their ruined farms.

Okinawa City—Koza[16]—clings to the perimeter of the base, its narrow streets and riot of construction a stark contrast to the spaciousness of Kadena. As I drove through the city, I felt like a swimmer moving across an enormous reef, its vibrant, expanding fringes counterbalanced by vast expanses of rigid, lifeless coral. Okinawa City radiates out in the same way, the debris of the modernization projects of past generations embedded in its concrete body. Tightly packed buildings lined the wide, asphalt highways linking the island's military training and storage complexes with the airfields at Kadena and the military harbour in Naha. Many of these buildings were vacant, their faded signs continuing to advertise bars, discos, restaurants, and souvenir shops long since closed. Narrow side roads led through crowded Okinawan neighborhoods where wooden houses with red-tiled roofs stood side by side with modern homes of polished concrete and glass. The crests of hills and slopes overlooking the sea were given over to tombs, neighborhoods of massive stone and concrete crypts inhabited by ancestral spirits. Beyond, entire districts of crumbling Western-style concrete bungalows mirrored the American housing areas on base. In fact, these were once the homes of the Americans who have now retreated to the communities constructed at Japanese taxpayers' expense within the base perimeter. Now they run to ruin, some occupied, most awaiting demolition and reconstruction. They stand as a kind of high water mark of the American military's physical penetration into Okinawan social space.

As always, my gaze was drawn to this Okinawan landscape—there seemed to be so much to see and to understand. And yet, I also felt as if I was searching for something that I did not see in the concrete neighborhoods,

fujiki hayato, the storyteller

the cane fields, the rocky hilltops. Did I imagine that, after half a century, the hillsides would give up the bodies of those who died by the thousands in the withering fire of the war? Did I think that I would glimpse a shell-shattered village, still smouldering? Did I expect the streets to be packed with Vietnam-era revelers or rioters? Or perhaps I thought that I would catch a glimpse of an earlier self, the young Marine infantryman that I had been more than a decade before?

My tiny, underpowered car labored painfully as I climbed along the mountain road, heading south. To my right, an American golf course occupied a ridge where Okinawan tombs once stood; to my left, the road winding down to the eastern coast was lined with flamboyantly designed "love hotels."[17] Every draw, every open field in the lowlands was planted with sugarcane, a legacy of the Japanese colonial administration still supported by modern state subsidies. I passed through a hilltop neighborhood of elaborate California-style ranches, home to the U.S. consul, the commanding general of the U.S. forces, and a number of wealthy businessmen. Towering above them, an abandoned Sheraton Hotel and several shuttered restaurants testified to the mistaken conviction that Okinawa City would become the center of Okinawan tourism and industry after reversion to Japanese rule in 1972. I followed the road as it descended through a jumble of construction sites and concrete houses, rose through a second public golf course and an evergreen forest. At last, I turned into a small parking lot that stood before the walled compound of a rural Okinawan villa.

I climbed out of the car, a cool breeze challenging the heat that still radiated from the asphalt pavement. It was sunset, the sky streaked with violet and crimson. A young woman, Fujiki's wife, met me in front of the main gate and we exchanged greetings. After receiving brief instruction from Mrs. Fujiki, an attendant led me through the gate and to the right of the hinpun, the massive masonry barrier defending the household from the direct assaults of intruders and malevolent spirits. Skirting a paved courtyard (the nā), we stepped up onto the veranda of a semidetached guesthouse. I slipped off my sandals and followed my guide through the guesthouse and into the public rooms of the main villa. Connecting doors had all been removed for the evening, and an open expanse of tatami stretched from the eastern side of the house to the kitchen on the west. With a smile, the attendant motioned for me to sit in an open spot before the ancestral altar. I nodded to the guests already present and joined them in facing the courtyard.

The sliding exterior doors of the villa had also been removed, affording guests an unobstructed view of the nā. Behind me, the doors of the ancestral altar had been opened as well, the interior shelves laden with flowers, fresh fruit, and water, providing a comfortable space from which the spirits could also observe the guests as well as the courtyard beyond. Smoke from newly lit mosquito coils mingled with the scent of tropical flowers and the lingering fragrance of incense offered earlier at the altar.

A low murmur of conversation and laughter filled the rooms as guests continued to arrive. By now, the rooms of the main house were filled and latecomers were forced to sit along the veranda of the guesthouse as well as the edges of the courtyard itself. Neighbors shared fans and passed cans of chilled Orion beer back and forth. The audience was diverse, most coming from the neighboring communities of Okinawa City and Nakagusuku, as well as some from Chatan on the west coast of the island and Urasoe and Naha to the south. They were socially and economically diverse as well: office workers and bureaucrats, university students, schoolteachers, construction workers, and electricians—a few still in their mint-green *sagyōfuku*, or working uniforms. There was also a smattering of tourists from mainland Japan—cognoscenti of Okinawan pop culture, as well as the odd anthropologist. Entire families sat together, toddlers on their grandparents' laps, groups of friends and coworkers next to young couples on dates.[18]

In many ways, this gathering resembled Okinawan household celebrations and feasts. Against this similarity, the differences are striking and important. Although our host had greeted us, this was not actually his house. In fact, save for the ancestral spirits whose names were inscribed on the tablets that stood on the altar and the various household deities, no one lived in the compound at all. The diverse group of men and women seated together was brought together by something other than the bonds of kinship. The villa—the Nakamurake—was one of the few structures in central Okinawa to have survived the Pacific War. The original house is said to have been built to house a retainer of the legendary Gosamaru,[19] whose castle lay in ruins on a neighboring hilltop. The compound had been rebuilt according to a geometry that integrated it into the kingdom of Ryūkyū and, beyond

fujiki hayato, the storyteller

that, the spatiotemporality of the Chinese court. However, courtiers had been absent from the guesthouse since the Ryūkyū kingdom was destroyed by the Japanese state at the end of the nineteenth century. The fields had been partitioned and sold, and the estate was now surrounded by a parking lot, a mental institution, and the ruins of a nightmarish hotel built during the American occupation to accommodate tourists who had never come. No pigs rooted about in the empty sties, the servants' quarters and kitchen were vacant, the storehouse depleted. In a valley to the north, the famous stream Chunjun Nagare still wound its way to the sea,[20] but dancers no longer greeted the spirits of the dead in the villa courtyard during Obon.[21] The one-time residence of the *jitoshoku*, or village headman, of Nakagusuku had been made into a museum, its only occupants a few visiting tourists.

Fujiki's choice of the Nakamurake for his *Hitori Yuntaku Shibai* was not simply an exercise in nostalgia. This is a space that represents the historical integration of the Okinawan household into a certain set of practices, a certain mode of being that was of course both social and economic.[22] It is a site saturated with daily life. As several members of the audience told me, it is a place that invokes a complex texture of their own childhood memories and images that they know only from media representations. In Lefebrian terms, it is a profoundly representational space, in which Fujiki's guests experience an uneasy recognition of the symbolic character of the everyday. Their comfortable experience of their surroundings is juxtaposed with their real unfamiliarity with the disposition of this residential space and the use of the agricultural implements ready at hand.[23]

Here, in the "now" of the Nakamurake, the audience confronts the contradictory spatiotemporalities of Ryūkyū and modern Japanese Okinawa. On the one hand, they cannot forget the quotidian calendrical cycle of daily labor, of salaries to be drawn, taxes to be paid, and loans to be repaid. Their lives are constrained and defined by the rhythms of the fiscal and academic years, by tourist and construction seasons; they await the punctual return of high school baseball championships and American military exercises. On the other hand, they are confronted by signs of Ryūkyūan spacetime. The full moon shining above the courtyard is a reminder of the continuing importance of the lunar cycle and *kyūreki*, the archaic calendar. And as Fujiki begins his performance in the *nā*, they are made to recall the *nenjū kuduchi*,[24] the rituals that punctuate and give form to the year. The elements of this event

Fujiki Hayato

resonate powerfully with the work of native ethnologists such as Yanagita Kunio, who observed that these rituals did not simply commemorate the passing of the year; they produced it, anchoring relationships with the invisible ancestors in the materiality of human praxis.[25] But what is produced by the practices of Fujiki's audience? What relationship do the nenjū kuduchi have to their everyday lives? What does a harvest festival mean to a construction worker who has never tilled a field or cut cane? How can residents of complex, diasporic settlements summon ancestors whose graves are scattered across Okinawa, across the Pacific, their native villages destroyed?

For the rural agrarian everyday evoked by the Nakamurake is no more—certainly not in central Okinawa with its American air bases, cramped urban sprawl, golf courses, and massive petrochemical storage facilities. And here, where the everyday has become unsettled, Fujiki has found the possibility of establishing transformative, dialogic communication with his guests.

It is not surprising that Fujiki should choose storytelling as the vehicle to effect this manifold transformation. In the context of interwar Europe, Walter Benjamin turned to a consideration of storytelling in order to explicate the crisis of modernity.[26] For Benjamin, the art of the story was predicated on an oral tradition, grounded in the common experiences of a specific community of listeners. Benjamin argued that at the very moment that folktales were valorized as a true sign of the folk, the actual practice of storytelling was becoming extinct. He called into question any kind of meaningful intersubjective transmission of experience, of memory free from the intervention of the fascist state, of the possibility of historical experience as commonly understood. Similar experiences of fragmentation and loss are evoked by Fujiki's Nakamurake performances. And yet, while Fujiki clearly intends to intervene in the crisis of meaning, his efforts represent more than a critical explication of its conditions. For Fujiki, storytelling continues to offer the possibility of a transformation in the lives of his listeners.

In order to understand this possibility, it is necessary to understand storytelling and its critique in the determinate historical and cultural conditions of Okinawa and Japan. Fujiki's mentor Teruya Rinsuke once told me before a performance that it was imperative to focus the attention of his audience on *kotodama*—the spirit of language, and to draw on this power in performance.[27] Here, Terurin explicitly evoked nativist and ethnographic discourses on language.[28] As H. D. Harootunian explains in his analysis of the Tokugawa nativist Hirata Atsutane,

> The reductive strategy that propelled restorationists' impulses . . . constituted a conception of the real that was rooted in specific social practices of the eighteenth century, since it sought to retrieve essential and tangible meanings no longer available to contemporaries. This impulse lay at the heart of the nativists' emphasis on words and representations, their search for a primary and natural language that was capable of expressing things tangibly and accurately, and their attempt to rescue the traces of *kotodama* itself—the spirit of language—which had preserved the true vehicle of expressibility. The principal purpose of this reductive strategy was not to invite the present to slavishly imitate the ancient past or even the original language, but to recall meanings and functions in their essential forms to serve as guides for the present and to demonstrate that tangibility and wholeness derive from naturalness, not contrivance.[29]

However, the most immediate reference for Terurin's remarks is the nativist ethnography that emerged in a dialogic engagement with the profound social and economic transformations of the early twentieth century. Horrified by the fragmentation of meaning and the destruction of everyday practices, these ethnographers sought to incorporate their work into the genealogy of Hirata's nativist formulations. For Orikuchi Shinobu, oral narration such as that practiced by female chanters held forth the possibility of a foundation for a Japanese national literature. For Yanagita Kunio, agrarian ritual, household practices, and the reproduction and narration of folktales could provide a bulwark against the relentless urbanization and industrialization of modern Japan.[30] And for these ethnographers, Okinawa promised to be a reserve of practices, beliefs, and traditions that had been extinguished throughout the rest of Japan.[31]

I will deal with Terurin and his relationship to native ethnography in the following chapter; at this point, I want to emphasize Fujiki's reconceptualization and redeployment of nativist formulations. While Terurin's insight is important in understanding the historical background to Fujiki's performances, it is not because Fujiki holds out any hope of recovering an authentic, originary form of practice. It is precisely the opposite. Fujiki is inspired to seek a form that is more adequate to the crisis of contemporary Okinawa, to build a complex secondary genre that incorporates elements as diverse as *rakugo* (monologue), *manzai* (dialogue), folk ritual, local storytelling, and the testimony of war survivors.

Fujiki is a well-known figure in Okinawan popular culture. While I worked in Okinawa, he hosted several weekly programs on at least two local radio stations, appeared regularly in local television shows and theatrical performances, published his own free newspaper, occasionally recorded and released music CDs, and was an almost ubiquitous presence in Okinawan advertising. In addition, he had appeared in a number of Japanese films, performed comedy routines in mainland Japanese venues and introduced Okinawan programs on NHK, the national television channel.[32] After I finished my fieldwork, Fujiki went on to write and direct his own theatrical productions, tour mainland Japan with the rakugo artist Tatekawa Shinnosuke, create his own musical group, and—most famously—play a supporting role in the popular NHK television serial *Churasan* and its sequels.

There is something compelling about Fujiki's staging of the *Hitori Yuntaku Shibai*, perhaps his best-known if least-seen performance. Although Fujiki has published an anthology of his earlier scripts, he only performs the *Hitori*

Yuntaku Shibai live. Given his intense involvement in radio, television, and recording, it cannot be that he has a general aversion to these media. Instead, he seems to have made an effort to bracket the *Hitori Yuntaku Shibai* from the rest of his work. Performances are small and intimate: the audience is limited by the size of the performance spaces. While he does advertise, notices are posted here and there in Koza, and sometimes noted in the local newspapers[33]—not places that would catch the eye of a conventional mainland tourist.

As I suggested above, these performances evoke the forms of certain practices coded as traditional. They also trigger associations with the popular theater, in particular the *uchinā shibai*—Okinawan theater—and community center parties that remain popular throughout central Okinawa. Of course, they also call forth associations with a host of televised comedy reviews, not the least of which would be Fujiki's own roles in Tamaki Mitsuru's[34] Shōchiku Kagekidan productions.[35]

Fujiki draws on his own experiences of growing up in Nakanomachi—the bar district of Koza (or Okinawa City, as it is now officially known) during the American occupation. His mother was born on the tiny, outlying island of Ihei, the birthplace of the founder of the final Okinawan dynasty. Fujiki's father immigrated to Okinawa from Amami Ōshima and opened a cabaret catering to American GIs. After a stint as a mailman, Fujiki began apprenticeship to his craft in earnest as a member of both Teruya Rinken's eponymous band and Tamaki Mitsuru's comedy troupe.

Many Okinawans fondly recall Fujiki's wildly improvisational manzai-style routines with Gakiya Yoshimitsu.[36] However, by his own account, he was neither a gifted comedian nor a talented musician: his career with the Rinken Band began as a member of the road crew. He still jokes that he had been a singer for some time before his microphone was turned on. Still, Tamaki Mitsuru described him to me as a tremendously focused student, and he spent long hours studying Okinawan history, folklore, and conversational patterns, as well as honing his skills as a singer, drummer, and comedian. His studies were eclectic: his teachers Tamaki, the seminal humorist and musician Teruya Rinsuke, the distinguished Okinawan historian and conservative political thinker Takara Kurayoshi, and the famous *rakugoka* and television personality Tatekawa Shinnosuke. By the time he began his solo career in 1993, he had appeared on several Rinken Band albums, completed a world tour with an omnibus of "world music" artists, and starred in *Owarai Pō Pō*,[37] a successful television series featuring Tamaki's troupe in an improvised review.

The possibilities of Fujiki's storytelling are many. On one hand, he seeks a substantive engagement with the crises of everyday life, to stimulate his audience's sense of contradiction and to foreground the possibilities ready to hand. At another level, his appropriation of the form of the *iwai* (celebration) is done in complete seriousness. His performances by night offer the possibility of a transformative practice within the everyday world.[38] He quite literally undertakes the production of a kind of value—karī[39]—that can be imparted to his audience. Several of my friends suggested that, in doing so, Fujiki drew heavily on the itinerant artistry of the *nā ashibi*[40]—the eisā and *chondarā*[41] performances that took place in courtyards much like that of the Nakamurake. Particularly in the case of eisā—Okinawan *bon odori*[42]—these performances would mediate the community's collective offerings of gratitude to the ancestral spirits; conversely, they also mediated the distribution of the karī received from the ancestral spirits to the households that composed the community. The karī imparted to these households would give them the strength to endure the vicissitudes of life in the agrarian villages of central Okinawa.

Here, Fujiki told me that he was inspired by Onaha Būten's and Teruya Rinsuke's postwar transformation of these practices. In the aftermath of the war, these two musicians and comedians carried their sanshin and a bottle of awamori from tent to tent in the internment camps and from house to house in the newly resettled neighborhoods of Koza. Entering each house, they announced their *nuchi nu sūji* (*inochi no oiwai* in Japanese, the "celebration of life"). They offered to dance and sing on behalf of the households that they visited, transferring karī to the residents. Shocked and angered, their neighbors asked how it was possible to celebrate while they were still grieving for their dead. Būten laughed and replied: "It's precisely because it is a time like this! Of course it's true that many people died during this war. Unless those of us left alive celebrate and get on with our lives, the spirits of the dead will never be raised. It may be true that one in four have died, but doesn't that also mean that three are left alive? Come on now, let's celebrate our lives with passion. Those left alive have an obligation to the dead to live joyously."[43] Būten uses the shock of everyday practices redeployed at a time when daily life has been thrown into chaos in order to forge a new continuity. Walter Benjamin observed that "to become part of the community of the story, we must be able to reproduce the story."[44] Būten's insight is that reproducing the story is perhaps a step toward recreating the community. In the aftermath of the war, the sequence of events to which traditions such as the iwai belong has been shattered. Reassembling these practices could not recreate the prewar form of Okinawan society; however, it could begin the process of reintegrating survivors into relationships with their ancestral spirits, and reestablishing a productive sense of community in what had become a mere contiguous collection of households and individuals. Following Terurin's and Būten's innovative practices, Fujiki appropriates these forms to produce a spiritual transformation adequate to addressing the problems of everyday life in contemporary Okinawa.[45]

Once the guests were seated, the lights of the house were extinguished. Conversation faded as the rising edge of the full moon illuminated the red-tiled roof of the storehouse and the paving stones on the western side of the compound. A recording began to play from speakers under the eaves of the house, a melody weaving elements of Okinawan folksongs and Indonesian gamelan in an electronic pop instrumental. As the full face of the moon finally broke out above the rooftop, a spotlight flashed on, illuminating our host as he bowed silently in the center of the courtyard. Fujiki stood, acknowledged the audience's applause, and greeted them.

Minasan, konbanwa. Yatte maerimashita. Uchinā mōsō kenbunroku, Nakamurake spesharu pāto tsū de gozaimasu ne.

(Good evening, everyone. Here I am again. This is the second edition of my special performance of "A Hallucinatory Record of Okinawa" here at the Nakamura House.)

Fujiki continued in this vein, addressing the audience in standard spoken Japanese. He selected a distal form of address (indicated by verb roots modified with -masu endings), using appropriate honorific terms in reference to the audience and humble verb forms in self-reference (maerimashita rather than kimashita, degozaimasu rather than desu). This manner of address is significant on a number of counts. It demonstrated Fujiki's proficiency in

Fujiki Hayato in performance

standard Japanese, the language of public oratory and intellectual debate in Okinawa, as well as the principal form of aesthetic expression in contemporary performance genres throughout Japan. This point is not inconsiderable, given the profound interventions by the state in the Okinawan educational system since the colonial era, aimed at eradicating local dialects and producing competency in standard Japanese. It also plays on the preconceptions of some mainland Japanese tourists who, Fujiki insists with some seriousness, know so little about Okinawa that they expect the residents to speak only English. At the same time, Fujiki was able to show his comfort with other forms of expression, making humorous asides to the audience, sotto voice, in contemporary Okinawan.[46]

This formal greeting also provided an explicit reference to Japanese popular performance genres, linking Fujiki to rakugo and manzai artists.[47] This linkage to popular forms, particularly rakugo, plays on the audience's familiarity with these genres and their expectations as to how they will be organized. Fujiki's opening and closing devices are central to this. The opening of the performance, with its theme music, spotlight, and formal greeting, has its counterpart in the closing. Fujiki bids the audience goodnight, bows, the spot is extinguished, and music plays as the audience departs. This device provides a kind of framework within which the performance can unfold, bracketing it in space and time.[48] However, within this framework, Fujiki has considerable latitude to improvise and experiment in ways that would be impossible within the conventions of rakugo.

Finally and most interestingly, the introduction provides an opportunity for Fujiki to again transform his relationship with the audience: in this case, he shifts positions from considerate host to performer. At the same time, the guests are invited to assume the role of his hosts, seated in the villa—and also as interlocutors in his conversations.

Although Fujiki had intially encouraged its identification with rakugo, his performance at the Nakamurake differs from it on a number of important counts.[49] Typically, Rakugo performances are highly formalized and the narrator is dressed in traditional male attire (*hakama*, etc.) and seated on a *zabuton* (cushion). The rakugoka may move about in order to indicate motion within the story, but cannot leave the sitting positon. At the same time, the rakugoka is restricted in the use of props and can only use a fan and a handkerchief or small towel to indicate the objects used in the narrative. Although Fujiki uses very few props, he does not restrict himself as rigorously as does a rakugoka. He walks about freely on stage and dresses in a style appropriate to the central character that he portrays.

Fujiki also departs from the conventions of rakugo on the question of address. In the case of rakugo, it is quite clear that the audience members are the addressees: the rakugoka begins by speaking directly to his listeners, then recounts the conversations that he has experienced through extended passages of reported speech. As I have noted, Fujiki himself follows this pattern in his opening. Once the introduction is complete, Fujiki continues to speak casually, touching on current events and his recent experiences traveling around Japan. Songs, jokes, and brief anecdotes—sometimes the kernel of as-yet undeveloped stories.

However, once he begins the storytelling set pieces that are at the heart of his performance, it is clear that Fujiki as performer no longer addresses himself directly to the audience. Rather, the explicit addressee of his performance remains within the framework of the narrative. In the case of the first sketch that I will discuss, it is a housewife who has been subjected to the efforts of a traveling salesman. In the second sketch, it is the grandson of an old man. What's more, Fujiki eschews the rakugoka's practice of repeating passages of reported speech, reprising the utterances of both interlocutors in order to enact this central encounter. Instead, he pauses after delivering one series of utterances and the responses go unspoken.[50] The effect of this strategy is to conflate the audience with the explicit addressee of the narrative. The audience is dialogically (if imaginatively) drawn deeper into the experience of the narrative, constantly struggling to recreate the unspoken statements that yield Fujiki's responses. This is not to say that Fujiki does not narrate conversations imbedded in the form of reported speech; he simply does so to different ends.

To return then to Fujiki's performance: After concluding his opening remarks, the stage and the house lights were extinguished. When the lights rose, Fujiki was again standing stock-still in the center of the courtyard. This time, his hair had been slicked back and he was wearing a tight, shiny, brown business suit and a pair of steel-framed glasses, a type particularly popular with ageing schoolteachers and politicians. His front tooth was capped in gold—a hallmark of the marginal figures that he often portrays. What's more, his entire bodily hexis had changed. From the easygoing confidence of his opening monologue, he had become stooped, constricted, diminished. Blinking nervously, he struggled to appear presentable as he clutched his battered suitcase.

He cleared his throat and began to speak. He was, it seemed, a traveling salesman. His products were Okinawan cultural artefacts:[51] the shīsā—lion-like rooftop guardians of the household; the ishigantō—character-etched tablets that obstruct the linear movement of evil forces; knotted blades of miscanthus and the hinpun; the mongoose and the gecko. Already intensively presented to tourists as markers of Okinawa's intransitive past-in-the-present, he was working a market already sadly overextended. But his customer was not a tourist. In a halting monologue, nervous, looping, and repetitive, he addressed the middle-class Okinawan housewife to whom he was trying to sell his wares. For his products were not simply the kitschy gimcracks, the cheap reproductions that are found in countless souvenir shops and hotel lobbies throughout the islands. Instead, they had been reconfigured and redeployed to meet the demands of an Okinawan life in the modern world. A hat-mounted shīsā to protect the Okinawan working in the mainland or abroad, a portable hinpun to safeguard a student from school bullying, an ishigantō to protect a smoker from the inevitability of lung cancer. With mounting desperation, he tried to convince his customer to buy these improvised protections against the hazards of the everyday. He endured the condescension of the housewife, the contempt of her husband, and a beating from her son. And to his surprise, he is successful—he makes the sale. There is an undeniable attraction to old things.

Once this first sketch had ended, the lights of the Nakamurake were again darkened. Members of the audience talked quietly among themselves for five minutes or so while music continued to play through the sound system. Then, the stage lights came up once more.

> Kazubō! Your grandfather has seen ghosts. And I've seen our ancestral spirits too, . . . Anybody who's tried as hard to die as I did during the war can't help but see them.

An old man is standing on a beach with his grandson on one of the Kerama islands, just off the coast of Naha. He begins to tell the boy a story about his experiences during the war, when he was the same age as his grandson. As in the first piece, Fujiki initially frames the performance as a dialogue, in this case between the aged protagonist and his young grandson, using long pauses to encourage the audience's dialogic participation. Then, he shifts to long passages of reported speech from the narrator's wartime experiences—conversations between the young protagonist and various Japanese officers and Okinawan villagers. The effect of these sustained passages of reported speech in Japanese is to draw completed events of the past, rendered in the perfective in the initial dialog between the protagonist and his grandson, into the "now," rendered in the imperfective, as if they were now occurring or about to occur. Once this pattern is established, it is repeated in phases of varying lengths. The protagonist reflects on the meaning of the events of the past—events that remain immanent in the present—and yet is not always able to present a coherent understanding.

Fujiki's performance is clearly influenced by the genre of war remembrances.[52] Themes common to collections published in Okinawa appear throughout the narrative: a description of the militarization of civilian life, reflections upon the narrator's youthful naiveté, discussion of the problems of *tennōsei* and the system of imperial education,[53] and finally, the traumatic experience of war. Published accounts are generally based on interviews, and attempt to capture the immediacy of the narrator's utterances. However, given the structure of the ethnographic interview, the resulting text tends to be written in a distal style that indicates at least some deference on the part of the narrator. It is also not uncommon for accounts to be edited rather heavily, removing nonstandard locutions and producing a final account that is much more aligned with written conventions. Both published accounts and spoken performances also use direct quotation to a considerable extent —this use of reported speech clearly influences Fujiki's performance. However, the device by which Fujiki conflates the audience with his silent interlocutor has the effect of creating a much more intimate tone, an atmosphere that is both intense and confidential in a way that published accounts do not seem to be.

As the American forces approached Okinawa, regular soldiers and conscripted civilians struggled to prepare for the inevitable invasion. A young man—Fujiki's character—is filled with admiration for the brave Japanese soldiers and begs the commander of the local garrison to allow him to become a cadet. His wish is granted, and he joins the daily routine of constructing field fortifications and training for combat. However, the idyllic camaraderie of shared military service is short-lived:

It was the year that the war ended—it had started on March 26th of Showa 20. There were air raids until the 23rd, then it changed to naval bombardment after the 25th. Shells fell on the mountainside like rain; the ground looked like there had been an earthquake and the whole island shuddered.

When we went out to dig shelters, we thought that a message would come telling us to gather in the trenches that we had dug in the red clay and then commit suicide [*gyokusai*] to die an honorable death.[54]

However, when we reached the front of the shelter, everyone had hastily been assembled into a formation of assault troops. Of course, although I was only a cadet, I joined in too. I had a sense of the ground, so I led the route.

I was sixteen—the same age that you are now.

fujiki hayato, the storyteller

During the course of preparations, he is praised by the garrison commander for proclaiming his willingness to die in defense of Japan—to kill ten American soldiers before sacrificing his own life for the emperor. This willingness to die was a constant part of their everyday lives and every soldier and cadet carried a manual to study in their spare moments: the numbers one and ten were even the challenge and password for night patrols.

"One kills ten"—when you are going to die, you take ten of the enemy with you. Gyokusai—that's a word that you learned on the battlefield. Unless someone could reply "Kills ten" when you challenged them with "One," they were your enemy and we thought that it was OK to fire on them.

To tell you the truth, I didn't really completely understand it either. We had a notebook that we carried around with us. It just came into my mind. But when I started to get the drift of it, it was natural to think of it seriously.

[As if he is putting his hand on Kazubō's shoulder]

"Are you afraid of dying?"—I was shocked. Even in those days, your grandfather was surprised.

When I answered, "I can't imagine that when everyone fights for this island, for Japan, with no thought for their lives, that I would be the only one left alive," I was praised. After that, I realized that I should always respond in the same way to that kind of question.

That expression was our bread and butter.

Yet his satisfaction at this accomplishment is short-lived: when he returns to his quarters, Lieutenant Someya (his immediate superior) furiously upbraids him for his ridiculous response, for regurgitating a stock answer without even considering its implications. The lieutenant gave him a second book—a pocket dictionary—telling him to make sure that he was clear on the meaning of all orders, to take nothing for granted.

[The old man speaks as Lieutenant Someya]

"Here—I'm giving this book to you."

That's what he said and, in those days, I was at the age when I wanted anything that I thought I could get my hands on.

"Thank you very much. I'll always treasure this as a memento." But, as I said that, I felt kind of uncomfortable.

fujiki hayato, the storyteller

"What do you mean, treasure? Just don't kill yourself as you've said you would. What is it that you think death is?"

Ah—here it comes. That discussion again. I just said that I'd been waiting for it.

"How can I think that I alone will be spared when everyone unhesitatingly fights for this island, for Japan?"

When I said this, his face suddenly flushed bright red and—enraged—he smacked me: "You idiot!"

"Forgive me," I apologized immediately.

"Why do you apologize? Oh yeah—you said something that made me angry. If you're apologizing, what is it that made me mad? I think that you know exactly what it is. Why don't you try and answer me?"

"How would I know?" I asked, but he made no reply. All I could do was stare at him.

"Get rid of this conceited idea of yours. You're not the kind of person to throw your life away so senselessly. What good does it do mucking around with war-games when the country is falling to pieces all around you. You have to keep on for as long as you can—don't throw away this precious life that you received from your father. The fact is, if you're a soldier, you ought to protect your life as much as you can."

Somehow, as he said this, his strength seemed to wane and his words trailed off. Then, he looked at me and spoke haltingly.

"Are you hurt?"

I was an idiot. I should have thought more before answering, but, without thinking, I replied, "No."

"*No?* It's not *no!* Be more honest. Do you want me to hit you again?"

Enraged once more, he hit me again without waiting for my reply. And it hurt! I bowed my head and, tears streaming down my face, apologized.

"I understand. Please forgive me!"

He stood up and seemed to lose focus for a moment. Then, after a time, he turned to me and said: "Death just isn't that way. Take care of your life. Understand?"

And with that, he asked if I was hungry. Now, if this were you Kazubō, how would you answer? If you're wrong, you might get smacked again. Yes. If it were you, what would you say?

I didn't know either, so I just kept my mouth shut. The lieutenant only apologized for hitting me and said: "Here—eat this."

fujiki hayato, the storyteller

Now, I don't know where he got it from, but he pulled a chunk of brown sugar from his trouser pocket and gave it to me.

[Returning to present]

This is a disorienting experience for the young man who admires the dedicated Japanese soldiers and desires the approbation of both the garrison commander and Lieutenant Someya.

The invasion begins, and the young cadet begs Lieutenant Someya to allow him to join in the attack against the Americans coming ashore. However, his unit is pinned down by a savage bombardment and arrives on the battlefield after the skirmish has ended. Here, in the ruins of his familiar village, he confronts the horror of war. The bodies of villagers and soldiers are scattered everywhere:

The carnage was horrific—I got sick and vomited. Pigs wandered about, rooting in the rotted, decomposing bodies of the dead, their entrails strewn everywhere.

Renewed bombardment scattered the soldiers and they fled to the mountains; the lieutenant disappeared in the fighting.

There was a pause in the assault and an unnerving calm settled on the island. Each morning an American patrol boat passed the shore, urging the villagers to surrender. Before returning to the American position on Zamami, the boat landed, leaving supplies for the starving villagers. Still, the Japanese garrison was relentless in its defense. An elderly couple from the village was found with American supplies and executed as spies.[55] American efforts to force a surrender continued, and his missing mentor, Lieutenant Someya appeared in the company of the Americans, urging the garrison to give up its futile resistance. American reconnaissance patrols landed openly on the beach and Japanese sentries, terrified of combat and of reprisals from their own leaders, ignored their presence.

Finally, the American patrol boat returned, this time carrying the captured commander of another Japanese garrison in the Keramas. He called out to the young cadet's leaders, and the American ship landed a small party on the shore. The boat withdrew and the soldiers were assembled by their commanding officer. Convinced that they were about to receive orders to commit suicide, the young cadet made his final preparations. However, the soldiers were simply told to gather on the beach. The American patrol boat returned, this time carrying a meal for the islanders. Everyone—Japanese and American soldiers, and the Okinawan villagers, sat together and voraciously consumed the feast of sliced pork and canned rations. With gestures and a few halting words, the soldiers tried to speak to each other as they ate.

The meal ended and the soldiers stood. Before anything could happen, an American chaplain offered up a prayer for peace, a prayer that was translated by a Nisei interpreter.[56] Then, the Americans returned to their boat and the Japanese soldiers to their fortifications.

At this point, Fujiki's performance again differs dramatically from rakugo. True to its name, rakugo performances tend to end with a dramatic utterance—the *ochi*, or drop—that knits together pieces of the narrative that have gone before, bringing them to a striking conclusion. Fujiki's story ends on a much more ambiguous note. Although clearly framed by the closing devices, the performance itself trails off. The passages of conversation presented through reported speech end, the protagonist's vague responses to unspoken questions make it more and more difficult to evaluate their meaning, utterances fade away into confusing fragments.

THE PHILOSOPHER AND THE STORYTELLER

I would like to contrast Fujiki's narrative with the argument that Tomiyama Ichirō presents in *Senjō no Kioku* (Memories of the battlefield). Tomiyama's argument is deployed to counteract the stultifying effect of discourses on Japanese victimization, and to attack the ideological conflation of Japanese victimization with the victims of Japanese aggression. His objective is to develop an adequate account of the complicity of individual subjects—individual Okinawan subjects—in their own oppression. Tomiyama sketches out the colonization of the everyday by disciplinary practices that produce Okinawan subjects willing to sacrifice their lives on the battlefield for the emperor and the fascist state. He is particularly concerned with the enduring nature of these practices, taking his inspiration from Tsurumi Shunsuke's observation that an individual's history is inscribed on the body like a tattoo that cannot simply be washed away and forgotten. Tomiyama explores the ongoing effect of this subjectification, particularly in the terrible tension between the continual impulse for improvement and the recognition that Okinawans can never completely become Japanese subjects.[57]

Fujiki's performance could be seen as a perfect complement to Tomiyama's argument. Like Tomiyama he is determined to explore the role of the individual subject in the war and its aftermath. Tomiyama carefully explicates the metonymic link between the desire for self-improvement (*shusse*) inculcated in the individual and the modernizing dynamic of the imperial Japanese state. Through this argument, he exposes the seeming contradictions of preparation for war within the everyday, preparations that subjects hope will lead to a future peaceful existence as Japanese citizens: "In the event that we win this East Asian War, we Okinawans will be put on the same level as the Japanese. So, if we win this war, we'll be able to go to Japan and live happily ever after with our families."[58]

In performance after performance, Fujiki portrays Okinawans who have made these sacrifices—in the Japanese colonial period, in the Pacific War, in the Koza riots, in the base land crises—and, years later, are driven to reexamine the consequences of their actions. He is particularly concerned with their determination to communicate their critical reflections to successive generations.

Like Tomiyama, Fujiki is also fascinated by the persistence of the effects of the creation of imperial subjects. In 1997, I spent some time studying standup with Fujiki: one of the first things that he had us learn was a series of routines that he developed during his days with Tamaki Mitsuru's Shōchiku Kagekidan.[59] In *Remembrance of White Sands*, Fujiki creates a brief interlude by the overt quotation of one of these earlier sketches, directing attention to the problem of the emperor and daily life. Here is his earlier routine:

OLD MAN: Doctor, my right arm won't raise up so I've come to see you. Please have a look at it.

DOCTOR: So it's your right arm, eh grandfather? Well, if that's it, let's have a look. [Examines the arm]. Well—this right arm—it's just old age!

OLD MAN: What? This arm—*old age*? Doctor, you're a liar, aren't you!

DOCTOR: What kind of a thing is that to say—calling a doctor a "liar"! Grandfather!

OLD MAN: What are you talking about—you're lying! "Right arm—old age!" I'll spell it out for you. My left arm and my right arm are the same [age] but it [the left arm] goes up without any problem! [The old man raises his left arm for the doctor.]

Fujiki transforms this manzai-style performance into the following passage:

> The effect of the education under tennōsei that I had in those days was profound. What was tennōsei? It seemed like whenever the least thing happened, we'd all shout, "Tennō heika, banzai!—Ten thousand years life to the emperor!"
>
> [Caught up in his recollections, the old man tries to throw up his arms as he shouts. He stops abruptly, grimacing in pain.]
>
> Ah! I can't raise my arm any higher than my shoulder! When I go to the doctor, he tells me that it's just old age. Kind of strange, don't you think? If it's just age, my left and right arms are both the same, aren't they? Then why is it that my left arm is fine? These days, it's getting to be that you can't even believe doctors! Ouch!
>
> [When the pain subsides, he returns to his reminiscences.][60]

As he reminisces about the war years, the old man cannot simply explain the imperial system to his grandson. Even after the passage of so many years, his account becomes more immediate and he cannot help but give physical expression to the cry of "Tennō heika, banzai!" The interlude becomes an opportunity for a manzai-style joke about aging—an interlude that actually serves to highlight the gravity of the moment. Yet, for Fujiki, this continued physical embodiment of commitment to the emperor is also accompanied by persistent pain. Fujiki's concern with the moments of inscription is also interesting and complex. Though he shares Tomiyama's interest in the ongoing effects of discipline, Fujiki also wants to direct attention to the already existing subject onto whom these technologies were inscribed and to the irresolvable tensions that this inscription produces.

In addition to the jarring use of a manzai reference to discuss the lingering embodied elements of fascism, Fujiki uses the circulation of set phrases from the utterances of the Japanese military officers to those of the young cadet in order to demonstrate the ideological inscription of the Okinawans. Thus, phrases such as "Gyokusai,"[61] "Ichinin jūsatu,"[62] and "Minasan ga kono shima no tame, nipponkoku no tame ni inochi o oshimazu, tataitte iru no ni jibun dake ikinokoru ki wa arimasen"[63] circulate from character to character in the imbedded dialogs, and weave into the aged protagonist's recollections. It is clear that the young protagonist does not adopt them for reasons of understanding and agreement with their meaning in relationship to discourses of Japanese fascism. Quite the contrary—he does so because of the situation of these utterances in the social field of wartime Kerama. It is less his understanding of *gyokusai* as such than his desire for the approbation of his senior officers that leads him to deploy the phrase in his own discourse.

The young cadet's earnest efforts as a laborer for the Japanese garrison parallel this: he works with great dedication to excavate a trench in which something called a *marure* can be hidden; however, in discussion with the garrison commander, Major Noda, the cadet admits that he has no idea what a marure is. Major Noda's explanation that the marure is a torpedo boat in no way clarifies his confusion. In fact, it is never clear that the cadet recognized that these torpedo boats were the maritime equivalent of kamikaze aircraft such as the Ōka.[64] Perhaps this is why Someya presents him with a dictionary. For whatever reason, he is simply proud that Major Noda took the time to speak with him, a common Okinawan conscript, and to praise his efforts.

Unlike many commentators, Fujiki avoids a facile reduction of Okinawan culture to some functional principle by which practices are structured—for example, by Okinawan *yasashisa*, or gentleness. In fact, he goes to great lengths to show that his character embraces militarization, that it is his desire that drives him to become a soldier. An existent Okinawan subject is not simply overwritten by Japanese military discipline; instead, there is a profoundly important element of enjoyment to the process of transformation.

But there were good times too! It's not very interesting if all we do is talk about death. Listen to this funny story. This is my favorite one. We didn't actually shoot, but we practiced aiming in, crawling, etcetera. My heart pounding, I practiced as hard as I could. Once, we stood in formation while Major Noda, the commander of all island forces, addressed us. I was elated when he told us:

"You lads look like fine Japanese soldiers too."

And so, one time I got permission to take my rifle home with me. Bursting with happiness, I immediately grabbed it and went home. Lietenant Someya was there drinking at my house—in fact, he was already drunk. When he saw that I was carrying a rifle, he came to his feet and drew down on me with his pistol.

"Don't be so ecstatic because you are carrying a gun. If you want to die, I'll be more than happy to kill you anytime."

fujiki hayato, the storyteller

Saying this, he holstered his pistol—but the sickening feeling remained. That wasn't enjoyable at all. . . . What was that? . . . I did say that I'd tell you a funny story, but. . . .

In the person of the young Okinawan cadet, Fujiki recalls the earnest admiration and longing that characterized prewar songs like "Tsuyoi Nihonjin" and "Hadashi Kinrei no Uta,"[65] a sense of affect that is often missing from their ironic performances today.

At the same time, Fujiki points to the impossibility of finalizing these networks of practices for producing a totalized imperial subject. Tomiyama draws a similar conclusion, with the exception that this imperfect transformation continues to motivate subjects' commitment to the imperial project. For Fujiki, Okinawan culture—the same culture that somehow articulated with Japanese militarization—also empowers the recognition of the peril of becoming Japanese. Neither Lieutenant Someya's rational argumentation nor physical intimidation can convince the cadet of the profound flaws in the imperial project. It is the cadet's participation in the counterattack against the American landing force that foregrounds these contradictions. The Okinawan cadet is not simply brought around by the horrors of war—he has, after all, already seen his own neighbors executed for accepting food from an American patrol. Rather, it is the specificity of the carnage in his village that shocks him. There, among the wreckage of his neighbors' houses, he sees pigs tearing at the bodies of the dead. In a rural Okinawan community, this would have been the ultimate inversion of the accepted life cycle. It is man who eats the entrails of pigs on festive occasions, not pigs who are to feast on the entrails of man.[66]

In one expertly constructed image, the contradictions of the entire project of Japanification are revealed. The prohibition against quartering pigs in outdoor privies, an important tenet of Okinawan seikatsu kaizen, was more than an attempt to subject Okinawans to Japanese hygienic regimes. It was an intervention that interrupted the recovery of that portion of residents' mabui (spirit) that was traditionally thought to be discharged along with excrement. If not recovered by the household's pigs, this spirit could not be returned to the household through the periodic consumption of pigs' flesh. Over time, this spirit would be lost. In Fujiki's narrative, these practices lead not so much to the production of a Japanese subject but to the destruction of

fujiki hayato, the storyteller

an Okinawan one. Tomiyama argued that many Okinawan soldiers believed that the sacrifice of their own lives could enable subsequent generations to become Japanese; in Fujiki's narrative, becoming Japanese requires this sacrifice. It is a process that yields the extinction of the Okinawan way of life, not its transformation.

Insofar as Fujiki's performance presents a critique of the destruction of a way of life, it does so through a narrative that is profoundly influenced by traditional forms. In Okinawa, there are a host of myths that deal with the human mediation of the relationship between the autochthonous deities of sea and land. This mediation often involves the efforts of the islanders to eke out a living in an environment where neither the land nor the sea can, by itself, sustain life. Once, during a visit to Kudaka Island with the poet Takara Ben and the native ethnologist Akamine Masanobu, I mentioned Fujiki's *Remembrance of White Sands* as a thoughtful engagement with memories of wartime responsibility. As we discussed his performance, they suggested that one of the myths of Kudaka resonated powerfully with his example of mediation.

Long, long ago, as they say, a young islander on the eastern shore of Kudaka sees a ceramic urn carried along by the waves just beyond the surf zone. Frustrated in his attempts to catch it in his fishing net, he walks to one of the sacred groves. His prayers to the deity of the grove are answered, and he is given detailed instructions that must be followed exactly if he is to catch the floating object. He returns to the beach and hurries through the prayers before again trying to catch the urn. But he has been careless in his recitation and fails once again. A second time he returns to the grove, a second time he fails to correctly perform the ritual, a second time he fails to catch the urn. Finally, he returns to the grove for a third time, pays careful attention to the instructions of the deity, correctly performs the required prayers and offerings, and succeeds in catching the crock. He drags it up on the beach and cracks it open. Inside are the grains—barley, millet, and wild rice—that will allow him to begin to cultivate the sandy soil of Kudaka. In this myth and in most of the others, the act of mediation is complex, difficult, and fraught with dangers. If the required tasks are not performed, the mediation can only fail. And if the mediation succeeds, it does so only on a contingent basis—it only provides the possibility of survival for now.[67]

Fujiki's narrative unfolds in strikingly similar terms. The young cadet's survival depends on the successful mediation of the relationship between the Japanese entrenched in their inland fortifications and the American patrols arriving from the sea to the east. Again and again, the islanders try to successfully negotiate these two poles. In this case, the failure to correctly mediate the relationship produces catastrophe: after the food that the Americans unload on the beach is eaten, the villagers are executed by the Japanese soldiers. Even the commensal meeting of the Japanese (who come down from their fortifications) and the Americans (who come up from the sea) yields only a temporary respite: shortly thereafter, the battle resumes. It is at this point that the difference between Fujiki's narrative and the mythic narrative begins to emerge. In the case of the Kudaka myth, the young man learns that correct performance of the necessary rituals earns the beneficence of the deities of land and sea. In Fujiki's narrative, the young man learns that it is impossible to mediate the relationship between the Americans and the Japanese with any certainty of success; and yet, to fail to attempt this mediation will lead to more immediate destruction. What Fujiki's performance does is to shift emphasis from the correct performance of mediation to the absolute necessity for subjects to undertake action.

Considering the relationship between the Americans and the Japanese in Fujiki's narrative in terms of the deities of sea and land, of east and west, also serves to highlight their mutual incommensurability. Perhaps this is the work of Fujiki's performance—to recover the content once signified by Okinawan deities and to contrast it with that signified by the Japanese state. Rather than implying their authenticity, equating Japanese and American forces with these autochthonous deities immediately foregrounds the constructedness of their status. In the case of the Japanese state, it also emphasizes the role of the Okinawan people in its construction. Here, Fujiki's image of Okinawan volunteers energetically excavating Japanese fortifications is particularly poignant: it is Okinawan labor and Okinawan practice that have created the Japanese state in Okinawan social space. While Fujiki's narrative shows the possibility of an everyday in which one can mediate the relationship between humans and deities, it also shows an everyday in which the objectified structures of society are turned against the very laborers who produced them. The Japanese garrison, entrenched in Okinawa by Okinawan labor, proceeds to mobilize these same Okinawan volunteers and lead them to their destruction.

fujiki hayato, the storyteller

Fujiki's work is far from a nostalgic meditation on the past. In many of his performances, we are shown a relationship between the destruction of a traditional way of life and the production of the idea of tradition, a tradition that becomes suffused with a sense of longing and loss. Yet we also see that the Okinawan past has not yet been resolved to the totalizing practices of the modern Japanese state. At the same time, Okinawa is not shown as an authentic, utopian alternative to Japanese social organization. For Fujiki's Okinawa is not only at odds with the modern Japanese present; it is itself marked by inherent contradictions and conflicts that can no longer be resolved, that have had their future progress obstructed. The disquieting experience of these differing temporalities enables the cadet to recognize the contradictions in his everyday life. And yet, the ambiguities of this recognition made it difficult to resolve his choices to one form or another. He aspires to be a brave Japanese soldier, but he stops short of sacrificing his own life. He admires the ambiguous, militarized generosity of the Americans, but he does not follow Lieutenant Someya's defection. He sees the possibility of a resolution of conflict through traditional commensal practices, but he returns to military discipline. It is this emphasis on choice— even in the form of failed choices or the failure to choose—that is essential to understanding Fujiki's project. This is what the grandfather tries to impart to his grandson on the beach in Kerama. Individuals do not simply instantiate cultural forms; they are not merely interpellated into social structures. It is the action of individuals that reproduces these forms, and Fujiki's performances demonstrate that there are points at which the action of individuals have the capacity to transform them.

The careful explication of the cadet's narrative resonates with Fujiki's listeners' understandings of their own history, their memories, their experiences of the everyday. He opens a space to engage the contradictions that have been enacted, to work through them in a critical manner. Again and again, he returns to the practices of the past. As in the narrative of the traveling salesman, he shows that these practices have not been discredited by failure. Instead, the possibility remains that their potential can still be recovered in the context of the everyday.

Fujiki's own argument remains open. Solutions to the crises of wartime Okinawa that confronted the protagonist as a youth are not presented in the interpretations given by the aged narrator. Neither do they appear in Fujiki's own commentaries addressed directly to the audience. Rather, they are found in the utterances of Lieutenant Someya, Major Noda, and others. Fujiki can recall them, give them voice in the imperfect dialogs that he presents. He does no more.

His guests are encouraged to explore for themselves the possibilities of traditional practices; they are not provided with traditional answers to modern problems. Still, he is clear in the nature of his own choices. His performances are, as I have discussed above, critical interventions. They are also, in their own right, productive acts that transfer value—karī—to the audience, attempting to reconfigure traditional praxis in a manner adequate to the crises of the everyday. Where once karī enabled farmers and fishermen to persevere through the hardships of their daily lives, it is now imparted to Fujiki's audience so that they can struggle through life in the modern world. In this sense, Fujiki's performances are profoundly political, articulating an ethical practice configured around a politics of hope, hope in the transformative powers of the past.

And yet, as the lights came up and the audience rose to depart, I wondered how many people were reached by this message and how they would respond. Throughout the performance, I had watched faces of the people who sat around me—excited, actively listening. I saw them laughing as they left for home, enjoying the final moments of a relaxing interlude in their busy lives. But what comes next? What do they take away with them? Are they inspired to act on the possibilities that Fujiki has described? Are they conscious of the karī that they have received, energized by its transmission? Or are his performances no more than moments of distraction, of no more import than his innocuous portrayal of an inoffensive Okinawan bar owner in the NHK television series *Churasan*.

the heritage of his times

teruya rinsuke and ethnographic storytelling

Perhaps I know best why man alone laughs: he alone suffers so deeply that he had to invent laughter. The unhappiest and most melancholy animal is, as fitting, the most cheerful.—FRIEDRICH NIETZSCHE, *The Will to Power*

It wouldn't be quite right if I were to say that because I am a fuyūnā [an idler], I do nothing but play—it is rather that all of the difficult things in the world overcome me, making me a troubled man. And because I am an indolent man, I cause great troubles. This is what it means to be a man of the world. But even if I say that I am a man of the world, it is not because I have accumulated experience and I really understand the way things are in this life. Rather, I have endured the punishments of the heavens and this has made me worldly. In order to escape from this worldliness, I cannot turn away from drinking. That is the curse of this life.—TERUYA RINSUKE, *Terurin Jiden*

In the months following Fujiki Hayato's performance at the Nakamurake, I continued to think about his work and his efforts to create a critical performative genre capable of addressing contemporary social and political conditions. As Fujiki was always quick to admit, he drew on a long tradition of performance and scholarship. Without the inspiration and the engagement of older Okinawan artists and scholars, he said that he would probably still be a mailman. For Fujiki, the most important of those older performers was Teruya Rinsuke (Terurin). Both Fujiki and Tamaki Mitsuru suggested that Terurin's engagement with the Japanese academic discipline of native ethnology, or minzokugaku would be of interest to me as well. As I began to learn about Terurin's work, I was fascinated by its depth and complexity. It seemed that Terurin was able to manipulate the conventions of minzokugaku in order to locate a sense of agency for the Okinawan people, and explore their culture as a powerful resource for operating in the modern world.

PERFORMANCE AND DEVELOPMENT

We stood in Teruya district of Koza at the crossroads—Koza Jūjiro—where two former military highways met, the wide asphalt pavement sticky in the summer heat. The afternoon sun was intense, pressing down on me like a weight and reflecting back up from the pavement. The wooden and concrete buildings that lined the street had a look of age and disrepair—paint faded, windows covered, signs darkened or missing. It was hard to believe that all of this had been rebuilt in the sixties, and that thirty years ago this was "The Bush," a maze of bars and clubs catering to African American GIs, a hotbed of Black Panther political activity, and neighbor to the warren of brothels that someone in either an optimistic or ironic moment named Yoshiwara.[1] In 1969, antiwar anger and racial tension between African American and white soldiers exploded here in rioting that left American military vehicles burning in the street and armed patrols maintaining order.[2] In the postreversion years all the life seemed to have been drained from the neighborhood. Although it was Saturday afternoon, the streets were deserted and the steel shutters had already been pulled down over the windows of the few remaining businesses. Across the street, a Self-Defense Force sergeant began to bring large advertising placards back into the recruiting office.

My wife Atsuko and I turned from Route 330 into a series of streets that had been enclosed to create a shopping arcade. Sunlight filtered down through the tinted panels that covered the street, casting a greenish glow across the glossy decorative tiles that had been used to repave the walkway. Banners promoting the businesses of the Gintengai[3] hung from the rafters. However, it was clear that business was slow throughout Koza. Most of the shops inside the arcade were closed, and those that remained open were largely deserted.

Okinawa in 1997 was in the grip of economic uncertainty. Postbubble Japan remained in recession, and Okinawa was one of the more profoundly affected areas. Although the actions of the central government had temporarily resolved the issue of renewing the leases of central Okinawan lands for American military use, the revenues directly generated by these leases as well as by on-base employment were inadequate to stabilize the Okinawan economy.[4] Unemployment remained high—double that of the national average—

the heritage of his times

Okinawa City Shopping Center

and underemployment an even more persistent problem. Plans to create primary industry in Okinawa had not been seriously considered since reversion, and Okinawan tourism was threatened by diminished disposable income among Japanese consumers and better value for the tourist yen in rival sites such as Hawaii.

Once considered untouchable, the reduction or elimination of the so-called *omoiyari yosan*, or "sympathy budget," was also being discussed in political circles. This massive subsidy from the central government was intended to address the injustice of having American military bases in Okinawa and to enable the prefecture to pay for labor costs and facility maintenance associated with the bases. Linked to this were enormous investments in public works projects in Okinawa. Okinawa has the highest level of dependence on publicly funded, capital-intensive development projects of any prefecture in Japan—an estimated five trillion yen had been spent since reversion.

The two main Okinawan banks were in crisis, rumored to be on the verge of collapse. At the same time, studies considering the feasibility of innovative prefectural development projects such as the creation of a regional free trade zone yielded ambiguous results. Experiments with a limited model in Naha were hampered by central governmental interference, as well as the inability to provide the necessary legal exemptions and attract viable businesses.[5]

Okinawa City was one of the more severely affected regions of central Okinawa. The massive sprawl of Kadena Air Base, the Awase Communication Facility, and ammunition storage sites occupied a significant amount of the physical space of the city. While the bases still generated revenues for landowners, individual and municipal, they blocked any other conceivable use of the land. The continued reduction in on-base jobs diminished what was once one of the primary sources of income in the area. At the same time, the service industry in Koza, catering as it once did to American military personnel from Kadena Air Base and the complex of Marine bases to the north, was deeply affected by several related factors. The recent rape incident, still fresh in the memory of many Okinawans and Americans, had a profoundly chilling effect on commerce in Koza. New policies had been initiated by the military command, restricting the hours that servicemen were free to travel off-base, and certain areas were placed off limits at all times. On the Okinawan side, a number of clubs and restaurants declared a "No Americans" policy, sacrificing American patronage for what they hoped was the security of their Japanese customers. Perhaps more to the point, the revaluation of the dollar against the yen during the mid-1980s had the concomitant effect of severely limiting the buying power of American servicemen and these effects became increasingly pronounced in the 1990s. Additionally, the American bases had undertaken projects (funded by the Japanese government) of increasing both on-base housing and services, and it had become possible for most servicemen and their families to spend their entire tour on Okinawa within the confines of the network of American facilities.

Okinawa responded to this economic crisis on a number of levels. The prefecture continued to press for state subsidies while struggling to set a timetable for the reduction of U.S. forces on the island. At the same time, they continued in their efforts to initiate projects such the aforementioned free trade zone. In addition, the recently announced plans to build an American helicopter base in the Nago region of Okinawa had sparked a new cycle of antibase ruminations, and the upcoming gubernatorial race promised to be especially acrimonious. The position of the incumbent governor, Ōta Masahide, had been compromised by his perceived equivocation in his opposition to base lease renewals and his credibility with the Left had been severely eroded. He was also associated in the popular imagination with the failure to either deliver a clear decision about the future of the bases or ensure the economic security of the prefecture, despite months of controversy.[6] His administration was open to a strong challenge from the candidate put forward by the coalition of Okinawan conservative parties and he had also become a target for conservative groups at the national level, who directed considerable funds into local political war chests.

A number of regional plans for development had also been put forward. Efforts to resuscitate cane production, establish innovative aquaculture programs, revitalize the tourist industry, and create local projects such as dam and highway construction that could articulate with prefectural projects were common. The question of development was of profound concern in Okinawa City, and the incipient mayoral contest between the incumbent, Arakawa Shūsei, and the challenger, Nakasone Masakazu, promised to turn on which candidate had the ability to bring a massive construction project to the east coast in Awase. The prefecture had already established a research center in the area for the purpose of exploring and exploiting the potential of subtropical islands. Now, Nakasone's platform called for the construction of an island in Awase Bay, on which a futuristic complex of high-tech industry, regional trade, modern entertainment, and residential centers would be located. Although it was unclear precisely what businesses would occupy this new island, the construction revenues alone generated by the project would have a profound effect on the regional economy: Nakasone claimed that it would create five thousand new jobs and generate three hundred billion yen in revenue. However, the project was already deeply controversial. In addition to the economic uncertainties noted above, construction promised extreme ecological damage, as well as the destruction of fishing, aquaculture, and salt extraction in the Awase Bay area.[7]

The Ryūkyū Broadcasting Company (RBC), one of the primary prefecture-wide mass communication services (radio and television), presented a series of broadcasts dealing with the regional development issues that I outlined above. In the case of Okinawa City, the RBC discussion[8] focused on the role of local cultural production in strengthening the economic base. Discussants noted the success of local events such as the "Peaceful Love Festival"—a two-day outdoor rock concert featuring local and national artists. Mention was also made of a proposal by Okinawa City to renovate the stricken neighborhoods Nakanomachi and Sentā—once the main entertainment districts catering to American servicemen—creating mixed residential and commercial districts organized around a central plaza featuring venues for Okinawan performing arts. And soon, the discussion turned to the concept of "Koza Dokuritsu Koku." Playing on the ambiguities of the Japanese formulation, the term could be translated as either the Independent Nation of Koza, or Koza, the Country of Independence. This formulation has been long attributed to the comedian Teruya Rinsuke, who had proclaimed himself its president, and his home both its capital and its embassy to the rest of Japan.

Given the emphasis on monumental, capital-intensive development throughout Okinawa, I thought that it was fascinating that the performances of artists such as Terurin were seen as part of this project. Of course, any scheme to build a tourist economy requires a product to market to visitors. At the same time, it seemed to me that recognition of local artists and practices was as much a part of *hondonami*, or "catching up with the mainland," as massive development schemes. The identification of the value of local culture could be read as opposition to the ideology of shusse—self-improvement—that Fujiki critiqued (as recounted in the previous chapter). However, it could also be seen as an index of the hopes of those anxious to catch up to the mainland that Okinawa was at least as culturally complex and sophisticated as the rest of Japan.

At the top of the main street of the arcade, the local community access radio station FM Champla[9] had opened a satellite studio in a vacant storefront and created a small performance space in one of the many empty buildings nearby. Several dozen people stood in front of the small auditorium as staff members and announcers from the radio station hurried back and forth to their offices.

As we joined the crowd, the station manager opened the performance

the heritage of his times

Teruya Rinsuke in performance at the Gintengai

space and let everyone inside. The room was small, with about fifty folding chairs set up in front of a raised stage. A blue plastic tarp had been spread between the chairs and the stage so that people could comfortably sit on the floor. Fifteen or twenty older people sat on the tarp while small groups of younger people found seats. Technicians from the radio station and a sound engineer checked the equipment on the stage. The room was plainly finished, the stage undecorated. A folding chair, two mike stands, and a kind of wheeled trunk that contained a floor monitor and a music stand stood on the stage.

At 4:30, the station manager stepped out on the stage and welcomed everyone to the Gintengai. He said that he hoped that events like this would help to attract business and bring popular entertainment back to the neighborhood. He was looking forward to FM Champla being a part of the revitalization of the community. Then, with a bow he introduced the featured performer, Teruya Rinsuke. The audience, now filling the folding seats and the space to the front of the stage, applauded heartily.

Because of ill health, Terurin[10] performed less frequently, usually in the small theater at the Terurinkan[11] or other venues in Okinawa City. His steps

the heritage of his times

were uncertain as his assistant helped him to his seat. He painfully adjusted his position and lifted a musical instrument from the trunk to his left. He connected it to a cable running along the floor and began to tune it. Unlike the three-stringed acoustic *sanshin* that is the mainstay of Okinawan folk music, this instrument had an additional string and an internal microphone. It was, he said, a *yonshin*.[12]

Terurin's appearance was remarkable. He was in his mid-sixties and heavy set. He wore a large, floppy beret—or perhaps a shower cap—decorated with white and yellow hibiscus blossoms, a bright red blazer over a tie-dyed T-shirt, and violet and white *kehan*[13] strapped over his jeans. And yet, despite his attire, he maintained an aura of solemnity, of dignity as he prepared for his performance. He spread several sheets of paper out on the music stand, settled the yonshin on his lap, and adjusted his enormous butterscotch-framed glasses.

"Well then, I think that I should like to begin today's class at once." Terurin spoke in a rich, mellifluous voice—famous throughout Okinawa, and recognizable in much of Japan. Formal, measured, the voice of one accustomed to public oratory.

STORYTELLING AND MINZOKUGAKU

It is striking that Terurin should choose an academic motif to present his musings on Okinawan history and culture. He is an accomplished performer, trained in Okinawa classical and popular genres, and could easily use Okinawan vernacular styles. In a career that spans more than half a century, Terurin has acted as the host and lead performer of a stage review and radio variety show, was an advertising spokesman in both regional and national campaigns, and a writer in newspapers, books, and magazines published both locally and nationally, and remains a popular recording artist (both as a solo performer, with other artists such as Noborikawa Seijun [or Sēgwa] and the late Kadekaru Rinshō, and in collaboration with his son Teruya Rinken, leader of the eponymous Rinken Band). In recent years, he had acted in a number of films, often working with the experimental film-maker Takamine Gō, whose *Untamagiru* received the Caligari Award at the Berlin Film Festival in 1990. However, most often Terurin chose to work within a genre that resembles nothing so much as a folklorist's lecture—a lecture whose seriousness is problematized through his dress and his choice of venue, but a lecture nevertheless.

In fact, the presentation of self as a scholar in general and a folklorist in specific has a long history in Okinawan performance. Terurin himself is certainly inspired by the work of Onaha Būten,[14] who regularly appeared as both a doctor and a teacher in his performances.[15] Terurin's student Tamaki Mitsuru and members of Tamaki's troupe[16] often appear in the role of doctors or professors at the University of the Ryukyus.

I learned more about the experiences that Terurin drew upon to create this self-representation when I appeared with him at a public forum concerning Okinawan culture held in November 1997 at the Koza Café in Okinawa City. In addition to Terurin and me, the panel included the comedian Fujiki Hayato and the musician and former drummer of the bands Murasaki and Condition Green, Miyanaga Eiichi (or Chibi); it was moderated by Tamaki Mitsuru—who was himself dressed as a researcher, wearing a white laboratory coat. Tamaki had invited me to join the discussion, and, although I knew the other members of the panel, it was my first opportunity to talk with Terurin at any length. He asked me about my fieldwork and my academic training. With a sly smile, he told me that he had a long-standing interest in anthropology. He mentioned a number of prominent anthropologists and folklorists at Japanese universities, as well as commentators and critics with whom he regularly corresponded. Then, he told me that he had a bit of formal training himself.

During the American occupation, several universities were established in Okinawa. The most prominent, the University of the Ryukyus, was built during the occupation. The campus stood in the ruins of Shuri Castle, which had been occupied by the Japanese army as headquarters for the 32nd Army and destroyed in the battle of Okinawa.[17] A number of other colleges were then built in central Okinawa, including Kokusai Daigaku (International University) in Koza.[18] Terurin told me that as soon as he heard that there would be a university in Koza, he made up his mind to study there. Initially, he was refused admission because he had never completed high school. Eventually, one of the professors, a fan of Terurin's popular radio performances, interceded on his behalf, and he was accepted as a special student. For the next eight years, he audited classes in folklore, anthropology, and psychology. Even now, his performances frequently contain references to the work of prominent Japanese native ethnologists such as Yanagita Kunio, as well as European intellectual figures such as Freud, Bergson, and Huizinga.

While this explains Terurin's familiarity with native ethnology, among other academic disciplines, I do not think that it completely accounts for Terurin's presentation of self as a native ethnologist. I would argue that his choice is also tied to the history of Okinawa as an ethnographic object, a history that has long been a deep and personal concern for him. Terurin has developed a new performative style that synthesizes elements such as popular song and storytelling with ethnographic research and the academic lecture. It also enables Terurin to recover the authoritative perspective from which to examine Okinawan culture, a point that I will return to later in the chapter.

From the moment of its incorporation into the Meiji state, Okinawa has been subjected to intense ethnographic analysis and nativist speculation. While these projects were, for the most part, directed from the governmental and academic centers of mainland Japan, they have also entailed ambivalent and complex levels of Okinawan participation.

The intellectual historian and cultural critic Tomiyama Ichirō opens a discussion of this problem in his study of the relationship between the ethnographer Torii Ryuzo and the Okinawan scholar Iha Fuyū.[19] Having secured the national boundaries of Japan, the early Meiji state apparatus turned its attention to the peoples that it had encompassed, focusing on those at the spatial margins of the state. Sponsored in his research by the Meiji government, Torii worked extensively in colonial Taiwan and Okinawa, parsing the physical characteristics and cultural practices of the people of these islands so that the difference that he knew must obtain between the Japanese and the non-Japanese could be documented. Tomiyama argues that in order to produce a naturalized, unmarked Japanese identity, Torii relied on the concept of "the Okinawan" to mediate relations with those outside the southern boundary of Japan, such as the indigenous Taiwanese. As a consequence of this displaced comparative project, it was as necessary to observe and categorize the Okinawans (who were to stand for the unmarked Japanese) as it was to observe and categorize the aboriginal Taiwanese, and to repress all similarity between these two categories.

Iha Fuyū worked closely with Torii, as both colleague and a kind of native informant. A subtle scholar, Iha recognized the tension and contradictions involved in Torii's project. Iha was skeptical of the possibility of creating a category of "the Japanese folk" to which the Okinawans—the Ryūkyūans—could be both included on the basis of equality while at the same time subordinated to the Japanese of the main islands. At the same time, he was committed to a project of modernization and development in Okinawa. However, he was concerned that the project to develop Okinawa could result in the categorization of Okinawans as more primitive than the rest of Japan, closer to the natives of the South Pacific on a scale of differing temporalities. He articulated the idea that both the contemporary Japanese and the Ryūkyūans (or the Nantōjin, the people of the southern regions, as he categorized them in a new formulation) were descended from a common people, a proto-Japanese folk. There is a kind of hope to this project, an optimism that the dynamic movement toward the future, through modernization, could also have a recursive movement back to an ideal common past. And yet Tomiyama argues that the effect was precisely the opposite, that the benefits of modernization were inseparable from incorporation into the space of modern Japan, and that Iha would be silenced, left unable to even communicate in his native tongue what it meant to be Okinawan.

Inspired by Iha's scholarly work, the seminal Japanese folklorist Yanagita Kunio also turned his attention to Okinawa. However, Yanagita was less concerned with the need to categorize the people who comprised the Japanese state than his determination to come to grips with the uneven experience of capitalist modernization.[20] For Yanagita, the practice of folklore research became a strategy to compensate for the profound transformations of everyday life that accompanied industrialization and modernization. It was his hope that a more authentic life might still be available in the countryside. At the same time, he tried to highlight the inequity of the material, social conditions that existed in rural Japan, the hardship and deprivation of the everyday.[21] Configured within the framework of social scientific research, these considerations led Yanagita to the margins of Japan, to the sites that the unevenness of modern capitalist development have left closer to his originary ideal.[22]

Yanagita felt that Okinawa was an inexhaustible resource of material that he could utilize in order to construct his ideal model of the authentic Japanese folk. He believed that traveling to this spatially distant edge of Japan would also enable him to move backward in time, to recover the past in the present. In spite of Okinawa's legacy of colonial subordination and social and economic deprivation, Yanagita made the startling observation that Okinawa was isolated from foreign contact, free from the accretions of Buddhism, "a preserve of the unconscious archaic customs that can no longer be seen in Japan, [that] holds the key to understanding the doubts and fears of the modern Japanese."[23] While Iha had developed a triadic set of categories— the contemporary Ryūkyūans and Japanese, both descended from the archaic Japanese—Yanagita collapses this into a binary: the contemporary Japanese in the main islands and the archaic Japanese still present in the customs and practices of Okinawa. Yanagita was convinced that the study of daily life in Okinawa would yield an understanding of the social forms of archaic Japan, practices and beliefs that could then be redeployed to restore meaning to the everyday of modern Japan.[24]

Still, there are a number of questions that demand a response. What of contemporary Okinawans, whose coeval existence is effaced by Yanagita's formulation? What of the status of folk practices—particularly those of the Okinawans—in contemporary Japan? The emphasis that Yanagita placed on the relationships that comprised his ideal of Japanese daily life produces a jarring sense of incongruity when one recognizes that the social conditions within which these practices and relations emerged had been irrevocably transformed. Is his project then one of nostalgia, albeit one that mobilizes nostalgia, as Gerald Figal argues, in order to shatter complacency with the conditions of the present?[25] If, however, these practices can be recovered, for whom and by whom?

During his Gintengai performance, Terurin began with a brief introduction in formal Japanese, emphasizing his long history as a storyteller in the tradition of mainland benshi[26] and as a student of Onaha Būten. Then, he paused to intone a brief prayer in liturgical Ryūkyūan, an invocation requesting that the local deities transfer karī or good fortune to the audience.[27] Having completed his prayer, he paused and addressed the audience:

It's often said that everything that Terurin says is a lie. However, the truth of the matter is that this statement itself is a lie. I want you to think that the contents of my stories are entirely made up, that they are nothing but a mass of lies. But that lie is different from an average lie. It is a real lie that's been packaged so that it looks like the truth. Out of self-interest, I've gone to great lengths to show that my remarks can't just be dismissed as being self-serving.

the heritage of his times

The truth is that there are so many liars nowadays that go around insisting, "The lies that I am telling are true!"—now, this isn't me that I'm talking about. When people other than me are telling you, "It's true, it's true," then they're lying. . . .

You must recall that the idea that I am a liar is, in fact, the truth. However, while acknowledging that I am a liar, you must see that this lie is entirely a real lie so there isn't a single thing in it that is true. The fact that there isn't an iota of truth in it is, in fact, totally true—this is what I think that I would like to get you to believe. So, here's a fabulous lie that might be of use to you in the future—if I were to say what that might be, I'll have to let you in on something. I can't say if it's true or a lie but, if I were to be pressed, I would say that it seems real but it might all be a lie.

More and more, this discussion gets to be unintelligible, doesn't it? The conclusion of my discussion must be that that which you don't understand must be the truth. Understanding that you must pretend to understand is a useful thing that no one understands. And all the more so if you don't understand the value of practicing saying, "Yes, sensei, I understand."

The audience reacts throughout Terurin's narrative with laughter, but a laughter that becomes increasingly uncomfortable as his locutions become more complex and contradictory. In interviews and conversation, Terurin regularly notes that he is fond of word games, and the constant playful inversions and reversals of this speech are perfect examples of his interest. However, wordplay alone is inadequate to explain his speech. Up until this point, he had worked to establish his credibility with the audience: he had recounted his personal history, demonstrated his linguistic mastery by switching effortlessly from standard Japanese to colloquial Okinawan to liturgical Ryūkyūan, and shown his performative grasp of public oration and Okinawan music and prayer. What purpose does it serve for Terurin to both evoke and challenge the authority that inheres in the work of ethnographers —the authority that he has practically produced?

If we understand Terurin's comments to remain within the performative character of the folklorist, the scholar, they are quite startling. Terurin's scholar exposes—confesses—his own failures to understand, his self-serving pretensions to knowledge, his uncritical subordination to authority. The laughter of the comedian and the duplicity of the scholar intertwine.

the heritage of his times

His remarks recall the tension that Iha Fuyū felt between his discomfort at Torii's formulations of Okinawan culture and his own support of the project of Japanese modernization. They also resonate with Harootunian's criticism of Yanagita's nativist ethnology and Yanagita's silence on its recuperation by the expansionist fascist state. Harootunian notes that Yanagita was moved to establish folklore studies because of his concern with the effects of capitalist modernization, the consequences of uneven development and the destruction of rural lifeways. However, native ethnology soon turned to practices and social forms defined by the putative absence of modern capitalist influence. As a consequence, this form of nativist analysis yields a historically indeterminate conception of the past, and a collective notion of the folk. At the same time, the work of ethnologists assumed a definite political valence when the ethnographic object was expanded to the contours of the Japanese state. As Harootunian argues, folklore studies then not only fail to provide a critique of modern capitalist society but were actually recovered by the imperial Japanese state through the logic of a "communal body" that could incorporate other members of the Asian community in its corporal form.[28]

Speaking as a native ethnologist, Terurin reveals not simply a scholar's dishonesty and stupidity, but his own awareness of this incompetence. It is a scathing indictment of cynical authority. How can traditional forms of satire and criticism, dependent as they are on exposing the posturings of the elite to ridicule, be effective against this kind of presentation? It is no longer enough to unmask the ideological constructs that distort social reality. This is precisely the situation that the critic Slavoj Žižek points to in his discussion of Peter Sloterdijk's *The Critique of Cynical Reason*: "The cynical subject is quite aware of the distance between the ideological mask and the social reality, but he none the less still insists upon the mask. The formula as proposed by Sloterdijk would then be: 'they know very well what they are doing but still they are doing it.' "[29]

And yet, having made this point, Terurin continues his performance, his ethnographic storytelling. One could perhaps argue that remaining within the compromised character of the folklorist simply instantiates Terurin's criticism, albeit to a point of absurdity. However, it seems to me that Terurin holds out an urgent hope for nativist ethnology, one that he maintains despite its failures in the past.

It is here that Terurin's intervention becomes particularly salient. Far from rejecting folklore, Terurin attempts to critically reevaluate its insights, shifting emphasis from the undifferentiated masses of the folk to a collection of cunning, active subjects. He speaks of Okinawans who can conform to the status quo, function in the world of labor and of Japan, and master the rules of the factory or the workshop. At the same time, they have another way of thinking that is grounded in a reserve of traditional rites, practices, beliefs, and expressions. They draw on their experiences of exploitation, hardship, and repression that they share with their neighbors and fellow workers. The way in which they bring these practices together continually exposes hierarchy and order to ironic criticism.

While this clearly resonates with the kind of Gramscian notion of common sense that has motivated Western scholarship since at least E. P. Thompson, it seems that Terurin is driven by his own practical rethinking of the nativist valorization of traditional practice found in the work of Yanagita and his successors. It is the ambiguous and contradictory dynamic of this appeal to and critique of ethnographic authority that is central to Terurin's project. He is urging his audience to consider that simply by identifying himself as an authority figure, he ought not to be automatically granted authority. At the same time, he suggests that the historical and political conditions of Okinawan society are constantly shifting and changing, subjected to intervention from many different centers of power. What is true in one context might not be so in another. Terurin's performance can be illuminated by Richard Bauman's observations about the narrative practices of dog traders that he has recorded in rural Texas: "The narratives that are the instruments of these negotiations do not fall into clear-cut categories of factual and fictional, truthful and lying, believable and incredible, but rather interweave in a complex contextual web that leaves these issues constantly in doubt, even susceptible to strategic manipulation whenever a trade is joined."[30]

It may be that traditional academic disciplines are compromised or inadequate to understanding the conditions of contemporary Okinawa. It may also be true that the performative styles of the past cannot express the criticism necessary to engage these social conditions. However, Terurin continues to hold out the hope that the complex, secondary genre within which he performs can somehow address these shortcomings. And, like any aspiring dog trader, the members of the audience had better keep their wits about them and follow Terurin's lead carefully and critically.[31]

the heritage of his times

NARRATING THE EVERYDAY

In 1998, Terurin published *Terurin Jiden*, his autobiography. This text was the culmination of a long performative engagement with his own life history. Virtually all of his public performances are framed by his experiences of everyday life in mainland Japan and Okinawa, experiences that bridge the Pacific War and American occupation of Okinawa. Lengthy interviews[32] and the published transcript of his discussions with the television anchorman and essayist Chikushi Tetsuya[33] allowed Terurin to give narrative form to his life story; it is presented in full in *Terurin Jiden*. It is by now a commonplace to note that a dialogic relationship exists between life histories of individuals and the narrative of the social groups in which they are situated. At the same time, representations of personal memories often have complex relationships to accepted historical narratives, marked by unexpected absences, additions, and surprising emphases.[34] On this count, Terurin's autobiography is extremely compelling.

He ties the narrative of his life to the collapse of the Ryūkyū kingdom and the Okinawan diaspora, particularly that of the Ryūkyūan nobility. Japanese colonial authorities disestablished the traditional class system, and the court positions and stipends of the former nobility—to which Terurin's family belonged—were abolished. Rinsuke's account of the vicissitudes of his family during the years following the destruction of the kingdom of Ryūkyū parallels the experiences of many former nobles who were forced to leave the capital at the end of the nineteenth century. The pattern is repeated in many other accounts of those days: the highest nobles were given titles in the newly established Meiji aristocracy, others were able to convert their estates to capital and enter into the modern Japanese economy. Many impoverished courtiers moved to the mountains of Yanbaru or other sites in northern Okinawa, sought work in mainland Japan or in the growing number of Japanese colonies, or immigrated to Okinawan enclaves abroad in places such as Brazil and Hawaii;[35] successive generations returned or began to move south as they accommodated themselves to the capitalist economy of modern Japan.[36]

Colonial administrators such as Governor Takahashi Takuya were convinced that the process of transforming Okinawans into Japanese subjects required making each citizen aware of his or her own equal subordination to the state and to the emperor. Continued reference to atavistic social relations, such as those between noble and commoner, could only interfere with this process. To these ends, Takahashi advocated dispensing with the category of "Ryūkyūan," using in its place the term "Okinawan," a citizen of Okinawa Prefecture. Thus, "Okinawanization" is a duplex process, producing both an imperial subject and an enlightened subject. Ryūkyū would become a negative symbol of irrational practices and relationships, of oppression and backwardness. Kano Masanao notes that while tremendous effort was expended to standardize spoken language, translate personal and place names into standard Japanese forms, and eliminate any quotidian practices that smacked of regional backwardness, the term "Ryūkyū" took on pejorative connotations, even in the Okinawan press. And the figure of the noble came to stand for Ryūkyū, instantiating all of these negative qualities.[37]

However, it is not the disestablishment of the nobility as such that gives form to Terurin's narrative. Neither is it the almost unimaginable trauma of the battle of Okinawa. Rather, it is the purposeful movement of these former nobles through space and time that organizes his text. Terurin focuses on the cunning of these déclassé nobles and the tactics that they deployed in order to make their way in a changing and hostile world. Events such as the Pacific War and the annexation of the kingdom of Ryūkyū by Japan become contingencies to which déclassé nobles must respond, drawing upon the resources of their culture and their experiences, as well as their inherent abilities. For while their social position had changed, the innate qualities that differentiated them from their fellow Okinawans had not.

Terurin begins his narration with the forced departure of his grandfather's family from the capital. He notes that disoriented courtiers were woefully unprepared for their introduction to competitive society and modern capitalism. Successful commoners from the countryside and merchants from Kagoshima became powerful in the urban commercial centers of Okinawa, establishing networks that extended into the countryside. And yet, impoverished nobles were not left without resources. Terurin returns again and again to this theme in his autobiography—former courtiers continued to rely upon their intellectual curiosity, thoughtfulness, aesthetic sensibility, and artistic abilities. These attributes would enable them to maintain their commitment to the Ryūkyūan performing arts, practices that had once been theirs exclusively.

the heritage of his times

Former household servants, now farmers in central Okinawa, interceded on behalf of Terurin's family so that they could obtain a plot of arable land and a site to construct a house. Terurin's grandfather Rinki settled in Uiichi no Iribaru (Uechi no Nishihara), one of the *yādui*, or communities of déclassé nobles, that were being settled on the periphery of older, established farming villages.[38]

Life was difficult for these former nobles, unfamiliar with farming and unused to the loss of their prerogatives. Terurin's grandfather, Rinki, lost the family savings on an ill-conceived plan to establish a rickshaw service. After the collapse of this venture, the rickshaw rotted in the farm's courtyard, a material reminder of the Teruya's lack of business acumen. Unemployed and withdrawn, Rinki squandered their remaining savings and continued to borrow money from local moneylenders to support his drinking.

In order to service the interest on the family's debt, Terurin's father, Rinzan, was indentured to their creditors, and he spent years laboring in their service. Eventually, he was able to marry and start a family, but he was unable to repay any of the principal owed to local moneylenders. Finally, at the age of thirty-nine, Rinzan moved to Osaka as an itinerant laborer. Securing a position as a carpenter on the construction of the new Kōshien (National High School Championship Baseball) Stadium, he built a small house for his parents in Okinawa and brought his wife to Osaka. After a time, he was hired as a factory worker for Nippon Senryō, a chemical plant in the Osaka area. The promise of secure employment was short-lived: Rinzan was injured in a chemical spill. Despite his status as a nonunion laborer and the absence of any legally mandated compensation, he negotiated a small settlement from the company. Using this windfall, he opened an awamori bar in the Okinawan community. Rinzan's bar was quite successful. By the time he returned to Okinawa in 1936, he had saved one thousand yen. His seven-year-old son Rinsuke, who had been born in the Okinawan ghetto in Osaka, returned home with him.

The diaspora of the déclassé nobility is one of the elements that gives narrative organization to Terurin's autobiography. At the same time, his encounter with Okinawan culture and society resonates in interesting ways with Yanagita Kunio's nativist ethnology. In order to understand this relationship, I would like to give a brief sketch of Yanagita's methodology. A critical sense of its structure enables one to grasp why it is that Terurin chooses to not only represent himself as a folklorist, but to perform in an ethnographic modality. I have noted that Terurin makes frequent reference to Yanagita. His performances and commentaries feature explicit discussions of *Kaijō no Michi* (The sea road), Yanagita's study of the role of the North Pacific ocean current known as the Black Current in the development of Japanese culture.[39] In fact, he was a commentator in a nationally televised NHK special about Yanagita and the Black Current, broadcast from the Great Hall of the Okinawa City Chūō Kōminkan. Terurin also frequently mentions Yanagita's *Meiji Taishōshi Seisōhen* and *Senzo no Hanashi*.

Yanagita felt that the methodologies of contemporary social sciences were inadequate to the task of understanding the Japanese folk, arguing that it was necessary to develop a kind of manifold hermeneutic in order to explore the nature of the archaic everyday in Okinawa and elsewhere on the margins of Japan. He proposed a methodology that could be understood as three complementary levels at which research would be conducted in order to achieve increasingly deeper understanding of its object—the folk.

> The first level concerns the external form of everyday life. It is visual collection: one could also call it the collection of a traveler. It is notes on the techniques of everyday life. What has come to be known as the traditional study of local custom is exemplary of this. Folklore studies of various nations have been concerned with this.
>
> The second level concerns commentary on everyday life. It is collection by the ear and eye. Once could call it the collection of a lodger. It is what one can study through the knowledge of language. From the naming of things to folklore —all linguistic arts are included. This includes the study of custom and folklore research.
>
> The third concerns substance, the knowledge of everyday life. One might also call this collection of the heart—by those of the same community. Excluding a few exceptions, outsiders cannot ever be relied upon concerning this. That is why there will always be local studies.[40]

It is not necessary for a folklorist to work through the first two levels in order to master the third. This final level demanded an inside perspective in order to learn about the community from within. Yanagita asserted that this perspective was, with few exceptions, equivalent to a kind of native competence and was, for the most part, unavailable to outsiders. H. D. Harootunian has termed the resulting methodology an "intransitive hermeneutic."[41] In Terurin's largely autobiographical Gintengai performance and in his autobiography itself, his encounter with Okinawa takes him through each level of Yanagita's manifold hermeneutic, culminating with the recovery of his native competence, his authentic authority.

Having been born and raised in Osaka, Terurin knew little of Okinawan society and was unable to speak anything other than the Japanese of the Osaka region. At first, the experience of everyday life in Okinawa was alien to him. He could only view it as a stranger, a visitor to this place that everyone told him was home. Tormented by neighboring children, Terurin avoided school and spent his days hiding in the countryside. At the same time, he discovered his mimetic facility, amusing his father's friends by performing manzai and rakugo routines that he learned from records that his father had bought in Osaka. When he was eventually forced to return to school, he surprised his classmates with his ability to perform these humorous monologues, and he later attributed his incorporation into the community to his ability to retell the stories that he had learned from his father's recordings.

During the American invasion, Terurin and his family fled to the isolated forests of Yanbaru in Northern Okinawa, once again drawing upon the hospitality of a farming family. As a counterpoint to the tales of death and suffering that characterize much of the published reflections on the Okinawan experience of the war,[42] Terurin insists that, for him, the war was a time of learning. He spent the battle of Okinawa in isolation, reading and rereading a boxful of books by famous Japanese authors that he had brought along with him.

After the war, Terurin's interest in Okinawan everyday life resonates with Yanagita's "collection by the ear and eye." His family returned to central Okinawa, and he began to work as a driver for the American occupation. In his travels to villages all across the island, he was amazed with the linguistic diversity that he found. Making pocket notebooks out of scraps that he salvaged from the typhoon of paper generated by American bureaucrats, he filled volume after volume with notes on Okinawan culture. He gathered notes on the words that he heard spoken, the songs that he heard sung, the stories that he heard recited.

In the villages and resettlement camps that he visited, several other factors came together to deepen his engagement with Okinawan culture. First, he became better acquainted with Onaha Zenkō—Dr. Būten. In recent years, Būten has experienced a resurgence in popularity with the release of a recording of his postwar performances and a series of articles in the Okinawan press. However, Būten as a character has been a long-standing fixture in Terurin's performances, and Terurin's discussions of Būten often become important vehicles to express Terurin's own thoughts on Okinawan culture and history. Like Terurin, Būten was also the scion of a former noble house. Although Būten's family had also moved to the countryside, Būten himself was an educated man. After attending a mainland Japanese university, a notable accomplishment in those days, he returned to Okinawa where he opened a dental practice.

In many ways, Būten was a master of traditional performing arts, studying classical dance and song, interested in court performances and seasonal rituals. He believed that before one could attempt to improvise or innovate, one must first master the traditional forms. With his encouragement, Terurin began to explore the musical traditions to which he was heir. For example, Terurin's father, Rinzan, was not only a sanshin maker but an important member of the Nomura school of classical sanshin performance who trained a large number of contemporary Okinawan musicians. While maintaining his interest in popular genres, Terurin would study classical Ryūkyūan music with his father and his father's students.

For Būten, it was not enough to be able to reproduce classical performances, regardless of their sophistication. The essential form of his art, he felt, was to first master the traditional form, then to smash (kuzusu) it. Būten was famous for his strangely syncretic performances such as the Nusubito Kuduchi, in which a thief's flight from a local constable is given the form of a classical dance, or the postwar performances that he gave at the Ishikawa Bullfight Ring, in which he appeared as Santa Claus and produced one beautiful female elf after another from his sack as he danced.

Terurin is particularly interested in the subaltern sensibility that Būten develops concerning humor. By citing Terurin on this count, I by no means mean to suggest that I subscribe to his assertion that Būten was the first to develop this perspective. A cursory study of modern and early modern comedic genres in mainland Japan would yield many similar themes. My interest here is to explore Terurin's interpretation and the consequences that it will have for his performances:

> Up until now, Būten said that laughter had been from the top down. This was the Japanese style of comedy. The elite laughed at the commoners. The rich laughed at the poor. Scholars laughed at the ignorant. You might be teased, "You're an idiot!" but no one will insult you by saying, "You're really fantastic!" Someone might say, "You poor bum!" but no one will sneer, "You rich person!" This is the Japanese way of comedy. But for Būten, laughter is based on the person on the bottom looking at those on top and laughing at them. Dismissive laughter. Subversive laughter.

Given Terurin's strategy of including long excerpts of performances in his autobiography, his discussion of Būten's work is interesting for what it omits.[43] Although he reminisces about Būten's uproarious performances, the text only includes a sketch of their basic themes. In place of a detailed retelling, Terurin constructs an exegesis of the levels of meaning that came together in Būten's humor—providing the reader insight into Būten's comedic genus as well as a glimpse of Terurin's own training in anthropology and psychology.

There is a similar pattern in his Gintengai performance. Terurin describes a song called "The Mikeneko" (The calico cat), written and performed by Būten before the war. At one level, the song is a kind of commentary on the social conditions of prewar Okinawa. Terurin explains that most young Okinawan men had been conscripted into the Japanese army, were working abroad, or had been consigned to labor units. Women of the same age had been pressed into working on the Japanese bases. The song is a lament about the interruption of everyday life, the inability of young Okinawan women to marry within their own age group of Okinawan men.

However, Terurin explains that the song has a deeper meaning highlighted by its performance in venues frequented by Japanese soldiers. Sung in Okinawan, the mainland Japanese were largely unaware of these inflections. Terurin suggests that the song provides a commentary on the conduct of the Japanese soldiers whose behavior was that of an occupying army in prewar Okinawa—ostensibly a prefecture like any other, not a colony or a

the heritage of his times

conquered territory. While the conscripts, the average soldiers, were con-signed to life in miserable conditions, the officers appropriated the best houses, demanded the best sake, and spent their time strutting around, chasing women.

In another song that he performed at the same time, Būten adopted the guise of a traveling storyteller to lampoon consumer society. Terurin re-counts how Būten told of the conspicuous display of affluence in the new high society, of how one must even buy water in order to have a drink because it is far too humiliating to be so rustic as to fetch a bucket from the well. Būten's narrator is amazed to find that there is a wide variety of water available, with names like the varieties of sake. Many varieties of sake end with the suffix -toki. However, Būten pronounces this as teki, which indicates enemy. Terurin reveals the deeper meaning of Būten's critique: while sup-posedly enumerating the varieties of imported products available to the Okinawan consumer, he is actually listing the number of enemies cultivated by the aggressive Japanese state.

Again, the emphasis is on Terurin's understanding and interpretation rather than on Būten's performance. Readers and listeners are given no more than a sketch of the surface or manifest form of the performance before Terurin reveals the deeper or latent meaning. Perhaps Terurin's per-formance is intended allegorically—stories about the arrogance of an oc-cupying army and the thoughtlessness of capitalist consumer society are explicated, criticisms that resonate as well with the social conditions of their current retelling as they do with the historical context of their original performance.

Both Būten's and Terurin's performances turn on the relationship be-tween the categories Japanese and Okinawan. Certainly the Japanese, as they appear in Terurin's account, are stereotypes—arrogant occupiers, superficial consumers, monolingual dupes. However, I do not think that Būten and Terurin are directly concerned with illuminating the Japanese character or correcting Okinawan misapprehensions. Rather, it is the Okinawan charac-ter that they explore. Unlike the Okinawans of Iha's formulation, these Okinawans have not had their native voices silenced by integration into the Japanese state. It is the ability of Būten's audience to understand both Japa-nese and Okinawan that enables the wordplay so central to his humor.[44]

I would like to suggest that this interpretation does not exhaust Terurin's commentary on Būten's storytelling. It is not enough to reveal the meaning that is concealed by the form of the performance; it is also necessary to ask why social commentary takes the form of popular performative genres.

In his autobiography,[45] Terurin describes how he became one of the leading popular performers in postwar Okinawa. He began to write and perform in musical reviews that were presented in live venues in Koza, on whirlwind tours through the countryside, and on the fledgling Okinawan radio stations. Within a few years, his *Watabū Shō* (Fat boy show) became a runaway hit and he was known throughout the islands. However, his performative prowess was counterbalanced by his fiscal irresponsibility, and he accumulated a massive amount of debt. With no warning, he disappeared, abandoning his theatrical troupe and his family. This is a motif that Terurin will deploy again and again throughout his autobiography. For every moment of success, every brush with fame, Terurin seems always to suffer setbacks and failures. Terurin readily attributes these failures to his own actions: unreasonable optimism, financial irresponsibility, stubbornness, shyness, laziness, or drunkenness.

Living a marginal existence on Ishigaki Island, Terurin met the famous ethnomusicologist Kishaba Eijun.[46] At this point, his project begins to correspond with what Yanagita called "the collection of the heart." After their introduction at a local performance, Kishaba and Terurin began to meet at the inn where Kishaba lived. Terurin recalls that ethnographers and folklorists from all over Japan would gather there—most of the guests were scholars of one kind or another. Terurin was asked to join them. He remembers that the level of the conversation in which he had been invited to participate initially overwhelmed him. Having only graduated from middle school, he felt that he had been given a second chance at education.

Kishaba told Terurin that he intended to do whatever he could to help him learn about Okinawan culture. Having said this, he produced a collection of bound notebooks in which he had written the results of research that he had conducted as a young man teaching in schools throughout Okinawa—his fieldnotes, not his published works. The material was both detailed and diverse: studies of local traditions, folksongs, and community performances. Kishaba told Terurin that his writing might be a little hard to decipher, so he wanted Terurin to read aloud from the notebooks. Whenever a passage would prove difficult for Terurin to read, Kishaba would decipher it for him.

the heritage of his times

Whenever an account appeared that Terurin didn't understand, Kishaba explained it to him. With Kishaba's permission, Terurin recorded these sessions and, little by little, he began to develop deeper insights into Okinawan culture. They met frequently and their discussions would last for as long as three to four hours.

Terurin and Kishaba playfully manipulate one of the central genres of ethnography, the interview, and one of its most overdetermined artifacts, the fieldworker's notes. Rather than soliciting information from Terurin as a native informant, Kishaba presents Terurin the performer with the textual record of decades of research in Yaeyama. However, this is more than a kind of satirical role reversal. The generosity of Kishaba, who opens his archive to Terurin, is profoundly moving and reflects a remarkable level of concern and respect. The appropriation of the form of the interview is also particularly powerful. A genre used not only by scholars but by police and military authorities, the interview resonates in complex ways with Okinawans of Terurin's generation. Tomiyama notes in his essay that the Japanese ethnographer Torii conducted interviews at gunpoint throughout Taiwan and Yaeyama. Terurin and Kishaba take a genre that, at its least reflexive, is organized to extract information for use by the scholar, and transforms it entirely.

Terurin's dialogic engagement with Kishaba brought him into contact with primary materials that Kishaba had gathered throughout the Yaeyama islands. Under Kishaba's tutelage, Terurin developed a deep, affective relationship with the object of ethnographic investigation. He also engages with Kishaba's interpretations, the accumulated analysis of decades of research. As a performer studies a script—memorizing, internalizing, questioning, interpreting—Terurin makes this material his own.

More to the point, Terurin seizes the final level of Yanagita's hermeneutic. Along with Kishaba, he inverts the traditional pattern of folklore research: the scholar who formalizes and interprets the practices of the rustic informant, under the authority of a presumed shared native competence. At the same time, the directionality of the hermeneutic is reconfigured. The result of the process is not a textualized exegesis, available only to the cultural elite.[47] Rather, Terurin uses his insights as a scholar in order to transform his performances as a singer and storyteller, performances like those that were the original objects of investigation.

the heritage of his times

After briefly traveling through Yaeyama, conducting his own fieldwork and meeting with other scholars, Terurin returned to Koza. As I mentioned earlier, he enrolled as a student at Kokusai Daigaku. After auditing classes for several weeks, the professor asked him to talk about his own experiences as an Okinawan performer. This gave him the opportunity to experiment with his new performative modality. Eventually, he was given about twenty minutes at the end of each class as a forum for his ideas. Terurin drew on the research that he had done on folksongs, folktales, and myths and tried to integrate the lessons that he had learned from Kishaba. At the same time, he reflected on his training with Būten, and created a complex performative genre that synthesized elements as seemingly disparate as popular song, storytelling, ethnographic interpretation, and prayer.

CHANPURU RHYTHM

In his performance at the Gintengai, Terurin paused for a moment, cleared his throat and then resumed his lecture.

> Mindashimun—mezurashī mono, an amazing thing, it must be something that has yet to be seen by anyone. Where will you find that kind of a thing on a small island? It is said that amazing things sometimes fall from the skies. But what that really means is that they came from beyond the sea. When someone says Ama kara or amakudari,[48] to descend from the heavens, it really means to come from beyond the sea. Our traders went to the islands and nations that ring the Pacific and found new and interesting things. To say that these things are new—it might be the same kind of crock, but something about it, perhaps the way of making it, makes it seem different.

Terurin explains that scarcity of resources in the archipelago kept Okinawans constantly on the alert for unusual things. This was not merely inspired by curiosity: the unusual and the exceptional were the favored objects of exchange. Terurin notes that a villager who found some unusual object, perhaps washed up on the beach near his community, would present it to the lord at Shuri. In return, he would be richly rewarded.

This model, Terurin argues, was to bring the kingdom of Ryūkyū great fame and success in its relationship with the Chinese court. Although China

the heritage of his times

was the center of the world, the most expansive kingdom on earth, there were still things that could not be found there. Terurin suggests that this lack inspired in the Chinese emperor a desire for the unusual.[49]

Offerings made to the Chinese court were to be objects that were unique to the domains from which they were presented. In Terurin's formulation, the Ryūkyūans manipulated this system in order to enjoy the benefits of a relationship to the Qing court. Okinawa was a land of scarcity and had few resources that could capture the imagination of the Qing emperor. Ryūkyūan emissaries were delighted to find that the emperor prized the seashells that lined the beaches of Miyako—and an object that was entirely useless to the Ryūkyūans became money at the Chinese court.[50] The Ryūkyūans went on to establish a far-ranging maritime network to search for objects that would catch the emperor's fancy. It seemed that the more ridiculous an object, the greater it was valued. Even whale excrement (ambergris) was brought to the court, to the delight of the emperor.[51] As a result of this relationship, the kingdom of Ryūkyū became prosperous.

Terurin earlier deployed the motif of spatiotemporal movement when he discussed the Okinawan diaspora following the incorporation of Ryūkyū into the Japanese state. He described in general terms the movement of déclassé nobles from the capital to the countryside and recounted the specifics of his own family's experience. To this he now adds a discussion of presentations from villagers in the Okinawan countryside to the court at Shuri, Ryūkyūan participation in the Chinese tribute-trade system, and the exchange of offerings with Okinawan ancestral spirits. It would be possible to suggest that Terurin's work is structured around some dominant motif such as the quest;[52] or that it could be utilized to elicit a generalized theory of gift exchange. However, in this context, it is not the constituent elements that concern me, but the way in which Terurin organizes them in his narrative. It is the technique of emplotment that he chooses that draws attention to his concern with the cunning of the Ryūkyūan people. In the case of the Chinese tribute-trade system, the emperor expected and demanded strict compliance with his edicts. However, the Ryūkyūans manipulated imperial protocols, misrepresented themselves and the objects that they traded, played on the emperor's benevolence, arrogance, and gullibility, and gained the patronage of the court. In each of the cases that Terurin describes, it is not the event as such, but the clever response of the Ryūkyūan, the Okinawan people, that distinguishes it.

In his performances, Terurin ascribes this cunning to an essential feature of Okinawan culture—what he calls *chanpuru rizumu*, or chanpuru rhythm. He argues that Okinawan culture is comprised of forms that are "all jumbled up and mixed together."[53] Terurin takes the term *chanpuru* from a popular style of Okinawan cooking, one that he suggests Okinawans learned during the Ryūkyū kingdom's trade with Indonesia. In culinary terms, chanpuru is a stir-fried dish made up of several ingredients—a skillful combination of whatever is ready to hand. Popular variations include *tofu chanpuru*,[54] *fū chanpuru*,[55] *māmina chanpuru*,[56] and the most popular, *goya chanpuru*.[57] However, Terurin argues that the production of the meal instantiates an important principle governing Okinawan culture.

> Okinawan culture is a chanpuru culture. And if I were to say what the origin of this special point is, it lies in our history of poverty. All of you who eat chanpuru and say, "Ah this is so delicious!" have forgotten its origin. We perfected chanpuru because our ancestor's lives were so wanting, so poor. As you know, Okinawa is a hot place. Things here can't help but spoil. And leftovers end up being thrown away. But in the old days, we couldn't afford to throw away the scraps. They were kept and mixed with new ingredients for the next meal.

The anthropologist Ota Yoshinobu has written on the transformation of the notion of chanpuru, from its original use generally restricted to culinary production, to its more generalized reference to Okinawan culture.[58] He dates this extension to the late 1980s, when chanpuru became associated with the popular performing arts, an extension driven by Terurin and his students. Ota draws on the work of Mary Louise Pratt and Homi Bhabha[59] to suggest that a kind of "third space" of hybridity was created through Okinawan appropriation of elements of the dominant Japanese and American cultures.

Ota discusses the indigenous notion of *chanpuruizumu* or chanpuruism, a movement to consciously reflect on and to affirm the culturally syncretic practices of Okinawa, and one that is popularly associated with Terurin. In his ethnography of the work of Terurin's student Tamaki Mitsuru and his troupe, Shōchiku Kagekidan, during the late 1980s and early 1990s, Ota finds the possibilities of a third space that can authorize challenges to nativist formulations and modernist discourses. However, I think that it would be a mistake to associate Terurin with this valorization of a "third space." In Terurin's work, the notion of "chanpuru rhythm" is highly suggestive on this count. It is less the production of a "third space" than an attempt to reclaim nativist insights into the authenticity of Okinawan culture, the dire consequences of capitalist modernization under the Japanese state, and the related effects of acculturation or Japanification. While superficially it might resemble the Certeauian tactic,[60] a moment of free expression seized from within the structuring contours of the Japanese state, this explanation fails to grasp Terurin's real concern.

Terurin's focus is on the transformational logic that governs these operations. "Chanpuru rhythm" denotes the Okinawan practice of appropriation, of seizing varying objects and practices drawn from Japanese, Chinese, American cultures and beyond, and resetting them into an Okinawan pattern. His argument is not that these influences have led Okinawans to invent a new culture, but rather that a characteristic of Okinawan culture is its capacity to accept and transform these diverse elements.

He suggests that the same mode of patterning may have once existed in Japan, but it has been effaced by the social and cultural transformations of modernization. While Terurin recognizes that the power of the military as an institution has been eclipsed in postwar Japan, he argues that Japanese culture remains deeply militarized, restructured by the disciplinary practices initiated during the imperial era. In particular, he focuses on the perduring consequences of the militarization of language. The result of this has been Nihongo, a language of convenience and expedience, suitable to convey orders but no longer adequate for dialogic interaction. He distinguishes this from Yamatuguchi, the language of archaic Japan—a language that still resonates with Uchināguchi, the language of Okinawa. It is apparent that he retains an organization identical to Iha's tertiary framework, incorporating the historical recognition of the consequences of the Japanese project of modernization.

Terurin explains his notion of chanpuru rhythm by turning to Okinawan expressions. First, he says, "Shin-gwachi-kara-yamu-nun-shī-nun," translating it into Japanese as "Shigatsu kara wa mono mo sueru" (From April on, things start to spoil). Terurin suggests that the Okinawan version maintains the archaic rhythm as well as alliteration (tōin) that is lost in the Japanese. He then restates it as "Shīmī kara munun shīnun" (Things start to spoil with the festival of cleaning the tombs [shīmī]). While this retains the temporal connotations of the original, it also produces a juxtaposition of purity and putrefaction—when things are cleansed, they start to spoil.

Given the emphasis on cultural authenticity and purity of the fascist Japanese state and its ongoing effects in modern Japan, it is difficult to see this as anything other than a critique of Japanification. In this formulation, the necessary and contingent engagement with the complex influences of foreign cultures in Okinawa has enabled—has demanded—that culture remains dynamic and transformational. In Japan, the obsession with the pure and the authentic has had the opposite result: culture has become stagnant and decadent.

Terurin has mobilized his thoughts on the transformative potential of Okinawan culture in a series of constructive interventions, such as the Nuchi nu Sūji that he performed with Būten. Perhaps more famously, he caught the imagination of Okinawan audiences during the early years of the occupation with his performances of the musical Handogwa. Terurin took the Sanrai Kigeki or Hiren Kigeki, one of the cornerstones of the Okinawan theatrical repertoire, a story of tragic love that culminates in the suicide of the heroine. After the war, this play was in constant performance in Okinawan theaters— a tragic play for tragic times, as Terurin described it. In affirmation of the will to survive that drove those who had endured terrible losses during the war, and in tribute to the "strong, beautiful lifeworld of the [Okinawan] housewives that kept active in the darkened villages, that did whatever they could to make money," he decided that order could be brought out of chaos, and that tragedies should be rewritten as comedies. In Handogwa, he was determined that the heroine would not commit suicide. Too many people had sacrificed their lives, had committed suicide needlessly for their country and for the emperor. She must survive, he believed, if Okinawans were to believe that hope for the future remained. This is the pattern that organized his work through the present.

The question remains of the utility of Terurin's critique. Certainly, he has inverted the typical relationship between ethnographer and informant, recovering both the authority of the ethnographer and the competence of the native. He has also developed a creative mode of performance that attempts to effectively synthesize academic forms of expression with popular performative genres. His emphasis on the cunning of the Okinawan people also reclaims a powerful sense of subjectivity, of the possibility of meaningful activity. And yet, despite its inversions, his argument also remains within the framework of the nativist critique of modernity. Terurin's work remains centered on a concern with the relative valuation of culture, and the recovery or reconfiguration of native practices. Can this type of critique ever effectively engage capitalist modernity and unequal development, the very forces that produce the conditions of cultural transformation and social injustice against which the criticism has been deployed?

What of Terurin's influence? Although he has died since I finished my fieldwork, most Okinawans still recognized his face, his voice. Okinawans everywhere speak of chanpuru when they discuss Okinawan culture, yet they do so with a definition that is much more general than Terurin's notion of chanpuru rhythm. However, it is in practice that his influence persists. In the creative selection and combination of genres, in the sly appropriation of authoritative voices and restricted roles; in the continuing performances of his son's Rinken Band, Tamaki Mitsuru, Gakiya Yoshimitsu and Fujiki Hayato; in their willingness to explore tradition, to shatter convention, to innovate.

the classroom of the everyday

fujiki hayato and his "shima to asobimanabu" seminar

*It is not the object of the story to convey a happening per se, which is the purpose of information; rather, it embeds it in the life of the storyteller in order to pass it on as experience to those listening. It thus bears the marks of the storyteller as much as the earthen vessel bears the marks of the potter's hand.—*WALTER BENJAMIN, Some Motifs in Baudelaire

*That is why those metaphysical problems, said to be good for bishops who find their supper ready and waiting for them, are even more essential for those who set out every morning to find the work on which their evening meal will depend. Who is better suited than those who hire out their bodies day after day to give meaning to dissertations on the distinction between body and soul, time and eternity, or on the origin of humanity and its destiny?—*JACQUES RANCIÈRE, The Nights of Labor

STORYTELLING AND CRITICISM

On an autumn evening in 1997, another performance of Fujiki Hayato's Hitori Yuntaku Shibai drew to a close—this time, a benefit for local charities. A stage had been set in a corner of the Ton Ton House, a small carpentry workshop on the northern edge of Okinawa City. Fujiki, seated on an upturned box beneath the lone spotlight, wiped the greasepaint from his face and joked with the audience. He announced upcoming concerts by his friends and talked about new projects that he was working on. In a few weeks, he would start teaching a class on Okinawan culture and history at a continuing education program in Okinawa City, and he invited everyone to join him. With a laugh, he promised that the workload would be light and everyone would have a good time.

I was immediately reminded of the stories that I'd heard about Terurin's seminars—both the courses that he participated in at Kokusai Daigaku and the famous ongoing study group that he led for years in Koza. I wondered how Fujiki would bring his own performance style and his own distinctive perspective on culture and action to the class. How would he deal with the appropriation and reconfiguration of roles that could take place in the class-room? Would members of the audience be willing to take up Fujiki's invitation and join the seminar—to step down from their seats and take the stage themselves? The possibilities seemed very exciting. Later that week, I stopped by Tāchī Māchū, Fujiki's izakaya (pub/restaurant), to talk with him about the course. Tāchī Māchū[1] was located in Nakasone, near the newly completed Okinawa City Hall and the Nakasone ugwanjū (sacred grove). Once a district of love hotels and the U.S. Motor Transport Base known as Camp Koza, Nakasone had become a mixture of apartments and private homes, small businesses, and offices. The few hotels that remained catered to niche tourism, accommodating travelers who came to experience the popular culture of Okinawa City. Occasionally, I would also see American civilian base employees, renting a room while they looked for a permanent apartment.

Māchū differed from the hard rock bars and minyō pubs[2] that still stood here and there in the entertainment districts in Okinawa City. Presided over by a dynamic young chef who experimented with a kind of Okinawan fusion cuisine, the popular bar was furnished with hand-crafted wooden furniture and decorated with Southeast Asian textiles. The walls were hung with framed black-and-white photos of occupation-era Koza. An old jukebox stood next to the bar, its glass front plastered with posters advertising Fujiki's recent performances. The clientele seemed to be equally divided between workers from the city hall, local performers and their fans (often from the Japanese main islands), and young people from the Koza area. I found Fujiki sitting at the bar, dressed in an indigo samue (a two-piece garment resembling a judo gi) and rubber beach sandals, joking with the chef and his customers.

Fujiki was eager to talk about the seminar. He told me that when he was a novice performer in the Rinken Band and Shōchiku Kagekidan, he had the good fortune to participate in the informal workshop that Teruya Rinsuke ran at the Terurinkan. Over the years, he said, performers from China Sadao[3] to Tamaki Mitsuru had studied with Terurin; mainland scholars, reporters, and performers often stopped by to visit and to discuss Okinawan culture and performing arts. Fujiki felt that his studies with Terurin came at an important time in his life, and his work was transformed by it. He hoped that he could create the same kind of atmosphere in his class.

Fujiki laid a copy of the announcement for his class on the bar and pointed at the title. He explained that the phrase "Shima to Asobimanabu" really captured what it was that he wanted to accomplish. The use of *shima* was common enough—although it typically indicates an island or, more specifically, the island of Okinawa, it is also regularly used to connote a village or community.[4] Fujiki told me that the native ethnologist Yanagita Kunio also used *shima* to designate the idea of a rural utopia. The predicate *asobimanabu* is a neologism compounded from the verbals *asobu* and *manabu*. Of the two, *manabu* is fairly straightforward: it suggests the concepts to study or to learn, to grasp the object of inquiry. *Asobu* is more complex. It captures a wide variety of experiences: play and performance, idling, a sexual encounter. In this context, it implies a connection to the Okinawan nominal *ashibi*, which extends the concept of *asobu* to participation in a wide variety of ritual contexts from the solemn to the carnivalesque.[5] Widely recognized examples of this particular usage would be the *moashibi*, a common if vaguely illicit outdoor party between the young men and women of a rural community, and the *ashibinā*, the site of a *moashibi*. During the early twentieth century, the jurist and ethnographer—a kind of Japanese Lewis Henry Morgan—Okuno Hikorokuro saw the moashibi as a form of indigenous social practice capable of subverting the restrictive practices of the Japanese state, challenging the regulation and regularization of marital and sexual practices. Moashibi as a moment free from social and civic regulation, an opportunity for self-determination, has become a popular motif in Okinawan literature and performing arts.

Fujiki said that he chose *asobimanabu* because of its implication of a particular mode of learning, an unconventional form that emphasizes practical engagement and direct experience of the object rather than a rigidly academic approach. In the case of his seminar, he said that he wanted his students to have a less mediated, more immediate way to study, to experience Okinawa.

He told me that he owes his emphasis on play to the lessons that he learned from Terurin. I was reminded of this as I read a passage in Terurin's autobiography in which he discussed his discovery of the work of the philosopher Johan Huizinga.[6] Terurin was excited to find that Huizinga's thoughts on play resonated with his own strategy of artistic production.

the classroom of the everyday

Our personality is expressed through play. Human culture might be rational, but it is also playful. When you're a child, you sing while you play. Isn't that what they say in English—I play music? I think that it would be great to be that kind of an adult.

It would be one thing if this world were like the Olympics, where you lived in moments of extreme laughter or tears. However, Huizinga says that life is also a game and you must take pleasure in the things that chance brings to you. If you try to disregard chance and force your way through the world through dint of effort and preparation, life would be terrible. If that's the way things are, I want no part of it. On the other hand, maybe that's just something I say because long ago I decided to be a performer.

It isn't interesting to simply do extensive historical research and rummage through old archival documents in order to write a script. Instead, the best thing to do is to put it aside for a while and take another entirely different story and do your best to fit the two of them together. That's what interests me.[7]

Terurin suggests that it is an improvisational or compositional challenge for artists to synthesize two seemingly different stories. At the same time, a clever solution to this problem allows the performer to fold a historical lesson or critical argument into the form of a song or play that is already popular with the audience. As I would learn, Fujiki's seminar was shot through with the influence of Terurin's insight—and long-standing practice —of rethinking, recombining, and redeploying genres.

"I WONDER JUST HOW MUCH WE KNOW ABOUT THIS ISLAND?"

Between the Koza elementary school and the ruins of Goeku Castle, the Okinawa City Citizens Meeting Hall and Central Public Hall stand out in stark contrast to the other remains of the Ryūkyū kingdom and American occupation. Built in the massive vernacular style of contemporary institutional construction in Okinawa, these buildings synthesize the sharp, unadorned lines of Japanese modernist architecture with fragments of traditional Ryūkyūan style: tiled roofs, courtyards, shaded verandas. A lone shīsā[8] stands atop a column in the courtyard, his angry gaze directed to the south.

The compound includes a beautiful great hall, the site of events ranging from the public hearings on Japanese land appropriated for military use,[9] nationally broadcast musical and variety shows, and local productions. Next to it, a smaller venue accommodates more modest productions, as well as a small library. Beneath the halls were a number of classrooms and the offices of the Okinawa City municipal workers who coordinated the activities.

On a damp and cool evening—October 30, 1997—I wound my way down into the lower levels of the Central Public Hall for the first of Fujiki's classes. In other classrooms, groups met for city-sponsored educational programs such as beginning Spanish, signing, European folk dancing, music of the Okinawan court, introduction to the ocarina, and Western cooking.

In our designated classroom, several rectangular tables had been arranged in the form of an open box. As students arrived, they found seats around the tables. Most of the students had notebooks and pens or pencils, a photo-copied schedule of the course, and a copy of a book containing annotated transcriptions of Fujiki's performances. There was no fee to enroll in the course: the only expense that students incurred was the cost of Fujiki's book at eighteen hundred yen per copy.[10] In all, there were a dozen students. A young office worker and her boyfriend, a businessman; an electrical contractor; two women undergraduates from Okinawa International University; two nursery school teachers; two middle-aged female office workers; a young male bureaucrat from Okinawa City's Department of Education posted to the Youth Seminar; a young woman working at the City Hall; and two anthropologists—including me. Students ranged in age from their early twenties to mid-thirties. Although Youth Seminar classes were to be restricted to those who either lived or worked in Okinawa City, participants came from Urasoe to the south, as well as Kadena and Yomitan to the northwest. With the exception of the other anthropologist and me, everyone identified themselves as Okinawan. Almost all of the students were either enrolled in a local university or already held a two- or four-year degree.

The head of the public education office was present to welcome Fujiki. A middle-aged career bureaucrat, he wore a dark suit, white shirt, and striped tie. He delivered a brief greeting in formal Japanese and urged all of us to make the most of the opportunity to learn from Fujiki. Then, he introduced Fujiki to the class and excused himself. Dressed casually in a batik shirt and khaki trousers, Fujiki stepped to the front of the class and welcomed everyone, thanking them for coming. After we all introduced ourselves, the class began:

Let's start with the idea of culture. I've always thought that culture is hard to describe because it seems so natural to us. We live in culture like fish in water—it surrounds us, makes everything that we do possible. But normally we can't see it.

Fujiki paused, then offered a different analogy:

The things that make up culture are like the tools of a *daiku*, a carpenter. When we use them properly, we don't have to think about them at all. However, if they're broken or they don't work as we expect, we're forced to think about them.

Since the end of the Ryūkyū kingdom, life in Okinawa has been like the experience of the carpenter whose tools no longer are enough to get the job done. Again and again, Okinawans have had to think about new ways to make the old things work, and to think about new ways of acting when the old ways fail. This is not simply the result of the inevitable changes that come with the passage of time. Rather, it is because Okinawan culture has been subjected to so much interference from the Japanese state. From the most basic elements of the Okinawan language to the simplest practices of everyday life, Japan has attacked every aspect of Okinawan identity.

Fujiki then suggested that the mainland media had a powerful effect on Okinawan perceptions of the world:

They make everything that comes from Yamato [from mainland Japan] seem like it's better that what we have here. Maybe it's time to try and think more clearly about the tools that we have left, to try and understand them while we still can. You have to learn to trust your sense of difference. What does it mean to be Okinawan in modern Japan? What does it mean to speak Uchināguchi when people look down at you for using anything other than standard Japanese?

One of the students nodded intently. "While I was living in *Naichi*,[11] I was shocked when I realized that my Okinawan friends and I got embarrassed when we spoke *hōgen* [dialect] in public." Fujiki replied that she had gotten right to the heart of the problem. "When you realize that there are still interesting and important things about Okinawa," he said, "you can regain your pride in being Okinawan."

the classroom of the everyday

Fujiki said that he had found an intriguing contradiction in his work: "Ryūkyūan history is very long, but Okinawan memory is very short." Why are there so many treasures in the Ryūkyūan past and yet so much is forgotten? Why have so many moments of beauty and accomplishment, meaningful practices, and admirable figures been obscured by the shame and anxiousness of life in a world dominated by the Japanese state? Over the next few weeks, he wanted us to consider why this might be. He also wanted us to sharpen our sense of contradiction by focusing on current events, culture, and history. What happens when the line that divides what is forgotten from what is known becomes blurred, when you can catch a glimpse of both together? He told us that we need to realize that life is complex and filled with these kinds of contradictions. We should trust this sense of strangeness to guide us to a better understanding of the life that we lead.

Fujiki's example of a fish swimming in water fails to capture the complexity of culture; however, it is this failure that enables him to expose the naturalization of the historical. For culture is not a timeless, unchanging field: it is the result of definite historical events and processes. The perception of regularity is only possible when a person's intended actions conform to the objective chances with which she is presented. In other words, practical activity can only proceed free of contradiction and conscious regulation when objective and internalized categories, when social and mental structures correspond.[12] As Fujiki is at pains to show, this harmony is impossible to maintain. With simplicity and clarity, he asks: What happens when your projects don't match the objective world? What about the tool that no longer works, the tool that becomes an obstacle to our progress, the tool that we need but do not have? At this point the discussion turns to a world of interrelated representations, to a world of praxis. It is a world that must be actively, critically, and creatively engaged.[13]

It is not simply a phenomenological account of practice that Fujiki is trying to articulate. His critique is situated in the historically determinate conditions of contemporary Okinawa. From the abstract, heuristic example of the daiku's tools, he moves quickly to consider the profound effects of the intervention of the Japanese state into every part of daily life. At the same time, he holds out the possibility that there is something that can still be recovered from Okinawan cultures and practices. In the moment between the failure of the tool and its total loss, it is important to grasp it, to think about it, to see what it can still do. The seminar was organized around his consideration of this possibility.

He told the students that he uses his sense of the unfamiliar to guide his own collection of material about Okinawan history and culture. A voracious reader, he keeps a series of files filled with clippings from newspapers and magazines that he finds interesting. He showed us one as an example. Newspaper articles were cut and pasted to sheets of paper. These sheets were, in turn, organized and attached to either side of a manila folder with binder clips. He showed us a series about shishimai,[14] about newly discovered ugwanjū,[15] and about Yanagita Kunio's long engagement with Okinawa. He also showed a notebook in which he—like Terurin—wrote interesting pieces of information that he heard during conversations, in his travels throughout Okinawa and the rest of Japan.

Fujiki argued that it was also important that ordinary people be familiar with the tremendous body of scholarship about Okinawa. He suggested that we go down to a neighborhood bookstore and examine the books about local culture and history. He said that Okinawa had the second highest number of publishing houses of any prefecture in Japan, and the second highest number of published volumes of local history (a fact that he often mentions in his performances as well). Students should take advantage of this. Fujiki urged us to begin with the work of the historian Takara Kura-yoshi[16]—he said that he had learned so much about the Ryūkyūan past from Takara's books.

He also encouraged us to begin our own fieldwork. Projects could be open-ended or vaguely defined—so long as we were actively involved in investigating the world around us. He thought that interviews with friends and relatives were a good place to start. He said that he's always working on some kind of oral history project. Whenever he hears an interesting anecdote or rumor, he decides to investigate it and writes a short narrative based on his research—a narrative that will become the basis of one of his performances. He starts out by going to the library to check written records. Then, he contacts the people involved if he thinks that it would be appropriate. Many times there are things that they might not want to discuss, but he has found that people are generally willing to share their experiences with him.

He gave us a couple of examples: one about a beach party that supposedly happened between Japanese and U.S. troops. During the war, they had a barbecue—the U.S. soldiers unloaded material from ships and took pictures of the proceedings.[17] However, he was no longer able to locate the person who had originally told him the story. He had heard that a former Ryūkyū Daigaku (University of the Ryukyus) professor was working on the story and was rumored to have sold the rights to Big Comics.[18]

The other story was about a small island where he said that the residents respectfully refused to allow the Japanese army to establish a garrison there during the war. The islanders argued that fortifications could never defend against an American invasion. Rather, if a garrison were established, the U.S. troops would surely come to destroy it. When they came, there would be fighting and, whatever the outcome, the local people would lose. On that basis, the Japanese troop commander agreed, and the base was built elsewhere at an uninhabited site.

Fujiki paused and laughed, saying that it wouldn't really count as a class if he didn't give us some homework. He told us that we should remember what we had talked about in class as we read the daily newspapers and listened to the news on the radio or television. We should trust our instincts and select something that seemed to be strange or inexplicable. He asked us to make a note of it and bring it to the next class.

At this point, Fujiki said that he thought that he had covered enough for one evening. Rather than continue to lecture, he said that he would finish with a short performance that he hoped we would be able to relate to his earlier discussion. With that, he stepped into the center of the room, the open space left by the boxlike arrangement of tables. He pulled a chair out with him and sat down. For a moment he was silent, his hands spread out on his knees, his head down, his eyes closed. We all became very quiet, leaning forward expectantly, pens ready. Then, Fujiki lifted his head and began to speak.

THE RED CAT FROM THE HEAVENS

Fujiki's narrative began with a young Okinawan art collector searching the ceramic stores in the Tsuboya (Chibuya in the Okinawan pronunciation) district in Naha. For nearly four centuries, Tsuboya has been the artistic center of Okinawan ceramics. Drawing on techniques learned in missions abroad to China and Korea during the days of the kingdom of Ryūkyū, the artists of Tsuboya have developed distinctive styles famous throughout Japan. Exhausted from the summer heat and tired from his unsuccessful search, the narrator retires to a small noodle shop to eat his lunch and relax. The restaurant is small and dirty—it looks like nobody has cleaned anything since the end of the war. The elderly owner appears, and the young collector soon begins to suspect that he is mad. Service is slow and erratic, the utensils are dirty, and the whole room reeks of cats. Sneezing, the young man finds cat fur in his soup. As a joke, he asks if there aren't cats around in the restaurant. The owner replies that, yes, there are seven or so living in the shop.

Surprised and nauseated, the young man is about to leave when he notices the cats' dish of food. Here, in this tiny, filthy restaurant, the cats are eating their meal from a dish clearly recognizable to the young man as being made by the Living National Treasure Kinjō Jirō.[19] In fact, Jirō's signature is clearly visible on the plate. With a shock, the young man realizes that the dish from which the cats are casually nibbling their scraps of meat is worth at least 500,000 yen.

Returning to his seat, the young man begins to sound out the shopkeeper. Feigning an affection for cats, he confides that he is actually looking for a pet himself. Might these cats be for sale? The young man offers the shopkeeper 20,000 yen each for two of the cats. Protesting that the price is too high, the old shopkeeper says that he and his wife would have been happy to offer the young man one at that price and another for free—but, since he seems intent on paying, they accept his offer. Two cats for 40,000 yen.

Slyly, the young man says that he has never kept a pet, and he doesn't have any dishes at home from which to feed them. Would it be possible to get a dish from the shopkeeper? The old shopkeeper readily agrees and calls to his wife to bring down another bowl from the shelf. The young man responds that he doesn't want to put her to any trouble—he would be happy to take the old plate that the cats are now using. The old man hesitates—although the young man has bought two cats, there are five more left. A large bowl like this is useful when there are so many cats to feed.

The young man responds that the cats are surely used to this bowl, and he thinks that they would be more comfortable in their new home with a nice large dish. The old man agrees—and calls to his wife to bring down another large bowl for the young man. Finally, the young man is exasperated:

"It's *that* bowl that I want," indicating the cats' dish on the floor.

At this, the old man sadly shakes his head: "You really are an idiot, aren't you! Let me tell you something so that you can wise up—maybe it'll help you out in the future. *That* bowl was made by the Living National Treasure Kinjō Jirō and would surely sell for about 500,000 yen."

Now, the young man realizes that the trap has been sprung. He protests that he's been tricked, that the old man has taken advantage of him. The old man responds that he never once suggested to the young man that he buy a cat, never tried to force him to do anything. It was the young man who saw the plate and tried to come up with a scheme to get it.

The young man asks one last question: "Why do you use such an expensive plate to feed your cats?"

"Well, it seems to make the cats more valuable," the old man replies. "Since I started doing it, I sell three or four cats each day at just about the same price you offered me."

Fujiki's performance of *Red Cat from the Heavens* is much more closely related to the narrative conventions of rakugo than the performances that I examined in chapter 1. This is not accidental—he has often said that he likes to select a popular or interesting rakugo script and try to rewrite it in a way that would be appropriate to Okinawan cultural conventions. This performance is the result of one such exercise.

Like many rakugo stories, Fujiki's tale recounts an engagement across generations: in this case, an avaricious young man and his older interlocutor.[20] I will return to this point; for now I simply want to note its resonance with the conventions of rakugo. Like rakugo—and unlike most of Fujiki's narratives—this story has a definite conclusion, an *ochi* or a "drop" as it is called. In the final moments of the performance, the narrator recognizes that the old man has turned the tables on him. With that realization, the story comes to a conclusion. Thus, the performance is both thematically and compositionally finalized. In most of Fujiki's other performances, the narrative simply fades away, leaving a feeling of openness and indeterminacy that is only partially resolved by the formal closure of the entire performance.

In other performances, the question of address is much more problematic. Fujiki often enunciates only one of the voices in a dialog, forcing the audience to be quite consciously engaged with his performance in order to follow its direction. As a consequence, the audience is required to provide an imaginary discourse to which Fujiki's spoken discourse can articulate. However, in the case of the *Red Cat from the Heavens*, Fujiki selects from the performative conventions of rakugo, playing both roles in the represented conversation, and using variations in his voice, gestures, and bodily hexis in order to indicate characters. Also, as in rakugo, he remains seated, relying on a much more circumscribed vocabulary of gesture and movement in order to express himself.

Later, when we discussed the sketch, I told Fujiki that it seemed to me that he guided the audience more than he did in the *Hitori Yuntaku Shibai* performances that I'd seen. I wondered if it was intentional—a way to make sure that we caught the points that resounded with his earlier lecture.

"Hmm—that could be," he said, pausing for a moment to think. "But this sketch was also one of my first attempts at writing. I wasn't as comfortable with putting this piece together as I was with my later ones. That doesn't mean that your interpretation isn't right, but I can't say that it's something that I was thinking about at the time." As we finished up and got ready to leave, Fujiki asked us to think about why he chose this particular performance to end our first class.

When we met the following week, we took up this question. Shimabukuro Kenji, an official from the municipal department of education, had a convincing answer. "What could be more Okinawan than a bowl from Tsuboya?"[21]

At one level, the bowl does appear to be a kind of synecdoche for the objects and practices of a traditional lifeworld. We talked about the web of images of Okinawa that continue to populate the Japanese social imaginary. Okinawa is envisioned as a refuge from the world of capitalist modernity that is contemporary Japan. It is a place where spiritually attuned peasants live in wooden houses with red-tiled roofs; farmers till the fields with plows drawn by plodding water buffalo and fishermen ply the coastal waters in *sabani* (wooden canoes); musicians while away the hot afternoons, playing slow, exotic melodies on snakeskin-covered sanshin; wise grandmothers dispense advice gleaned from their communication with the spirit world; and late-night revelries in moonlit clearings or along the beach hold out the promise of another way of life.[22] Despite all historical evidence to the contrary—or perhaps because of it—this dreamlike vision of Okinawa is perpetuated in Japanese popular culture, especially advertising campaigns for Okinawan tourism, sentimental films, and television programs. The bowl could stand for all of this.

And yet, the very existence of this specific bowl shatters any utopian vision of Okinawa. Kinjō Jirō's status as a Living National Treasure is a sign of the exceptional character of the Tsuboya pottery that he practices. The category of Living National Treasure was created through the efforts of Yanagi Soetsu and others to ensure that folk crafts would not be completely abandoned in favor of industrial production and that profitability would not be the sole criteria for the evaluation of a mode of production.[23] However, not all Okinawans appreciated Yanagi's intervention or sought to maintain practices and preserve objects explicitly marking difference from mainland Japan. Intense debate over assimilation raged in prewar Okinawa and continues into the present: to many, the costs of marginalization were all too clear. Still, one could say that Yanagi's efforts have been successful—the practice of Tsuboya ceramics has not been entirely abandoned, and it is still possible to identify exemplary practitioners such as Kinjō Jirō. However, given the intensive modernization and urbanization of contemporary Okinawa, the transformation of its economic base, and the conditions of everyday life, Tsuboya pottery is now a marginalized and exceptionalized product of the prefecture.

In its contemporary context, the bowl is also a commodity, embedded in networks of production and exchange including potters, merchants (like the young man), tourists and collectors, curators and academics, shopkeepers, wealthy benefactors, museums, galleries, and publishing houses. The bowl's complex character creates its exceptionality. It is at once an object both quotidian and unique, a folk artifact and an artistic *objet*. Fujiki's narrative turns on the tension between these two competing understandings. However, in the case of the young man searching for inexpensive treasures in Tsuboya, this juxtaposition does not produce a kind of Benjaminian dialectical image that shocks him into recognition of the crises and contradictions of modern life. For him, sensitivity to contradiction simply figures a form of expert knowledge that enables him to select an item that would fetch a high price on the Japanese market, a market that caters to those with a desire for objects rescued from the brink of the abyss.

In our discussion, several of the students were intrigued with Fujiki's decision to make both of the characters Okinawan. It might have been easier, they thought, to suggest that a sophisticated Japanese collector has come to take advantage of a naive Okinawan merchant. Fujiki said that would be too obvious a choice. He wanted to show that Okinawan society could be divided against itself. It seems to me that these two figures do signal the profound nonsynchronism of life in contemporary Okinawa. While it might be difficult to argue that the young man's sneeze at the lunch counter is a nod to the famous standard for assimilation that the prewar intellectual and journalist Ōta Chōfu suggested,[24] it is clear that the young collector is in other ways caught up in his efforts to meet the standards of modern Japanese society. He has committed himself to a life of rational calculation as he understands it, to a orientation toward profitability. In doing so, he objectifies those with whom he comes into contact—the old man is simply an obstacle to be overcome, to be cheated for the sake of a profit. He has lost the ability to appreciate the other voices, the other positions that create and are created by contemporary Okinawan society. He is deaf to the heteroglossia of everyday life. A reified, fantastic image of rural Okinawa pervades his sense of his fellow Okinawans. He imagines the shopkeeper to instantiate the characteristics of the folk Okinawan—albeit with a negative valuation. For him, the shopkeeper is ignorant, dirty, careless, unaccustomed to modern business practices, and unaware of the value of the objects that inhabit his world. The sure sign of the shopkeeper's lack of sophistication is his inability to recognize the artistic and commercial value of the bowl, marked by his employment of it according to a kind of simple use value—using the bowl as a bowl.

"Ryūkyūan history is long, but Okinawan memory is short," says Fujiki. Influenced by the popular media, by a Japan-centric educational system, or by local prejudice, Fujiki's art collector completely misunderstands the shopkeeper. While they might, in Ernst Bloch's formulation, exist in different temporalities, with different senses of their own futures, the collector's failure to understand the shopkeeper has its inverted counterpart in the shopkeeper's ability to understand him quite clearly. What the collector takes to be folk idiocy is a historically situated cunning, a practical knowledge forged through the experience of the Japanese colonial era, the Pacific War, and the American occupation. It is worth noting that Tsuboya is not only the traditional site of Okinawan ceramic production; it abuts the *kosetsu ichiba*—the public market, a maze of streets and vendors, once the heart of the black market economy of Okinawa.[25]

It is the old man then who is situated in his times, and the young collector who is a kind of remainder. The young man echoes the indigenous Ryūkyūan elites who inhabit Terurin's narratives, nobles whose sense of entitlement and social position has been dislocated by incorporation into the Japanese state and the modern capitalist economy. His only response is to imitate the calculating, businesslike manner of the modern Japanese while turning to the formal remainder of distinction that characterized the Ryūkyūan tribute-trade system. All he can do is hold onto the notion of finding unusual things to market in the metropole; it is the old man who lives by a cunning built up through critical, historical experience.

STUDENT STORIES

During one of the following classes, Fujiki asked if we had given any thought to contradiction in our daily lives, if anything had caught our attention. Uechi Chieko, one of the nursery school teachers, was quick to respond. Once she had become attuned to this way of thinking about the world, she said that she couldn't think about anything else. She began to find contradictions everywhere.

> A couple of days ago when I was driving to work, I heard a strange news report on the radio. The announcer said that public phones were being installed in a really inaccessible region that used to be part of Soviet Central Asia. There had never been any phone service there before. I couldn't tell whether they were coin-operated phones or not, so I wondered how people would pay for their calls. And who would they call if nobody has their own phone?

Next, Yamazato Ruriko, a young office worker from Urasoe, described a picture that she noticed when she visited her grandparents over the weekend.

> My grandmother keeps a couple of old framed pictures on top of a chest in their living room. One shows several children walking together to school—my grandmother and her brothers and sisters. It was taken in Nago sometime before the

the classroom of the everyday

war. All of the children were wearing the same working kimono that they wore on their farm. However, the boys stood out because they wore sharp military-style school caps with their old clothes. And all the kids had shiny new leather randoseru [rucksacks] on their backs. It seemed strange that back then people didn't even have enough money to buy decent clothes, but they still had to spend their money on the rucksacks and caps that they were required to have.

After a number of other students related their experiences, Fujiki closed the sequence with a story of his own—one that he acknowledged might not have actually happened. The story concerns the famous activist Chibana Shōichi. By burning the Japanese flag, the Hi no Maru, at the kokutai (national sports festival) in 1987, Chibana interrupted the unity of what always seemed to me like the perfect Barthian moment—the former colonial Okinawans respectfully standing at attention as the Japanese flag was raised above the stadium.[26] Chibana was also in the news for refusing to renew his lease of land to the Japanese government, land that was located in the center of the American Sobe Communication Center, the notorious Elephant Cage (Zō no ori).[27] However, Chibana also had a quotidian existence away from these moments of public opposition to the Japanese state. He was a local entrepreneur, the proprietor of the Henza Store in Yomitan. His everyday practices, not his public actions, were the subject of Fujiki's story.

According to Fujiki, his friend was going to the beach in Yomitan and stopped at a local store to buy some necessities—soda, snacks, and so on. When he entered the supermarket, he realized that it belonged to Chibana. As he walked up and down the aisles collecting the items that he needed, he tried to catch a glimpse of the famous radical at work.

He found Chibana sitting at a table near the checkout counter. The table was covered with a variety of bentō, prepared lunches ready for purchase and consumption. Chopsticks in hand, Chibana was picking up boxes one at a time, opening them, adjusting their contents, replacing the lid and returning it to the table. Looking more closely, he saw that Chibana was using his chopsticks to remove the crimson preserved plum from the center of the rectangular portion of steamed white rice, and moving it to a corner.

Overcome by curiosity, Fujiki's friend asked Chibana what he was doing.

"Hi no Maru bentō [Rising Sun lunches],"[28] Chibana replied without pausing or looking up.

Fujiki's friend blurted out, "Then why don't you just burn them?"

"Mottainai [That would be a waste]," countered Chibana.

I thought that Fujiki presented two important points in this simple joke. First, he demonstrates his sense of conjunctural intervention. While it might be possible to change the course of political events through a series of powerful moments such as Chibana's flag burning or his refusal to renew base leases, there is also an important political character to the everyday. It is through regular action at this quotidian level that the effects of ideology are disrupted. At the same time, the appearance of a conjunctural moment can only be established after the event. Hence, the need to decenter the rising sun, to disrupt the image of the Japanese state, manifest even in the lunchbox. Each moment might be *the* moment.

Second, Fujiki argues that there are material constraints to every action. Chibana burned the flag at the kokutai and endured the consequences of his actions. Okinawa has an unforgettable history of hardship and deprivation. Even acts of political resistance must be circumspect: it might be possible to burn one flag, but it is inconceivable to burn a hundred lunches.

After our discussion of the Chibana joke, Fujiki told us that he had a group project that he wanted us to do. He asked everyone to take out his book. He had already selected one of the performances and divided it into short sections. Each one of us was assigned a section and asked to memorize it. He would begin class next week by calling up the student assigned the first section of the text. That student would recite the assignment, and then be replaced by the student assigned the following section. In this way we would not only perform our own section in front of the class; we would also work together to construct an entire performance.

The play that we were assigned was the second of two short pieces that Fujiki had written about Okinawan food. The first was entitled *Okinawa Soba*—Okinawan noodles; the second *Pōku Tamago*—Spam and eggs. He spent little time discussing the story itself, focusing his instructions on advice about learning and enacting the performance. He suggested that we read it several times in order to fix the sequence of events in our minds. Then, he urged us to find someone to help us learn about the character. We were all to enact the part of the narrator, an older Okinawan man. Fujiki suggested that students get together with their grandfathers or with any older relatives that they might have. In the absence of older relatives, per-

the classroom of the everyday

Fujiki Hayato in *Pōku Tamago*

haps an elderly neighbor or someone from work. He recommended that we read our assignment with them, and possibly get them to record it for us. Then, we could replay the passage over and over, learning to imitate their intonation, the rhythm of their speech, their spoken idiosyncrasies while we practiced. He also suggested that we note their gestures and their physical habits. All of these things would go into our performance of the assignment. If we only focused on accurately memorizing the text, he said that we might as well just read a *shōgakkō nikki*—an elementary school journal. Instead, he wanted us to broadly consider all elements of the performance and practice it until we really know it. Here, Fujiki used the expression *nomikomu* to indicate understanding. *Nomikomu* is literally a compound of the verbals *nomu* (to drink) and *komu* (to fill). Selection of this locution clearly implies an embodied, physical process of internalization.

Here again, I think that Terurin's influence has been extremely important to Fujiki. When I later read Terurin's autobiography, his account of reading Kishaba Eijun's fieldnotes reminded me of our exercises in Fujiki's seminar. Both Terurin and Fujiki advanced an innovative, experiential methodology in order to develop a creative and affective relationship with the object of their inquiry—to take it in, to make it their own. In Terurin's case, he was the student, exposed to the ethnographic texts that Kishaba had assembled; in Fujiki's case, he was the teacher, presenting the texts of his own performances to his students.

the classroom of the everyday

There are also notable differences. As I argued in chapter 2, Terurin's project involves the hermeneutic recovery of native competency. However, Fujiki's work is far less concerned with claims of authenticity. In part, this is a consequence of their times. Perhaps the difference is also due to their differing positions in Okinawan society. As a déclassé noble himself, Terurin always seemed to be concerned with his own ontological security. For Fujiki, this issue is at once more complex and less relevant. As the son of an immigrant from Amami Ōshima, now part of Kyūshū, the characters of his family name clearly identify him as being other than Okinawan—although he could (and does) assert that he is Ryūkyūan by ancestry and Okinawan by birth. Nonetheless, the nonsynchronous aspirations of the impoverished nobility are not of immediate concern to him.

William Hanks has noted that, for Bakhtin, all speech is dialogic and to simply refer to speech as dialogic tells us little or nothing about it.[29] Let us then consider the differences in these two dialogic encounters. Terurin uses his dialog with Kishiba and his texts to uncover the native voice, silenced or obscured by the polyphony of voices originating in the modern Japanized world. Fujiki uses the encounter with his text—a complex, secondary genre, ethnographic and historical material mediated by his own creative efforts— to encourage the students to recognize the possibility afforded by heteroglossia. In this engagement, their complacency with a world of doxic regulation, of categorical stability can be shattered. He wants the students to be open to the possibility of change and of transformation, even when the spark is found in the words of marginal, disreputable figures—in the speech of old men, criminals, and fools.

I couldn't think of any elderly neighbors who would be willing to help me with the assignment, so I walked up to the community center in Sonda[30] and got one of my friends, himself a musician and occasional collaborator with the humorist Gakiya Yoshimitsu, to read through it with me. Most Okinawan actors that I knew had a stock character of an old man that they could do, and my friend went through the script in that voice so that I could get a sense of what the performance might sound like. What follows is a translation of the section that I was assigned to prepare. The scene is a diner in Okinawa City. An elderly Okinawan man is intently explaining characteristics of the spoken language to his young mainland Japanese companion.

Tēki auto means "take out." I don't have any intention of making you laugh. . . . Tēki auto. . . . That's pathetic. Your words have been poisoned by the fast food era. Do you think that those words of yours will get through to the Americans? If you are thinking about trying to live in this island, then you have to learn the Okinawan Gairaigo.[31] That's right. Okinawan foreign words. These are words in Uchināguchi that foreigners can understand too.

So, do you think that this is interesting? Will you learn? "Please teach me!" you ask? Ah—you're good at appealing to my heart, aren't you. Well then, let me initiate you into the secret mysteries. First off, let's start with my introductory course.

Tūnā—do you have any idea what that means? You probably don't, do you. This is what people like you call shī chikin—sea chicken.

These days, the Japanese influence on this island has gotten a lot stronger. Now, lots of people say shī chikin, but the truth is, that's just a brand name. I've got lots of American friends, but if I were to say to them, "Do you guys know about sea chicken?" they'd just respond, "What? Are there chickens in the ocean?" And there aren't any, are there! That's right. The fact is, we're talking about tsuna[32] [tuna]. Now, if you were to say tsuna to a foreigner, do you think that they'd understand you? That's why, here in these islands, it's tūnā no matter what.

Ripīto afutā mī [Repeat after me], tūnā [tuna]. Could you remember it? It's hard, isn't it. So let's try to chant it with some rhythm.

Actually, there is another word from these islands that it resembles—chūnā. It sounds just like the way you would say rajio chūnā [radio tuner]. The meaning is "Is it today?" So, if you were to say, chūnā tūnā, it would mean something like "Are we having tuna today?" Now, if we make a rhythm game out of it, you will be able to remember these things, little by little. Let's try it wun moa agein [one more again, or one more time]. Chūnā tūnā chūnā tūnā.

The old man continues to practice the phrase with his companion, suggesting different mnemonic techniques. At one point, he even suggests that they sing the phrase to the tune of a well-known song.

You see? If you do it like that, you'll remember. Now there are lots of other similar words like chuinūnā[33] and achānā,[34] but it is pretty hard for you to remember that all at once. So, for today—chūnā—let's just "eat" tūnā. So then, for review, Today we will eat . . .

the classroom of the everyday

What are you talking about, tūnā? Today, we are eating pōku tamago [Spam and eggs] aren't we? Is this too tough? Too tough for you? OK—I understand, I understand. A young person like you should use this frustration as a springboard to remember these island words.

Fujiki's argument resonates with an observation about language that anthropologists have been attentive to since Boas noted it in his essay *On Alternating Sounds*.[35] A subject hears the sounds produced by the speaker of another language in terms of the sounds available in his own; his own production is limited by the same constraints. The old man in Fujiki's narrative explains that the idea of a fish is expressed by a native speaker of English as tuna, it is heard and produced as tūnā by an Okinawan such as the old man, and tsuna by a young mainland Japanese.

However, it is the historical and political implications of this observation that Fujiki explores. "Do you think that those words of yours will get through to the Americans?" the old man asks his companion. For Fujiki, the question turns on the exigencies of everyday life in Okinawa. The word tūnā produced by the Okinawan speaker would be, he argues, intelligible to an American listener, but not so to a Japanese. The word tsuna produced by the Japanese speaker would be intelligible to an Okinawan, but not to an American. Words appropriated into the Japanese language do not index a kind of heteroglossia, with its possibility of diversity: they are recovered by a monologic process. They are transformed so that they are no longer intelligible to a speaker of the language from which they were appropriated; at the same time, they remain marked in Japanese written expression through their representation by the katakana syllabary and their designation as Gairaigo. The Japanese speaker who tentatively advances their use in attempts to converse with, for example, an English speaker, will inevitably be confounded by their unintelligibility.

In his notes on the performance, Fujiki writes that the old man learned English exclusively through conversation with Americans; he would have learned standard Japanese in the public schools and Okinawan at home. He is able to produce and comprehend sounds from both Japanese and English sound systems. However, Fujiki does not argue that the Okinawan language is uniquely structured to mediate exchange with English and Japanese.[36] Rather, he observes that the necessities of everyday life in Okinawa have required Okinawans to overcome whatever impediments their language might impose on communication and to work toward proficiency in the languages that have been used to rule and to exploit them.

How then does this argument articulate with the themes of the entire performance? As Fujiki envisioned it, we would meet during a subsequent class and perform each of our assignments in succession, allowing students to both participate and to observe. As each piece was added, the whole performance would become clear.

Unfortunately, it was at this point that the pressures of the Okinawan everyday intruded into the seminar. When we met during the following week, it was obvious that it would be impossible to stage even a reading of *Pōku Tamago*, let alone a performance. Because of a new contract taken on by his company, the contractor Gima Shunji was forced to withdraw from the course. He came all the way to the class to apologize to us for any inconvenience that his absence might cause, and he thanked Fujiki for his generosity. The two students from Okinawan International University didn't even come: they had called the Youth Seminar office and told them that they were too busy with school and would have to drop out. Sheepishly, several of the other students present also apologized to Fujiki and the class. While they had read their assigned sections of the script several times, the demands of work had kept them from spending the time to perfect their performances. They were willing to read through their assignments, but they weren't confident that they could do even that very well.

Most students had envisioned this course as something to be incorporated into their leisure time, their hours away from work. However, this is time that is also filled with a myriad of other activities—management of the household, meetings with friends and associates (for an example, *moai*, or cooperative loan associations, account for several evenings of each month for most Okinawan adults), community activities, and sleep. A single set of practices such as studies in the Youth Seminar cannot expand infinitely—and certainly cannot cross into that segment of the day devoted to work. The requirements of Fujiki's assignment brought the students to the limit of their ability to manage their time. And if they were serious in following Fujiki's suggestion to be attentive to contradiction in their everyday lives, surely this was another excellent example.

the classroom of the everyday

There was a pause for several moments as Fujiki waited to see if anyone else was going to speak up. Then, he laughed and agreed that it was hard to find time for something as demanding as learning a complicated performance. Maybe the assignment was too much. For the final assignment, it might be better, he said, to pick a shorter text. Then, he brought up the young electrical contractor who had just left.

"Can you imagine that he came all the way up here from work just to tell us that he didn't have time to participate? And look—he brought this for us as well," Fujiki said, holding up a box of fresh pastries from a popular local bakery. "That's some consideration. He is a really good person."

Everyone agreed with Fujiki, and conversation turned to how busy people had been at work. Clearly many of the students were embarrassed that they had come to the class unprepared. They were relieved to find that they weren't alone, and that Fujiki wasn't upset with them. Gradually, Fujiki guided the conversation to a discussion of work and leisure in contemporary society. Before long, we were forced to end the class because Fujiki and I had a schedule conflict—both of us were participating in a panel discussion about Okinawan culture that Tamaki Mitsuru had organized at the Koza Café. The rest of the students thought that the performance sounded interesting, and they decided to come along with us.

However, Fujiki returned to *Pōku Tamago*. During one of our last sessions, he took advantage of a break in rehearsals for the final performance to enact it, much as he had performed *The Red Cat from the Heavens*.

PŌKU TAMAGO—SPAM AND EGGS

Fujiki noted that the story normally begins with taped narration introducing the performance; this time, he simply read it aloud. The narrator explains that this meal holds the key to many things in Okinawan culture. Although it differs from other, more famous items in Okinawan cuisine, there is a kind of simple purity to it, served on a white platter: "Okinawa's history was bound up in this simple dish."

As the performance begins, an old man is talking to his unseen interlocutor, a young Japanese man who has come to live in Okinawa. They are sitting together in a *taishū shokudō*—a kind of working-class diner. Fujiki's character is typical of old men who haunt the shops and restaurants of Okinawa City. Retired or unemployed, drunken or mad, they are constantly searching for a companion to whom they can hold forth.

> Those feelings that you've brought up now are an insult to pōku tamago! Understand? Think of how much you've improved the way you think about Okinawa soba.[37] . . . Of course, it's the first time that you've seen or eaten them. . . .
>
> So, why don't you judge pōku tamago on neutral territory? I don't know what tourists these days are looking for, but they've turned the pōku tamago here into a thing for their amusement. They come here and take commemorative pictures with pōku tamago—they laugh it up. Just a while back, six of them came and ordered one plate—they all passed it around and had their picture taken with it. I think that's pitiful . . . pitiful. Pōku tamago isn't something that you show off like that!
>
> That's right. I think that kind of jerk should be thrown out. Those are my feelings exactly. Thrown right out. So when they are about to press the shutter I just want to yell, "What do you mean OK, Cheese!—there's no cheese in pōku tamago! It's not peace! It's pork!" But they just ignore me—I get so enraged.

On the pretext of teaching his young companion about Okinawan culture, the old man cadges a plate of pōku tamago from him. For his part, the young man is curious about the old man and wants to hear the stories that he has to tell.

The old man warns his young friend that he has to be attentive to the differences between Okinawan and mainland Japanese culture, differences that inhere in the most quotidian practices. When ordering a meal, for example, a mainland Japanese tourist will inevitably order the teishoku, the set menu. This way, he is certain that he will receive soup and rice in addition to his entrée. Japanese meals have been rationalized, so that the only way one can obtain a complete meal is to order it item by item. However, in Okinawa, it is still common sense to think that a meal is not complete unless the entrée is supplemented with at least rice and soup. So, when one orders an entrée, it is unnecessary to ask for soup or rice—it simply goes without saying that you'll get it.

The old man goes on to say that Okinawan culture continues to bear the traces of contact with other cultures. There are many loan words in Okinawan that represent words borrowed from English. And, unlike mainland Japanese, Okinawan speakers attempt to pronounce them so that they can be understood by American listeners. At the same time, Okinawan culture reveals the effects of participation in the Chinese empire, and of trading missions throughout Southeast Asia.

And the old man returns again to canned pork, to Spam, in order to show the influences of Chinese culture and learning, as well as the continuing effects of Okinawa's situation in networks of global capitalism. But for the old man, pork is so much more than an instantiation of trade networks. It represents a moment of tremendous importance.

The old man skewers a slice of Spam on a single chopstick. The young Japanese man tries to follow the old man's lead and do the same thing. Watching him struggle, the old man stops him and begins to tell a story:

You don't have to kill yourself imitating me. Just listen to this story. I'll never forget it—it was December 20, 1970. It was just like a war, with the helicopters flying over our heads. Don't say anything—just listen. In those days, we were under American rule. The people's endurance of the various kinds of treatment that they suffered at the hands of the military had reached its limit.

Over and over, we'd set the time to start a riot and try to carry it out. But, in the end that dream didn't come true. That's "Okinawa time"[38] for you. When you add our feeling of terror, the meeting never quite came together. In the end, only a few people met at the gate and one after another they were caught. A few people just missed the assembly time and didn't make it at all. I was one of those.

But lots of people had gathered together in Nakanomachi for Christmas and bōnenkai[39] parties. And when it looked like MPs were going to help an American get away after he hit an old lady with his car, the people's rage exploded. Everyone started setting fire to the American cars—that was the famous Koza Riot. Nobody could do anything to stop it until all the cars were burned up.

I didn't run. I joined right in. If everybody does it, it isn't frightening, is it? It was great—just like a beach party in the winter.

Why quarrel with the American soldiers? . . . Absolutely. . . . Don't say such crazy things. The Americans those days were so strong. Have you ever seen the movie *Terminator*? That's what they were all like. Now, if you put a Japanese person in the role of the Terminator, he'd get killed at that time in the middle of the movie when the Terminator gets hit by a car. The movie would be over in the first hour.

the classroom of the everyday

That's why everyone took on the cars. I was OK. We ran away as the sun was rising. I was a master of running away [hingibisā], so there is no way that they were going to catch me. If I was identified, I would have been in trouble, so I took off.

Why does pōku tamago remind him of this moment? He returned to his house in the early hours of morning as the riots ended. His mother had just served breakfast of Spam and eggs. As he began to eat, an American helicopter dropped to a low hover over his house, making the building tremble to its very foundation.

When I ran back to the house, my mother had just set out the breakfast—and it was pōku tamago. It's a strange feeling, isn't it? I had dropped one of my chopsticks, so I skewered the slice of pork with the other one and was about to put it in my mouth when the helicopter hovered above the house. The sound of those propellers roared in my ears. Without thinking, I started to spin the slice of pork on the end of the chopstick as I ate it. Even now I remember it. So if I spin it like this, I remember that day just like it was yesterday. The only thing that hasn't changed is the pork. . . .

But it is more than the individual content of memory that draws him to pōku tamago. So many things were bound up in that simple meal.

NARRATOR: Life was difficult during the occupation and any conflict only served to further the Americans' purposes. They were just intruders who took advantage of openings provided by the selfishness of so many Okinawans. It's kind of ironic that it was none other than the Spam that the Americans offered to us that was served for breakfast that day. It's really something when you think about the content of memory that relates to this brand of pork luncheon meat.

OLD MAN: The Americans who taught us about pork, corned beef, and stew were certainly generous.

Huh? I guess you could say that too. Maybe they tried to use canned food to make us into their allies. But when it comes down to that, we're just a little bit better than they are. America—its history is just different. Do you understand? Since long ago, the kingdom of Ryūkyū had been able to create long life through its climate and through pork. After the war, we finally succeeded in using the abundant, delicious meat from America to build a perfect "Kingdom of Longevity."

That's right. Was I that persuasive? *Sensei*? Who—me? You're talking about me? You know, you are really good at getting me going. What's that? I was just saying it the best that I could. I'm serious—I didn't have anything else in mind. It was really that persuasive? Well, if we're saying that much. . . . Next time, you should pay attention to the claims of old people. That's right, that's right. If you're interested in this kind of thing, there's lots that I can tell you. Listen? Okay—

Okinawa cleverly took just the good points from many different countries. We absorbed American democracy and were able to produce a unique kind of freedom here. Only this island, mind you. If your superior says that we're going to have a burēko [a kind of free give-and-take session] you can say: "Hey, boss, if you do this, it isn't going to work. Stop it right now." And it's just a regular worker who can say this too. There are people who work on base who said, "Even if it means cutting my own throat, the bases must be withdrawn!" Also, when the crown prince came to Okinawa, someone yelled, "How's your dad?"

The old man sees pork and the other canned goods as signs of the kindness of the Americans who fed the starving Okinawans after the end of the war. After discussing it with his young friend, he realizes that it could also reveal the calculating nature of Americans who feel that a person's loyalty can be bought at the price of a can of food. With his reference to selfishness, Fujiki also recalls the black marketeers who profited from the sale of canned goods while others suffered. However, pork also suggests the strength of Okinawan culture. Since long ago, the kingdom of Ryūkyū had drawn on its relationship with China and its productive local climate in order to build a society of peace and longevity. The abundant, delicious meat that they received from America was used to supplement indigenous pork so that Okinawans could overcome the hardships of war and occupation, so they could once again lead long, productive lives.[40] For the old man, this is the essence of Okinawan culture: take something of value from the cultures that you come into contact with; put these elements together in order to make something that is specifically Okinawan. Democracy, freedom, all these things have contributed to the Okinawa that exists today.

The old man stops and addresses his interlocutor again:

Did you get a good feel for Okinawan culture? All I have to give you is the wisdom of an old man that I feel in my bones, the lessons of a lifetime that I've built up without realizing it. A responsibility comes with the gift of long life. Responsibility to reflect on Okinawan history and culture, and to share these lessons with others.

VIOLENCE AND DEMOCRACY

On a winter's night in 1997, I sat at a table in Māchū with Fujiki and Onga Takashi, a historian at the Okinawa City Hall Peace and Culture Promotion Section. Fujiki's seminar was nearly finished. As the anniversary of the Koza Riot approached, I had been seeing retrospective articles in the local newspapers and journals and hearing occasional comments on radio programs. These reminders came together with memories of Fujiki's performance, keeping the uprising in my thoughts. It seemed that Fujiki and others had been thinking about it as well.

On the table in front of him, Onga had spread out the contents of a thick folder. There were clippings about the 1970 uprising from Okinawan and mainland Japanese newspapers, both contemporary and historical; photocopied selections from the memoirs of Ōyama Chōjō, the mayor of Okinawa City during the incident, and Yara Chōbō, the first governor of Okinawa Prefecture after reversion to Japanese sovereignty; a stack of black-and-white photographs; critical essays copied from the journal Shin Okinawa Bungaku; transcripts of round-table discussions between antiwar and reversion activists; a special edition of Fujiki's free paper that featured a map for a walking tour of riot-related sites; and interviews with musicians and artists about the uprising and its influence on their work.[41]

After thirty years, the Koza Riot still looms large in Okinawan memory—the one incident of Okinawan mass violence directed against the American occupation. As we looked through the documents piled on the table, Fujiki and Onga mused that while many have tried to establish the causes of the riot, no one could really say for certain what happened. The documents suggested many things: fear of renewed Japanese control, of resurgent Japanese nationalism;[42] opposition to the war in Vietnam, rehearsed in Okinawan jungles and launched from Okinawan runways and warehouses; fury over chemical weapons stockpiled in Okinawa;[43] concern that the American bases will remain after reversion or be replaced by Japanese garrisons; fear that the bases would be closed and that thousands of on-base jobs would

The Koza Riot

disappear; and anxiety that the land will be returned and revenues from the leases will be lost. Fujiki said that most people believe that Okinawans had finally had enough of the unfair way that they were treated whenever they were caught up in a dispute involving Americans.[44]

Only days before the riot, an American serviceman who had killed an Itoman woman in a violent automobile accident had been found innocent in a military court, all evidence to the contrary notwithstanding. One could imagine that another auto accident, another injured Okinawan, another example of American insensitivity could spark an incident. Still, Americans were taken by surprise at the ferocity of the uprising. Perhaps, after twenty-five years of an unfair and negligent occupation, Americans felt that Okinawans would put up with anything.

I owe my own interest in the Koza Riot to my conversations with Tomiyama Ichirō in the months before I went to the field. In 1995, he urged me to consider the place of the uprising in the Okinawan imaginary, introducing me to a number of Okinawan essays and suggesting that I try to learn more from Onga in Okinawa. Tomiyama himself takes up the question of the riot in *Okuni wa*, his ruminations on Okinawan politics, identity, and popular culture. However, in his text, Tomiyama evidences little interest in providing anything like a conventional historical account. In fact, discussion of the event itself is almost completely absent. The most expressive representation in the text is a black-and-white photograph: several young men running away from a pair of burning cars, one looking back over his shoulder at the flames that blaze like a star against the dark background of the image.

the classroom of the everyday

Tomiyama writes that it is the ambiguity of the incident that fascinates him. He quotes the Okinawan poet and social critic Kawamitsu Shinichi, who witnessed the uprising as an *Okinawa Times* reporter: "the riot was neither planned nor executed by any known group or organization. It went beyond the doctrines of all the established movements."[45] Tomiyama argues that it would be impossible to create a conventional account of the riot. While many things can be said about the popular sentiment of the time or particular incidents during the evening, any narrative that attempts to establish causality can only impose a false sense of order. Tomiyama settles for a simple exegesis of the characters that compose bōdō, the Japanese term for riot: *violence in motion.* That is all that can ever really be known. The rest speaks only to an urge to fit the incident to comfortable categories and established concepts.[46]

But the images endure: Okinawan men and women crowd the streets, pulling American servicemen from their cars. Angry demonstrators hurl rocks, debris, bottles of burning gasoline. Okinawan police and American soldiers struggle ineffectively to restore order. The gates of the base are torn down, a guard post destroyed, an American elementary school burned. Heavily armored phalanxes of American soldiers advance on the crowd, bayonets fixed. The wreckage of dozens of cars burns in the streets.

Terurin suggested that a creative performance is crafted by wrapping a historical lesson or critical insight in the guise of a popular story. *Pōku Tamago* is an example of Fujiki's attentiveness to Terurin's methodology. Okinawan comedy reviews often deploy a sketch in which a disinterested young man is trapped and forced to listen to an old man's harangue. The old man is aggressive, confusing, insistent—and yet, in the end, the young man realizes that there is wisdom in the old man's words. In his days as a member of Tamaki Mitsuru's Shōchiku Kagekidan, Fujiki often appeared in this type of manzai-style performance. In those days, Fujiki would portray the young interlocutor, while Gakiya Yoshimitsu appeared as the old man.

In *Pōku Tamago*, Fujiki's aging character does not hesitate to explain the Koza Riot. For him, it is tied up with democracy. Throughout the performance, he argues that, compelled by the exigency of everyday life, Okinawans have learned to overcome the received categories that configure their speech, their actions, and their understanding. They have learned to cunningly appropriate, adapt, and utilize that which they find ready to hand.

Innovation and determination have enabled Okinawans to survive. They adopt the language of their American occupiers—as well as the national language of Japan. They accept Spam—a completely militarized food and an object of ridicule in America—and, drawing on customary ideas of pork consumption, use it to recreate their world. And they have appropriated democracy. But what kind of democracy is this?

Okinawans learned about peace, freedom, and democracy from the Americans. However, these lessons were learned in their negation. Okinawans became familiar with these concepts, only to sacrifice them so that they could be enjoyed by others elsewhere. For Okinawans, freedom was illustrated by the confiscation of their land, the restriction of their liberty, and the destruction of their customary way of life. Peace meant that their island would remain a military garrison, involved in every Asian war since the battle for Okinawa. Democracy meant repression, lack of representation, and a political environment dominated by decisions made in Washington and Tokyo.

This is why the Koza Riot took the form that it did. All was well so long as the Okinawan people were content to quietly and respectfully wait for the reversion that Japanese and American politicians had arranged on their behalf. When Okinawans questioned their conditions, demanded to be treated fairly, doubted the ability or the desire of the authorities to provide justice, they were met by a volley of rounds from American rifles. For Fujiki's character, the Koza Riot meant that Okinawans had seized the moment to act on their own behalf. This is their appropriation of democracy. As the narrator did during the days leading up to the Koza Riot, there are times when the opportunity to act is allowed to slip away—not everyone can be as vigilant as Chibana Shōichi, continually preparing for the decisive moment to arrive. However, like the old man on one December evening in his youth, like the construction workers arguing with their boss, like the base workers who campaign for base closure knowing full well that it will mean their jobs, there are times when they will assert their autonomy and seize their freedom.

KOBANASHI TAIKAI

The five sessions of Fujiki's seminar had been completed by early December. Constrained by the limitations of time and subjected to the pressures of labor and everyday life, our meetings still provided an important opportunity

the classroom of the everyday

Members of Fujiki's workshop at his club

for discussion and exchange. Many of us were reluctant to see the seminar end, and someone suggested that we organize a *moai* (a cooperative loan association) so that we could continue to meet.[47] Once or twice a month, we met for several hours at Fujiki's izakaya, drawn by the possibilities of discussion, laughter, and profit, and obligated by newly established friendships and by debts. Fujiki also encouraged us to join him for a performance at the Okinawa City Youth Festival, acting in a series of blackouts at an event that showcased local performing artists. A much better ending to a class than a report or an exam, Fujiki joked.

Several students told me that Fujiki had inspired them to continue with their interest in Okinawan history and culture. Shiroma Eriko, a young bureaucrat at the Okinawa City Hall, joined the "Shima Masu Juku."[48] A year-long seminar run by local artists, intellectuals, community activists, and entrepreneurs, membership was quite prestigious in the Okinawa City area. Other students continued to participate in informal research projects with Fujiki. In the summer of 1999, I returned to Okinawa to do some additional fieldwork. While I was filming the *eisā ōrāsē*[49] I met Yamazato Ruriko on a

the classroom of the everyday

crowded street in Koza. She had joined Fujiki and a group of tourists—Okinawan and mainland—to study eisā. For several days during Obon, they traveled across central Okinawa, watching performances in a number of different local communities.

One of the moments that remained with me, affecting my sense of what we had accomplished, took place during the final formal meeting of the seminar. Instead of a formal graduation exercise, we had a short performance in which everyone participated. Like the Youth Festival, it was comprised of a series of sketches. Most of us used stories from a handout that Fujiki had given everyone earlier in the course, although some of the students wrote their own scripts.

Fujiki opened the performance, clapping to set up a rhythm. Once everyone joined in, he began to sing a parody of the famous Okinawan melody "Tōshindoi."[50]

> Kobanashi doi, yuntaku doi,
> Minna kīte, waraimashō!
> Ane une, ane une, ane une une une!
>
> [The short stories are coming! The monologues are coming!
> Let's all listen and laugh!
> Ane une, ane une, ane une une une!]

One by one, each of the students stepped forward. There were no lights, no sound systems, no stage—just a space cleared in front of the cluster of the chairs where we all sat. Some of the students were quite good—well-rehearsed and confident. Others started well, only to become confused as they approached the punch line. A few students were still extremely nervous and uncertain—perhaps hadn't given enough time to rehearsal.

Of all the stories told that evening, Shimajiri Yoshiko's performance was the most arresting. Yoshiko was a nursery school teacher in Yomitan. She had joined the seminar with her friend and coworker, Uechi Chieko. At the beginning of the class, they told us that singing Okinawan children's songs and telling folktales to the children at their nursery school had awakened their interest in Okinawan history. Both of them were fans of Fujiki's *Hitori Yuntaku Shibai*: when he announced the seminar, they joined right away.

"This is a true story," Yoshiko told us. She said that she had been inspired by Fujiki's discussions and decided to start her own fieldwork, however modest. Over the past few weeks, she spent her free time interviewing her older relatives—parents and grandparents, aunts and uncles. She asked each of them to tell her about their experiences during the war. One of her grandmother's stories inspired the sketch that she was about to perform.

When the American soldiers came ashore in Yomitan,[51] her family and their neighbors took refuge in a nearby cave. For what seemed like an eternity, the battle raged all around them. Eventually, it became quiet—the sound of bombardment far away like distant thunder. Everyone huddled in the cave, unsure of what they should do. No one knew how much time had passed when there were sounds heard from the mouth of the cave. An American patrol stood outside, calling to the Okinawans to come out. Unfortunately, the Okinawans couldn't understand them at first. They thought that the soldiers were calling for Kamadō, a common girl's name:

> U.S. SOLDIER: Kamu auto, Kamu auto! [Come out, come out!]
>
> FIRST OKINAWAN: Eh—Kamadō? [What—Kamadō?]
>
> U.S. SOLDIER: Kamu auto! [Come out!]
>
> FIRST OKINAWAN: Inai sa, Kamadō wa. Kamadō wa inai yo. [She's not here—Kamadō. I'm telling you that Kamadō isn't here!]
>
> U.S. SOLDIER: Kamu auto! [Come out!]
>
> FIRST OKINAWAN: Eh—Higa—Kamadō yonde'ru yo. Inai te itte, ne. Inai wake sa. [Hey Higa—they're calling Kamadō. Tell them that she isn't here. 'Cause she isn't.]
>
> U.S. SOLDIER: Kamu auto! [Come out!]
>
> SECOND OKINAWAN: Kamadō? Kamadō ja nai sa. Kamu aotu te, dete koi to iu imi. Dete koi to yonde'ru yo! [Kamadō? They're not saying Kamadō. *Come out* is what they are saying. It means to leave the cave. They're telling us to come out.]
>
> U.S. SOLDIER: Kamu auto! [Come out!]
>
> OKINAWANS: We understand! We're coming out! Don't shoot!

Yoshiko stepped in front of us, dressed simply in jeans and a collared blouse. She was visibly nervous as she began to speak—her body rigid, her head lowered, her hands pressed tightly against her sides. However, it was clear that she knew her lines, had rehearsed them again and again. Gradually, her voice became more confident, a smile spreading across her face, her gaze reaching out to us. As her confidence grew, she began to move and to gesture, to enact the sketch with more and more enthusiasm. When she spoke as an American soldier, her voice became deeper, louder, accentuating the phonetic phrasings of the English commands. When she spoke as an Okinawan, she slipped into the lilting, Uchināguchi-inflected rhythm, the gentle tone of an older man. When she finished, she immediately became self-conscious and seemed a bit embarrassed. Still, she was obviously very excited, and moved by our response to her story.

The memories invoked in Yoshiko's story were intensely personal, drawn from her family's wartime experiences. At the same time, they touch on themes familiar to many Okinawans. Powerful traces of the Okinawan past condense in the image of the *gama*, the caves in which Yoshiko's characters took shelter. Before monumental tombs became popular in the seventeenth century, the remains of the dead were often given shelter within the caves, buried in the cliffs and caverns near Okinawan communities. These caverns were also thought to be the dwellings of Okinawan deities, the places where prayers and material offerings were exchanged. During the Japanese colonial era, shrines at Naminoue and Futenma were built over the openings of caves in an attempt to appropriate the power and prestige of sites associated with indigenous deities for state Shinto.

The gama are also sites of terror. In some communities, their presence is like a raw wound in the landscape, interrupting the unity of everyday life. Some have been blocked, others avoided until the efforts of local historians and peace and antibase activists opened them to discussion and to visitors once more. Still, memories of the caverns are shot through with the horror and violence of the suicides and massacres that took place during the war. These are the incidents so shockingly depicted in Norma Field's *In the Realm of the Dying Emperor*, and in films such as *Gama*. Okinawans were repeatedly told that anyone taken prisoner by the Americans would be horribly tortured and killed. Driven by fears of the American army, commitment to Japanese imperial ideology, threats by Japanese soldiers, and simply by desperation, countless Okinawans killed their own families and took their own lives. Many of those who did not were murdered by the Japanese soldiers whose mission had been to protect them.

Although more than half a century has passed since the end of the war, the

the classroom of the everyday

survivors of the gama and their descendants are still haunted by their experiences. Bitter, still-unresolved conflicts smolder over narration and public commemoration. This is the terrain that Yoshiko negotiated. She reached into the past, not for the native capacities and aesthetic sensibilities valorized by Terurin, but for perhaps the most horrible thing possible—the traumatic experience of wartime genocide. She made herself into a witness, searching out her relatives' experiences and opening herself to their narratives. She summoned the courage and creativity—if only for a fleeting moment—to enact what she had taken in, to share it with her friends.[52]

The voices of Yoshiko's Okinawans sheltering in the caves at Yomitan echo the cunning and resourcefulness of Fujiki's old man in Pōku Tamago. They are Okinawans who have borne the weight of the Japanese colonial era and the American occupation. They have struggled as itinerant agricultural laborers in Hawaiian cane fields, as warehouse workers on American bases built on the ruins of Okinawan farms. They have been driven from their homes by the savagery of the battle of Okinawa, from their streets by American riot troops. And yet, they can act on their own behalf, wielding the tools that they were forced to adapt. Enduring hardship, braving the dangers of combat, they struggle with the constraints of their own language in order to communicate with an American patrol.

Representations of experiences such as this are fraught with hazards. There is a tension between the need for expression and the inadequacy of language and gesture to capture the actuality of the experience. What's more, there is always the possibility that one could misappropriate the suffering of another or diminish the tragedy of the event. These concerns shadow Yoshiko's performance, and yet she presents it with respect and restraint, with lightness and a sense of play. She shapes her narrative in a way that is sensitive to the enormity of what her family endured and to the courage and resourcefulness that they demonstrated. It also a performance that bears the imprint of her own life, her own experiences, what she learned from the workshop with Fujiki.

We were all moved by Yoshiko's attempt to bear witness to her family's experiences. At the same time, I felt that in her words and gestures, she created a kind of allegory to her grandmother's account of past efforts to overcome the constraints of language, imperial ideology, and wartime propaganda. Many Okinawans had never been able to accomplish this, had been destroyed by their experiences. However, Yoshiko's performance demonstrated that some Okinawans—under tremendous pressure, with great courage, and with consequences that are still unfolding—have chosen to act. Perhaps this is the most important lesson of Fujiki's seminar. His workshop did more than recall the tragedy of nightmarish caves or the violence of riots. It reminded students of the tools that were still available to them and the abilities that they still possessed. Playing on the rhythms of everyday life to create a moment for reflection and creative action, he showed us that we could resist the constraints and the complacency of the modern world by doing the same.

4.

in a samurai village

Winter comes even to Okinawa. Under darkened skies, the brilliant sunshine and high, white clouds of summer seemed like a distant memory. For me, there was an uneasy emptiness to the first few weeks of January 1997. It was my first experience of the time that lies between the celebration of the calendrical New Year and its echo several weeks later, when the lunar year began. According to my friends, it also marked the conclusion of my third passage through the twelve-year calendrical cycle and my entry into a period of possibility and danger.[1] And yet, I felt something more than the anxiety of aging or the routine strangeness of living in Okinawa for two years—it came to me in snatches of heard conversations, discussions with friends, and articles in the local newspapers. Perhaps it was the unsettled pause between the euphoria of a season of political foment and the stunning disappointment of Japanese state repression yet to come.

It began to rain as I parked my small Suzuki sedan in the lot of a Sanei grocery store in Ginowan City. Overhead, two Cobra attack helicopters banked slowly, returning to the runway of the Marine base at Futenma, gray against the gray sky. I watched them—uncomfortably nostalgic—until they disappeared beyond the rooftops across the street. Turning up the collar of my jacket, I hurried down the street to Books Jinon, the rain falling more heavily. I stepped under the store's awning and shook myself off. The front door was propped open, and the manager waved to me from the counter where he was sorting books. The tables and bookshelves that filled the first floor were jammed with new publications and antiquarian treasures, everything imaginable about Okinawa or by Okinawan authors. Books Jinon was a kind of touchstone for Okinawan scholars. When I visited, I always felt that its shelves held the possibility of answers to the questions that had been turning in my mind, and the promise of projects that I had not yet even imagined. In its mute materiality, it could also seem like a challenge, the accumulated representations of events and practices that made up an everyday world that I would never fully understand. As I browsed along a shelf of books by Okinawan poets and novelists, a collection of poems by Takara Ben caught my eye.

Although I had briefly met him at an antibase demonstration and read several of his poems in translation, this was my first opportunity to read his work in its original language. I knew Takara to be an iconoclastic chemistry teacher at Futenma High School, an ethnographer, an activist for social justice, and a poet. His work brings together the classical songs of the Ryūkyūan court, Yamanoguchi Baku's[2] poems of the troubled identity and daily existence of working-class Okinawans in modern Japan, and Gary Snyder's poems of the turbulent interrelationship of action and existence in the contemporary world. Deeply informed by critical theory, native ethnology, and a concern with the quotidian experience of Okinawan history, Takara's poems are extremely personal explorations of the subjective demands of the political.

YĀDUI

As I leafed through the book, I found a poem entitled "Yādui"[3]—the rural villages of the déclassé Ryūkyūan nobility so central to Teruya Rinsuke's work. Yādui had been very much on my mind. Several days before, a representative of the local teachers association had told me that a group of local historians and anthropologists had been working on a study of yādui in Ginowan City that had been destroyed when American military forces seized local land for the construction of the Marine Air Station at Futenma in the early 1950s. He said that antibase activists would present the results of this research during upcoming public hearings—the kōkai shinri—into the impact of American bases on Okinawan society. Since I planned to attend the hearings and to also accompany the Okinawan sociologist Ishihara Masaie to a meeting of former residents of yādui within Kadena Air Base, I read the poem with great interest. It is stark and simple, its columns short and

in a samurai village

uneven against the white expanse of the page. Images follow one after another in a narrative present. The experience of the poem demands only moments of a reader, its lines descending across the top of just six pages.

Beginning with a scene from the narrator's daily life, the poem turns to an evocation of a moment in an unnamed yādui. Moreover, the precise temporality of this moment is ambiguous: it could be the early Japanese colonial period of the 1870s, the era of wartime militarization, or perhaps even a time after the reversion to Japanese sovereignty in the 1970s.

Dark night
Returning beaten by rain
Trudging with my daughter
Something is different
Just staring off into the distance
Bitter memories
Freezing waterpipes
In the foreign students lodging
The plover can't sing
Alone lone lone[4]

A ruined farmhouse
Summer grasses burn
Glittering in the salt spray
The old woman's back is hunched
Beneath the *yūna*[5] tree
She brings out a pestle
Mumbles as she crushes the bones
Crunch crunch
Alone lone lone

Roasts the dead old man's bones in the skillet
Break crush grind
Makes them into powder
Mutters something licks her fingers
Packs it into the amulet's pouch[6]
The old man will travel with her too
To the Land of the Sun[7]

in a samurai village

Uncremated bones cannot be taken
Threatened, the old woman
Roasts the bones night after night
Crushes them so that no one can see
Her white hair disheveled
Alone lone lone

The people who abandoned this samurai village
Crossing to the far side of the world
To Inca towns where the children of immigrants wait
Can't see the plover
Violet sash hazily floating
Hands kneading and pushing aside
The flower of the waves
Folded and crushed
Is the moon shining in the sky above the inn
Where an artist returned from the South Pacific
Haltingly confesses
That he can't paint the plover?
Alone lone lone

Somewhere in the world my wife is dancing again tonight
A coup d'état in Bolivia
A terrible earthquake in Peru
It's an outcast's village that sleeps at the bottom of the water
Is the old woman dead?
The rain runs down my neck soaks my back
News doesn't carry from the samurai village
(For Chijuyā)

Teruya Rinsuke often said that the measure of an Okinawan artist's virtuosity is his ability to draw upon the repertoire of classical and folk genres, transforming them in the performance of something new that still remains grounded in the old, the familiar. This dialogic mastery also demands a certain ability of the listener, whose relationship with the performer depends upon, and whose pleasure is enhanced by, the recognition of these intertextual moments. Takara's poetry is grounded in these same demands.

The spare constellation of images that he deploys calls upon readers or listeners to search and reflect on the contents of their own experience, to connect graphic and mnestic traces, linking the external records of their history with impressions of what they have learned and experienced. In turn, his artistry requires that he is sensitive to the social content of memory, to have a feeling for what and how much is available in his readers' archive.

The figure of the plover in the first lines of the poem, the later evocations of the dreamlike gestures of Okinawan dancers, the image of the narrator's wife dancing far away,[8] points the reader to "Hamachidori," or "Chijuyā" as it is called in vernacular Okinawan—a classical Ryūkyūan dance performed to the song of the same name. The title itself, "Chijuyā," is almost impossibly overdetermined. It refers to a dance remarkably ubiquitous in Okinawan performances: danced singly or in groups, at the National Theater in Naha, at neighborhood dance academies, family gatherings, and senior citizens clubs at community centers everywhere. It was a particular favorite of Yamanoguchi Baku, who often performed it with a circle of aficionados of Ryūkyūan dance that met regularly at the Okinawan bar Omoro near Ikebukuro Station in Tokyo. Takara Ben himself is also known to dance it occasionally. The minyō (folksong) to which the performance is set is famous in its own right. The late Kadekaru Rinshō,[9] an inveterate wanderer, is known for his haunting solo recordings of chijuyā and its variations. It remains extremely popular among Okinawan musicians, closing a recent recording of traditional minyō by the popular artist Ara Yukito.

Here are the first lines of this song of nostalgia and longing:

Traveling, I rest on a beach
Leaves of grass for my pillow
Although I sleep, I cannot forget
The times with my mother and father
On the beach, the plover cries *chui chui*.

Although the author of "Chijuyā" is unknown, the song is popularly understood to give voice to the experience of a Ryūkyūan traveler, perhaps a merchant sailor, his ship carried to distant shores by the Black Current.[10] A contemporary Okinawan dancing "Chijuyā" or watching its performance can experience a doubled longing: in recognizing the yearning of the sailor for his home, one feels a similar yearning for the lost world of the kingdom of Ryūkyū. This same imagery of the Ryūkyūan merchant and traveler abroad is crucial to Teruya Rinsuke's construction of a certain genealogy of Okinawan strength, cunning, and creativity.

However, Takara's poem is neither an elegiac depiction of a lost way of life nor directly suggestive of Okinawan craftiness. Certainly, the image of "freezing waterpipes in the foreign students lodging" provides both an unexpected seasonal marker (albeit a remembered rather than a currently experienced temporality) and a connection to a poetic tradition that ranges from descriptions of poverty and privation in the work of the Chinese ascetic Han-Shan,[11] to the work of the Japanese monk Ryōkan.[12] However, given Takara's interesting combination of classical influences and political concerns, one is also reminded of Gary Snyder's poetry—both his own translations of Han-Shan's *Cold Mountain* as well as personal works that forge a link between classical forms and concerns, and contemporary social and environmental issues. The negative image that Takara represents also contrasts with the equitable and promising lives of Ryūkyūan students living abroad in China before Okinawa's first brutal incorporation into the Japanese state.[13] And yet, the intertextuality of this image is historically grounded in the brutal specificity of Takara's poem: with a brilliant economy, he sketches the miserable experiences of thousands of Okinawan students like himself in prereversion Japan.[14]

The historical situatedness of the poem also serves to focus its affect. The gentle, generalized longing of "Chijuyā" is transformed: directed and intensified into a powerful sadness. Takara details losses that remain fresh and raw in Okinawan memory. When images of these losses are brought back to the reader for consideration, the pain is also recalled.

It is the trope of the yādui, the rural village of the impoverished Okinawan nobility, that is at the heart of Takara's critique of the consequences of reincorporation into the Japanese state. In Okinawa, memories of the yādui are complex and ambiguous. They are represented in the Okinawan press, in scholarly discourse, and in popular performance. Images are also circulated and reinterpreted in mainland networks, eventually returning once more to Okinawa: nativist ethnographies and seminars, tourist brochures and summer holiday packages, romantic films, and Marxist journals.

Yādui are depicted as authentic Okinawan communities, places of organic

in a samurai village

totality. Time passes in predictable cycles: crops planted and harvested, fishing boats launched, and festivals planned by the phases of the moon. Children are born, mature to adulthood, marry and give birth, die and join the ancestral spirits. The recognition of these cycles and the practices that produce and are reproduced by them anchor the community to the temporality of the Ryūkyū kingdom, and to that of China beyond.[15] Those that live in the communities are creative, not only bringing forth a life from the soil and the sea, but also producing works of art—music, dance, and ceramics. At the same time, they are temporally distanced in a way that a simple village could never be. Yādui, indexing the communities of courtiers sent down from the capital, suggest a place for those dispossessed of their land and their social position, between the old order of Ryūkyū and contemporary Japanese society.

Yādui are also represented as sites of privation and hardship. They signify the decline of the Ryūkyūan monarchy, no longer able to support nobles with court stipends, and the fragmentation of the Ryūkyūan social order under the pressures of Japanese colonial intervention. Sent down to the countryside, courtiers who have spent their lives as artists and bureaucrats struggle —often unsuccessfully—to farm desolate fields or to burn charcoal in the mountains. Farmers eke out a miserable existence, crops fail, and markets collapse. Parents sell their children, men and women look for work in the cities of mainland Japan—twenty thousand leaving each year during the 1930s, to become industrial laborers in mainland factories.[16] The Okinawan diaspora, driven from these villages, provides construction workers in colonial China, agricultural laborers on colonized South Pacific islands, and cane cutters in Hawaii. If the era is romanticized in rural idylls, it is also depicted as Sotetsu Jigoku (Sago Palm Hell): starving Okinawans boiling poisonous fruit, trying desperately to leach out the toxins so that they can eat.[17] The evenness of Okinawan space is fragmented; the continuity of time is broken.

The figure of the yādui is then a highly contested representational space— Henri Lefebvre's category to describe imaginative challenges posed to the material, practical activity that both produces and apprehends the social world (spatial practice) and to the dominant conceptual space that seeks to naturalize these contingent processes (representations of space).[18]

Remembered or imagined, depictions of the yādui are powerful interventions into the experience and understanding of everyday life in contemporary Okinawa. They challenge the quotidian experience of life: commuting to work via one of the broad highways that crisscross the island or threading one's way from home to office along a narrow, fenced road running through the wide expanse of an American Marine base; playing in a schoolyard beneath the routine flight path of American fighter jets; sharing the counter of a beachfront bar with laughing holiday travelers from Tokyo and a pair of Green Berets from Torii Station; filing directives from the national government in a municipal office; pouring concrete over a rebar skeleton in the framed foundation of a resort hotel; studying computer science at a local university; waiting for the annual payment from the Ministry of Defense for use of a parcel of land beneath the runway at Kadana Air Base that will help a struggling auto repair shop or electrical subcontracting business remain solvent for another year; waiting endlessly in a room shared with several siblings as another year comes and goes, hoping for more temporary work or for a temporary job to become permanent. They also contest the conceptual certainty of commercial roadmaps and street atlases; prefectural planning documents for extending airport runways, building dams, and eradicating fruit flies; architectural plans for a new duty-free shopping center or a new monorail station; a politician's proposal for a new industrial park; and defense planners' sketches and environmental impact studies for a floating airfield to which the American military aircraft at Futenma could be moved.

Politically charged deployments of images of rural communities such as the yādui are not new. As Alan Christy has suggested in his incisive reading of Yanagita's *Kainan Shōki*,[19] prewar nativist ethnographers such as Yanagita Kunio focused on ethnographic descriptions of the remote and rustic village, narratively purging the colonial present from Okinawa and representing it as a site where the timeless folk can dwell, where ancient Japan can be brought forth in the "now." A host of contemporary ethnographies—Japanese and American—have followed suit. There has been what can only be read as a deliberate focus on rural Okinawa; an overly credulous reader might never know that there are urban areas, much less American military bases, on the islands.[20] By contrast, Teruya Rinsuke, whose performances I discuss earlier, mobilized depictions of the harsh life of the fallen samurai to illustrate Japanese colonial repression and Okinawa resilience.[21]

In Takara Ben's poem, there is no background discussion of conflicted history, or the multiple layers of everyday life that had been lived in these rural Okinawan villages—all of that is left to memory, to that which is called to mind by the simple visual representation of the Okinawan vernacular word yādui in the title. So much is crystallized in this image. It is a familiar word now written in the phonetic hiragana syllabary, which signals that it is a word best spoken, expressed like a native Japanese term yet rooted in the local, Okinawa past. Takara eschews the katakana syllabary often chosen to represent Okinawan utterances, avoiding the strange effect of making a native Okinawan term appear to be foreign or otherwise marked. Were it to be written in kanji characters, the reader would be shifted to the terrain of a contemporary Okinawa struggling to find a place in modern Japan, imposing an unfamiliar image and an inaccurate voicing on a familiar phrase. All because of the anticipation of some imagined partner in a dialogue, a Japanese addressee who would, in any case, be puzzled by the context of this contingent locution.

Takara begins his poem in the aftermath of the destruction of the yādui. The houses are in ruin, the villagers about to be scattered. During the Pacific War, many of the yādui in central Okinawa were confiscated for the construction of Japanese fortifications and airstrips. In the battle of Okinawa, they were destroyed by American bombardment, their population caught in the crossfire of the Japanese and American armies, murdered by Japanese soldiers, or driven to commit suicide. After the war, return to many of the rural villages was made impossible by the American appropriation of existing Japanese bases; other villages, some already rebuilt, were destroyed as the bases expanded in the late 1940s and early 1950s.[22] Under the direct American rule that stretched from the end of the Pacific War until 1972, Okinawan landowners were compelled to lease their property again and again to the Americans, battling for the right to simply retain title to their lands. The movement for reversion to Japanese sovereignty held out the prospect that the bases would be closed and the land returned. This did not happen. While some installations were closed and the land restored to its owners, most land remained within base perimeters and most bases remained in operation.

If anything, reversion added another level of complexity to the organization of military land use. Instead of leasing land directly to the United States government, landowners found that their negotiations were mediated by the

Japanese state. Using Japanese tax revenues, the Ministry of Defense again renewed leases, providing it to the Americans for their continued use; American authorities now paid nothing for the use of their Okinawan bases. In the event that a landowner refused to allow the lease to be renewed, provisions were made for municipal or prefectural authorities to ratify the lease "on their behalf." This is a stunningly cynical manipulation of the idea of a proxy, depending on the complicity of local officials to support the interests of the central government regardless of the stated opposition, to say nothing of the actual presence of the landowners. Renewal of the leases was as good as compulsory until the prefecture refused to force ratification for a number of leases in 1995. Governor Ōta Masahide, a survivor of the wartime cadet corps, scholar, leader of the reversion movement, and politician, was seen as the driving force in defying the central government. As governor, he argued that Okinawans—Japanese citizens—were denied their rights in the forcible appropriation of their property, and that the Japanese government was in violation of its constitutionally mandated renunciation of war by providing this land to the American military.[23] It was at this time that popular indignation erupted, after the rape of a young woman by two American Marines and a sailor, driving mass demonstrations and a plebiscite challenging American occupation. And yet, by the time I first held Takara's poem in my hands, Ota's government had capitulated to pressure from the central government, shocking allies and opponents alike by reversing itself and renewing the base leases.

Takara once told me that, for him, art and activism were inseparable. He was a prominent member of the hitsubo jinushi (one-tsubo landowners), a visible presence at demonstrations and hearings.[24] He was also known for his public activity on behalf of the antibase movement, using his literary skills to publish essays, as well as write speeches and prepare statements for others. However, the image of the yādui was more than a simple trope that allowed him to articulate the history of base lands with the contemporary political struggles of base landowners. The destruction of the yādui opened a path to the profound interventions that the Japanese state has made into every level of everyday life. The yādui is a stunning synecdoche for life in contemporary Okinawa—it is representative of the experiences of all Okinawans who were thrown from their native villages into the crumbling, post-industrial, relentlessly reconstructed world of modern Japan. It speaks to the contradiction of Japanese citizenship: to serve the nation as loyal citizens, Okinawans must forgo the rights that citizenship should have afforded them. To live in peace, they must surrender their homes and harbor a foreign military. At the same time, the yādui remains a place of importance, a place lost to war and appropriation, but a place that calls for return.

Reflecting on the relationship of remembrance to the intertwined categories of life and death, the anthropologist Marc Augé has written: "The definition of death as the horizon of every individual and distinct life, while obvious, nevertheless takes on another meaning, as soon as one perceives it as a definition of life itself—of life between two deaths." Considering these twin horizons, the social self is compelled to locate itself on a spatiotemporal continuum. Constantly reminded of the death of others, one recognizes the inevitability of one's own death; whatever the uncertainties of the future may be, death is inescapable. At the same time—and this is more central to Augé's own work—one can never forget that both the life of the individual and the existence of society are built on the foundation of the deaths of those who have gone before. Death is the wellspring from which life—one's own life—emerges. This recognition is inseparable from a memorative obligation. And the dead, present and vigilant, insist that this obligation is met.[25]

Augé's observations also speak to the Japan in which Takara Ben has lived and worked. Most important here is the similarly complex and mutually transformational relationship that exists between the living and the dead. The living call upon the dead, seeking their blessing, their material support. The dead require, and receive, the remembrance and offerings of the living. They reward the diligent, remind the forgetful, and punish the negligent.[26] At the same time, I want to focus on the specificity of a life lived in contemporary Okinawa, a life building on the gift and the burden of all the lives that came before.

Ancestral spirits are thought to occupy an invisible realm coterminous with the world of the living. They appear in tombs and cemeteries, on distant mountaintops and forested valleys, in household altars and neighborhood streets, and yet they are whole, coherent, and intact. Active and engaged with their surroundings, they constantly observe and evaluate the conduct of the living.[27]

The experience of surveillance by the ancestral dead and the practices of self-discipline that it authorizes do not exist outside of history. In the prewar articulation of households with the imperial system, the emperor was cast as a kind of enduring ancestor of the Japanese people. A series of metonymic links produced an emperor who was both the exemplary head of the imperial house and the head of all households that composed the nation. As such, his was the ultimate authority to whose scrutiny each person would be subject, to whose standards all citizens must discipline themselves. In this formulation, the spectral desires and requirements of the ancestral spirits became manifest in the laws, policies, and regulations of the Japanese state. Compliance with the state was not simply analogous to submission to the patriarchal authority of the head of the household—it instantiated it. At the same time, the living were regularly reminded that they too would one day become ancestral spirits, receiving the devotion of their descendants and taking their place as arbiters of standards of behavior for future generations, insistent voices for the conservation of tradition.[28]

The imperial ideology was extended throughout the Japanese empire as well as in the home islands. However, a formal system of ritual practice and a hierarchy of practitioners existed in Ryūkyū prior to Japanese colonization. Countless historians and ethnographers have written of a gendered division of labor in which men were responsible for diplomatic and scholarly activities, while religious and ritual practices were the responsibility of women. The king had his counterpart in the kikoe ōgimi—a kind of chief priestess selected from the upper levels of the imperial household—and the system of dual authority extended to the village and household level.[29] An array of institutions and practices were deployed in order to mediate the ongoing relationship with the spirits of the ancestral dead, as well as propitiate autochthonous deities (the sun, the sea, various deities associated with sacred sites) and those that inhabit space transformed by human activity (the hearth, the well, the toilet). With incorporation into the Japanese state, these practices were proscribed as part of the elimination of the political and cultural apparatus of the kingdom.[30] However, despite the brutality and thoroughness of the colonial project, not all of these institutions were eliminated or articulated with imperial Japanese practice. In rural communities, shrines remained or were established, often with little to indicate their integration with the system of state Shinto. Many noro (local priestesses) continued to perform rituals in their native places, and other indigenous practices continued until struck by a renewed wave of repression during the final days of the Pacific War. After the war, in their efforts to rebuild a postwar world of everyday existence, Okinawans resuscitated many of these practices. It would, however, be a mistake to romanticize these gendered distinctions between diplomatic, scholarly activity and religious and ritual roles, even for their resistance to Japanese colonial pressure. There have been profoundly negative consequences to the persistence of this formulation: from the oppression of women in the domestic sphere to their exploitation as sex workers and low-paid laborers.[31]

While the regulatory aspect of the imperial ideology is said to have been disestablished by the postwar Japanese state, it continues to exert an uneasy influence, even in Okinawa. It cannot be simply dismissed as a melancholy object of the affections of the far right, or as the focus of leftist denunciation. It persists in spaces, in objects, in practices and in affect: in feelings still felt for the imperial family, in photos of the emperor displayed near household altars, in the statue of the Emperor Meiji that still stands in the courtyard of the shrine at Naminoue in Naha, as well as his spirit that remains enshrined there,[32] and in the enthusiasm that I have heard people express for a visit to Okinawa by Crown Prince Naruhito and his wife, Masako.

And yet, the architecture that once supported the imperial institution—the duties and obligations that characterize the relationship of the living to the dead—remains vibrant and certainly exceeds the repressive ideology that it once anchored. In their quotidian practices, Okinawans continue to maintain relationships with various household deities, particularly that of the hearth (the hī nu kwan or hī nu kan in Okinawan—the hi no kami in Japanese). At the same time, the spirits of the dead are widely thought to remain among the living, and maintaining the relationship between the living and the dead remains the most important objective of household ritual practice.

The dead communicate their desires to the living through dreams, through signs given in everyday life, through the intercession and mediation of yuta[33] or other ritual practitioners. They move in various ways through the world of the living, meeting them in both memorative spaces and sites of routine, quotidian practice. Although ancestral spirits sometimes manifest themselves directly—visually appearing, speaking, touching—these encounters are always structured around the practical interaction of two parties. Ancestral spirits receive daily offerings from their families at the household altar, accept the care and concern of the living, and listen to their requests.[34] They greet visitors at the tombs where they are sometimes thought to live, and accept invitations to return to their homes. They await their call, watching the world of the living from a distant place, perhaps *nirai kanai*, the other world.[35]

Interactions take the form of the intersection of what Nancy Munn has called mobile spatial fields—one centered on the body of the human participant, one on the body of the ancestral spirit.

> It is a space defined by reference to an actor, its organizing center. Since a spatial field extends from an actor, it can also be understood as a culturally defined, corporeal-sensual field of significant distances stretching out from the body in a particular stance or action at a given locale or as it moves through locales. This field can be plotted along a hypothetical trajectory centered in the situated body with its expansive movements and immediate tactile reach, and extendable beyond this center in vision, vocal reach, and hearing (and further when relevant). The body is thus understood as a spatial field (and the spatial field as a body).[36]

Like the human actor, the ancestral spirit is in some ways restricted to the same spatial boundaries that configure human interaction—gifts are exchanged, as if passed from one actor to another; prayers are offered and conversations conducted as if speaking to a nearby human interlocutor. Family members seated before the household altar or at the tomb present detailed oral reports, both formal and informal, as if the spirit is dependent on this encounter for its information. At the same time, it would be a mistake to view the ancestral spirit as limited to the spatial field as it radiates out from a human actor. I have often heard that, in the absence of a direct engagement with a human interlocutor before the household altar or in the courtyard of the tomb, spirits are able to range widely. Although their presence is diffuse, their perceptions of the world are able to take in distant and otherwise hidden events. They can exert their influence on their descendants through signs expressed in dreams or in embodied symptoms.

One could say that it is dialogic interaction that gives form to the ancestor's spatial field, that shapes it according to a combination of the conception of the limits of the actions and perceptions of a human actor—the being that the spirit once was, the expected and remembered powers of ancestral spirits, and the nature of the current interaction. Moreover, there is a perduring effect to these engagements. As practical engagements are repeated again and again, the situated spatial field of the ancestral spirit comes to be associated with these sites, leaving human actors with both the expectation that the spirit remains present there and that it can be engaged in predictable ways. This accounts for the sense among many contemporary Okinawans that ancestral spirits burn like the nativists' divided flame, at once present in any number of places such as the household altar, the tomb, and the nirai kanai. At the same time, I would argue that general contours of the spatial field, that which remains relatively constant from interaction to interaction and site to site, are largely determined by the transformation of the material substance of the dead that takes place at the tomb.

It is with this in mind that I want to consider the place of tombs in Okinawan everyday practice and in the way that space is understood, represented, and transformed. Through several centuries of documented history, tombs have been important centers of power through which the ancestral spirits exert their influence in the world of the living. They are sites through which a complex network of social relationships were created and maintained: with the spirits of the dead, within the families that comprise the kin group maintaining the tomb,[37] within the surrounding village, with neighboring noble and commoner communities, and with visitors from beyond. They are both fields of action in which mediational rituals were performed, and the basis of action, a reservoir of power from which the strength of the individual, the household, and the community derive and into which they invest their energies.[38]

"Critical dates interrupt the continuity of time," wrote Henri Hubert in his *Essay on Time*.[39] The continuity of space can also be disturbed. During the era of the Ryūkyū kingdom, rituals performed at the site of the tomb disrupted the regularity of the everyday. Mobilizing the material space of the tomb itself, these practices linked performances at this site with the monumental tombs of the royal family at Shuri, and with other tombs throughout the countryside where similar practices were taking place. In their physical orientation, they repeated geomantic principles governing the organization of social space, a space extending discontinuously to the continent and to the islands of Southeast Asia. Synchronized by the lunar calendar, these performances articulated with the cycle of calendrical rituals of the Ryūkyūan court

in a samurai village

Tombs in Okinawa City

and, by extension, to those of the imperial court in China.[40] Japanese colonization, the destruction of the kingdom and the suppression of relations with China, and the introduction of Western concepts and practices of time reckoning[41] fragmented the ostensive referentiality of these practices. And yet, to this day they remain important sites for regular performances.

Before the Pacific War, young men of noble descent living in the yādui throughout central and northern Okinawa spent summer evenings in the yards of community tombs, socializing, practicing sanshin and drums, and learning the eisā dances that they would perform during Obon, the festival of the dead. In many communities, ancestral spirits are still met at their tombs on the first night of Obon by a procession of eisā dancers and escorted back to their households. Families continue to gather in the spring for shīmī, a month of commensal feasting, prayer, and the presentation of reports about family activities to the ancestral spirits. In late summer, relatives meet at Tanabata to clean and repair the crypt—this is also the date that senkotsu (washing and preparing the bones of the dead) would probably have taken place. Regular communication with the spirits of the dead is also

in a samurai village

maintained through routine offerings of prayers, food, and flowers—even conversation—made at the door of the crypt. There is a comfortable sense of familiarity to the neighborhood tomb: children climb among them, playing games and relaxing atop their roofs. Elderly women cultivate gardens along their edges, taking a rest from their efforts in the shade of a stone wall. A drunken worker may be seen asleep on the paving stones of the courtyard in the evening twilight. Finally, tombs have been the sites of prolonged and complex Okinawan mortuary practice, from initial interment to the final mingling three decades later of the remains of the individual dead with those already placed in the communal ossuary.

The importance of the tomb to the household and the community is expressed in its monumental physical form. Since the introduction of the turtleback design in the early seventeenth century, tomb construction has been a visible sign of the affluence and the permanence of a household, and of its reverence for the dead. Present-day Okinawan tombs—whether those housing members of an extended clan or a more closely related group of families—are massive. Turtleback tombs remain popular, as do cubic, houselike structures. Built of cut stone or poured concrete, they open upon the nā (large paved courtyards) surrounded by stone walls and perhaps protected by a hinpun, or barrier. Okinawan tombs occupy hilltops and mountainsides or line a particularly picturesque spot among the homes of the living, perhaps with a view of the sea. These are often sites that have come to be prime real estate for tourist development or residential construction.[42] For hundreds of years, tombs were of far more solid construction than even the estates of the Shuri nobility. Rooted in the earth itself, they are protected from the elements, as well as from human and spiritual intervention.

Although tombs appear to be monumental and unchanging, this is clearly not the case. During the Japanese colonial era, social and political structures were shattered and reconfigured, the economy was transformed and the population of Okinawa thrown into motion. Immigration intensified to the countryside, to the cities, to mainland industrial centers, and to the colonies. Those displaced gave up hope of burial in their ancestral tombs.[43] The battle of Okinawa had an even more profound effect, not simply on tombs but on the totality of daily life. I've often been told that the bombardment that preceded the American invasion of central Okinawa was so severe that every square meter of land was struck by artillery. Homes, schools, municipal buildings, and tombs were all destroyed during these barrages—in some towns, there were no structures left undamaged. More tombs were ruined during the savage ground fighting that followed, burned or reduced to rubble. The living who took shelter in them were often killed, and the remains of the dead scattered.[44] Finally, the American occupation that swept Okinawans from their villages in the construction of new bases forced them to leave behind their tombs as well as their homes.

> The people who abandoned this samurai village
> Crossing to the far side of the world
> To Inca towns where the children of immigrants wait
> Can't see the plover.

Driven once again from their homes by their destruction or by economic necessity, Okinawan laborers again immigrated to mainland industrial centers, to Hawaii, and to Latin America.[45] These Okinawans were forced to reconstruct their daily lives in the place of another, in unfamiliar public and domestic spaces, without the objects and practices that they had used to construct their social world. The yādui and all that it contained was left behind. Most of those who remained in Okinawa were also unable to reproduce the form of their ruined agrarian communities in the new spaces where they lived and worked. Farms and villages were swept away; runways and control towers, ammunition bunkers, aircraft hangars, barracks, rifle ranges, communication sites, ranch-style residential subdivisions, swimming pools and elementary schools, shopping centers, bars, brothels, and hotels were constructed in their place. Fences—chain link and barbed wire— severed old paths, and new asphalt highways and oiled dirt roads connected spaces that had never before existed. New immigrants had displaced them as well: tens of thousands of American soldiers, sailors, airmen, and Marines, and their families and the contractors that supported them, as well as Chinese and South Asian merchants and laborers from the Philippines, Amami, Kyūshū, and Miyako. Agricultural production declined and economic development in general stagnated during the postwar period as the American bases paved over the most productive agrarian space on the island. The Okinawan population came to be concentrated in the intensely urbanized central section of the main island, in crowded communities clustered around the perimeter of the bases and in the dense neighborhoods of the capital. People found work in service—base labor, tourism, construction, and prostitution. Some attempted to build their new homes along the lines of those that were lost, stripped of the fields that once surrounded them. Walking down an alley in Okinawa City, I've seen tiny farmhouses with walled courtyards too small to do more than park the smallest of automobiles, standing row on row. Even more Okinawans abandoned the idea of the rural home entirely, adopting and modifying the cement cubes designed to house the massive influx of American military and civilian personnel. In the community where I work, concrete homes and crowded apartment buildings line streets so narrow that, in places, even a single vehicle cannot pass. And yet, the reconstructed tombs that shared the neighborhoods repeated the massive, spacious forms of prewar crypts. Tomb construction is expensive, and I have heard many stories of Okinawans who barely averted bankruptcy after rebuilding their family crypt. Several of my friends told me that tomb construction required their families to forgo home reconstruction or repair for years. Why, in this era of economic hardship, was such emphasis given to rebuilding the household tomb?

As David Graeber suggests in his ethnography of mortuary practice in Madagascar, tomb construction was a critical practice for the inscription of a certain kind of history into the physical space of the community. "What really knits a deme [descent group] together is not a human genealogy, but a genealogy of tombs. Older tombs are seen as generating younger ones, and the organization as a whole inscribes a pattern of historical memory in the landscape in a way that makes it seem like one of its most permanent features."[46]

In Okinawa, tomb construction is not the only such practice, but certainly the most visible.[47] Walking through a street lined with single household tombs in Okinawa City, I could see a kind of spatialized history of the neighborhood. Nothing exists that predates the battle of Okinawa. The oldest tombs were built in the 1950s, those of branch houses spreading out alongside those of the main household. Renovated and reconstructed crypts spoke to the prosperity of the family; fresh flowers and well-maintained grounds to their respect and affection for the dead. On tiny slivers of land between and in front of the tombs, gardens flourish. Potato vines curl on the ground; small bitter melons dangle like jewels from stick and wire frames;

in a samurai village

the scarlet, paper-like blossoms of bougainvillea run along the walls, the gold and green waxen leaves of ornamental plants lining their base. Neglect and disrepair suggest misfortune or absence—perhaps a line that has been extinguished or whose descendants have moved elsewhere in Okinawa or to the mainland. However, tombs are not merely material signs of history inscribed into the landscape but the sites of ongoing production of relationships and reinscription of memory.

The dead can only be transformed into ancestral spirits through a long, intensive process, mediated at every point by those closest to the dead in life, by those most bereft by their death. Regular labor, coordinated and precise, applied over time produces the complete and successful transformation of a decaying corporeal remainder in which the spirit of the dead inheres to an ancestral spirit with all of the expected capacities and occupying the appropriate spatial field. Many of these practices, such as the washing of the body, the wake, the periodic memorative acts, resemble those of mainland Japan. However, until recently, Okinawan mortuary ritual was distinguished by senkotsu—the washing of bones—which was very different from mortuary practice in mainland Japan.[48] In describing senkotsu, Kawahashi Noriko, a historian of religion, evokes Okinawan sentiment with the phrase *churaku nashun* (to make pure and beautiful). However, by the time I began my fieldwork in Okinawa in 1996, bone washing had been largely abandoned, replaced by cremation in all but the villages of the main island most remote from the capital at Naha, and some of the smaller islands of the archipelago. In discussions with my friends, the most recent senkotsu on the main island that anyone could personally recall was in 1987. Still, intense feelings about the practice persist.

In his ethnography of Okinawan religious practices under American occupation in the late 1950s, the anthropologist William Lebra provides a vivid description of bone washing.[49] After death, the casket containing the body of the deceased was placed in the center of the tomb and the door sealed. During this first period of interment, the spirit clung to the corporal remains of its body and it was confined to the vicinity of its crypt. As a being of both the material and spiritual worlds, its behavior was unpredictable. Sometime during the next three to seven years, the casket was disinterred and brought into the courtyard of the tomb, where the immediate family was gathered, sometimes under the supervision of a noro. The occasion for senkotsu could be the opening of the tomb for the interment of a new body; otherwise it would be held on Tanabata—the seventh day of the seventh lunar month.

While the body was exposed, a family member held an umbrella above it— Lebra explains that this was said to prevent the undirected spirit from escaping. Beginning with the closest relative, family members used large chopsticks to remove bones from the casket. If the body was still in an intermediate stage of decomposition, the women of the family would scrape away any flesh still clinging to the bones with a *kama* (sickle). The bones were then washed, first with water, then with awamori. Having been cleaned, the bones were carefully arranged in a funeral urn, reproducing the spatial organization of the body of the departed within the confines of the ceramic container.[50] Prayers were offered and apologies made to the spirit of the dead for any insult or unhappiness caused by the ritual. At this time, the personal name and birth rank of the deceased (for example, first or eldest son), the date of the senkotsu and the names of the women who washed the bones were recorded with brush and ink inside the lid of the urn. It was then placed in the tomb, on the lowest available position of the shelves that lined the walls. Older urns might be moved to higher shelves to create space; those reaching the thirty-third anniversary of their death could be commingled with the remains of the ancestors already filling the ossuary at the rear of the tomb. Lebra explains that the urn containing the deceased would be turned to face away from the entrance, discouraging the ancestral spirit from leaving the tomb uninvited. Finally, the door of the tomb was resealed.

Senkotsu is widely believed to have expressed the bereavement of the living, the respect and affection that they have for the dead. I have often heard it spoken of with a kind of nostalgia by women who had certainly participated in the senkotsu of husbands, parents, and children. Again and again, people told me that this practice was a material sign of their love for those who have died. Kawahashi Noriko writes that, in spite of the very real trauma engendered by the practice, it had widespread support in Okinawan society: "A woman in her early forties recounted to me her experience of having had her baby cremated several years ago. She explained that she found the simplistic and mechanical procedure of the cremation unbearable, and wished that she had been able to keep the baby's body in order to perform the bone-washing afterward. Others likewise admitted that senkotsu is a way of showing affection for the dead."[51]

Robert Hertz has famously observed that mortuary practice, particularly the kind of secondary burial that I am discussing, releases the spirit of the dead person from its physical form.[52] One of the members of the senior citizens club in the community where I worked explained that a body interred but never subjected to senkotsu would forever house an uneasy spirit, a spirit trapped in its now-useless flesh—unable to return to the world of the living, unable to take its place among ancestral spirits. And, as Augé suggested, the dead call to those who forget them. A restless and unhappy ancestral spirit would certainly make its displeasure known to its descendants, insistently sending them signs until answered.

Severing the material bonds that tied the spirit to its corporeal form also dislodged a kind of energy that must be recovered by the women of the household. The shape of the tomb is often compared to that of a pregnant woman, and the interior space of the crypt to the womb. Both are seen as important sites of productive power, necessary for birth. Sipping tea during an afternoon spent dancing with her friends at the neighborhood center, one elderly woman—a woman who had herself participated in family senkotsu— told me that it was crucial for women to capture the energy that was released while washing the bones. That is to say, it was necessary to recover, conserve, and utilize this power so that the next generation of children would be born with capacities equal to that of their parents. If the power were lost, Okinawan lives would become increasingly diminished as the abilities that helped them to survive the trials of daily life faded. "Isn't that exactly what was happening now?" she asked, to the agreement of the women surrounding her. "Now everyone ends up being cremated."

In senkotsu, creative, coordinated women's labor has transformed the ruins of the human body into a thing pure and beautiful. The same agrarian tools that are used to work sugar cane or rice, shaping, discarding, and retaining valued portions, are brought to bear on the remains of the dead. Rotted flesh is stripped away, bones cleansed, and the disorder and collapse of decay rectified. Their useless container discarded, the bones are carefully arranged—reconstructed—in a new vessel, strong and enduring. Standing within the funerary urn, itself a product of the creative labor of Okinawan potters, the ancestor is materially integrated with the community of the ancestral spirits, placed alongside the ranks of urns already in the tomb. Senkotsu transforms the decaying body, a thing of horror, to the subject of

in a samurai village

power encountered by human actors. It shapes and organizes the spatial field of the ancestral spirit, fixing it in place at the tomb, integrating it with the manifold presences of ancestral spirits already interred, while also recognizing it as a potential participant in the rituals and practices to be held at this site and at others.

And yet, even Lebra's normally dispassionate monograph makes it clear that the practice of senkotsu was a traumatic experience for those involved. It requires little effort to imagine the pain of a mother scraping the flesh from an infant child or a wife washing the bones of her husband. Lebra notes that even in the 1950s, many Okinawans were reluctant to participate in this harrowing ritual, and a number of young women in the Oku area refused to take part in it at all. The feminist historian Horiba Kiyoko links this resistance to her critique of gendered oppression in Okinawa. In a collection of essays published in 1990, Horiba argues that the role assigned to women in humiliating practices such as senkotsu was not only indicative of their general subordination to men in Okinawan society, but was actively productive of it. She urged women to reject these acts and embrace modern rationality in the interest of gaining a real equality with men. Her account of a group of women in Ōgimison who engaged in a kind of domestic revolt, challenging the demeaning role of women in household organization, suggests that her position was reflected in Okinawan social practice.

Although attitudes toward senkotsu were far from uniform, as reflected in the debate that raged in the letters columns of local Okinawan newspapers after Horiba's book was published, the practice has almost completely disappeared on the main island of Okinawa, fading throughout the rest of the archipelago. The consequences of the resentment and revulsion felt by women who were compelled to wash their family's bones were surely important. What's more, the effects of broader, sustained efforts by women to mobilize politically and effect social reform have also resonated with their attitudes toward senkotsu.

Senkotsu has also been subjected to the regulatory powers of the Japanese state and associated notions of hygiene and contagion. While American authorities evidenced little interest in the ways that Okinawans buried their dead, mortuary practice came under Japanese control after reversion in 1972. Cremation was mandated in urban areas and for those who died of any of a host of infectious diseases.

Beyond any direct prohibitions, Okinawans came under the practical discipline of public opinion. In the generations since the Japanese colonial era began, Okinawans have been caught up in a variety of *seikatsu kaizen*, or lifestyle reform movements. These early efforts demanded that Okinawans abandon their local dialects, stop going barefoot, eliminate bridal tattooing, and banish the household pigs from the toilet. As mainland industrial workers, many Okinawans denied their heritage, changed their family names, and tried to pass as immigrants from elsewhere in rural Japan. The onset of the Pacific War brought renewed attempts to integrate with Japanese society and to make sacrifices on behalf of the state. After the end of the war, during the era of global decolonization, Okinawans identified themselves with mainland Japan once more in their struggle to reunify with their former colonial state. Since Okinawan reincorporation into Japan, political and economic discourse has been marked with calls for parity with mainland development, and an ambivalent tension exists between interest in a distinct Okinawan cultural identity and immersion in an increasingly homogeneous Japanese everyday life. In all this, it is not difficult to find that practices such as senkotsu—stigmatized as grotesque, unsanitary, or backward—would become an embarrassment.

Finally, it is necessary to consider the commodification of death in contemporary Okinawa. The Japanese commercial mortuary industry has made deep inroads into Okinawa, taking advantage of the establishment of municipal crematoria and the extremely high price of land to build compact, modern cemeteries that many find an attractive alternative to traditional practices. Okinawan celebrities like the boxer Gushiken Yōko appear as spokesmen in radio and televison advertising, and home mailboxes are inundated with flyers urging the reader to investigate new, modern, and economical burial possibilities.

Consider then the moment into which Takara inserts his narrative. Whether by war, American occupation, or Japanese modernization, the yādui have been destroyed. Takara portrays an Okinawa in which the tomb, like every other site in the network of spaces in which Okinawans lived, has been scoured from the landscape, effaced as a center of power. The remains of the dead in their corporeality are thrown back into the hands of the living, stripped of any relationship to Okinawan symbolic networks and cultural references. The old woman, facing this cataclysmic change, stands at the margin of the yādui, about to travel to the "Land of the Sun," to make the monumental transformation to life in contemporary Japan. How does the old woman respond? Does she allow herself to be subsumed in the practices of new Japan? Does she surrender to the crushing melancholy of a loss that cannot be overcome, the loss of her home, her relationships, all the practices and places that have given her life meaning?

> Roasts the dead old man's bones in the skillet
> Break crush grind
> Makes them into powder
> Mutters something, licks her fingers
> Packs it into the amulet's pouch
> The old man will travel with her too

It is a stunning image that Takara has created. It is an image of sadness and desperation, but also of hope and creativity. The old woman lacks the banners and flags, the helmets and batons of organized dissent; she lacks the agricultural implements and ritual objects of traditional Okinawan practice. The powerful setting of the tomb has already been lost, and the specific practices of bone washing are beyond her capabilities. The collaboration of the community, already dispersed, is impossible. What remains is a deep reserve of memory where the possibility of all of these things still persists.

And so, driven by the urgency of the moment, with only the mortuary practices of the Japanese state and the domestic tools of an Okinawan housewife at her disposal, she acts. In absence of a proper place—the courtyard of a tomb—she relies on the content of memory to carry out her response in whatever space remains available. She struggles to cremate her dead husband, takes him with her, takes him inside her, determined to carry that which is of value with her to the new world. For she is driven by the conviction that her husband is not lost: it is the practices and the tools necessary to maintain their relationship that have been taken from her.

In one of his journals filled with notes for the *Passegen-Werk*, Walter Benjamin wrote, "It is my intention to withstand what Valéry calls 'a reading slowed by and bristling with the resistances of a refined and fastidious reader.' "[53] I not only share these concerns—I am afraid that my exegesis of Takara's poem may actually lead readers astray, encouraging them to busy

in a samurai village

themselves with the explanations and digressions that I have provided. Of course, it is too much to expect a reader to know what would "go without saying" for an Okinawan encountering the same material—the knowledge of Okinawan culture, of Ryūkyūan history, of the aftermath of colonialism and genocide. Without at least sketching that information, it would be impossible help a reader glimpse the tremendous archive of memory on which an Okinawan (or someone else deeply familiar with Okinawan history) can draw. Fortified with this introduction, perhaps readers can envision another way of encountering the text, an encounter built on long-established habit and knowledge, on the deeply familiar store of what has been heard, read, and experienced. It is this reading, a swift and unhesitating sweep through Takara's stark, economical constellation of images that will throw open the archive, letting it burst forth into the moment.

Takara's poem depends on this excess of memory. Michel de Certeau has written of the force that the spatial organization of contemporary society exerts on the autonomy of the actors that live within its ever expanding and transforming networks. Certeau argues that modern life is organized and regulated, fixed in appropriate places. Practices are observed, studied, codified, and coordinated, caught up in overlapping networks of the industrial division of labor, bureaucratic organization, and state surveillance. Their continued extension has the effect of ever increasing regulation, integration, and homogenization of everyday life. What interests Certeau is that this threat to a meaningful, autonomous life can also create the possibility for transformative action. As a new pattern of daily life is installed, it is constantly brought up against another everyday, increasingly lost to practice but perduring in memory: "Practical memory cannot be activated without the touch of the other, yet it atrophies in the autonomization of space and of the proper locus." It is in this moment that Certeau sees the possibility for action. Memory provides a resource for engaging the spatial transformation of the everyday, creating an opportunity into which new critical practices can be inserted. But the moment is fragile and fleeting, endangered by the force and the magnitude of the same transformations that illuminate the moment of contradiction.[54]

In order to understand the economy of Takara's narrative, I would like to consider the chronotope that structures the poem, its particular spatial and temporal organization. The use of imperfective predicates and indeterminate temporal references renders all of the events depicted coeval. While they exist in a detemporalized manifold, they are not all of a kind. Some seem to be like the places of abjection that James Ferguson has theorized: sites of oppression and exploitation, cut off from social and economic networks with which they were once articulated, isolated and mute:[55] immigrant villages, apartments filled with foreign students in an unfamiliar land, Latin American communities wracked by violence or stricken by disaster. However, other images do not depict simply spaces but spatial formations: sites of possibility charged with the potential for action: the old woman laboring in the ruins of her village; an artist speaking and reflecting on his craft, concerned with his failure; women dancing. All of these are punctuated by the repeated call of the plover—separated and joined by this image, suffused with sadness and longing.

While the spatial formations are depicted as capable of action, it is not clear that this activity can produce any lasting change or reconfigure the place in which they are situated. Neither is there any sense of progressive movement through these images, no protagonist traveling from situation to situation. It is the reader who negotiates each image before reaching the poem's narrative closure. The final lines come to a kind of compositional finalization with the samurai village lost—physically removed, severed from communication, the old woman's condition unknown—presumed dead.

But how final is this conclusion? What appears to be a deeply pessimistic ending carries within it the seeds of possibility. Here I return to the trope of the outcast village beneath the water. Without question, it references the ruined yādui in Okinawa as well as the isolated and poverty-stricken immigrant communities in Latin America. However, it is a powerfully overdetermined image, resonating with the trope of lost villages in Japanese literature and folklore. Like the hidden villages of defeated Heike warriors[56] or the mysterious mountain huts in Yanagita's *Tono Monogatari*,[57] there are places that endure at a remove from the spatiotemporality of modern life. Sometimes an unwary traveler crosses into this space; sounds and visions, chance encounters may occasionally touch the everyday world. In Okinawa, it is not only the shattered yādui that lie beneath the water: the Palace of the Dragon King may also be close at hand—a mysterious site, where strange powers can take hold, where a lifetime may pass in a day, a day unfold over a lifetime. In *Kaijo no Michi*, Yanagita argued that the Palace of the Dragon King was equivalent to *niruya* or *niriya*—nirai kanai, the Okinawan paradise.[58] Beings of great power, the *marebito*, come to Okinawa from nirai kanai, bringing good fortune and renewing the vitality of the communities where they visit. As Monika Wacker writes in her study of *onarigami* (the spiritual power of women), Ryūkyūan priestesses drew a force known as *seji* from nirai kanai, using it to "protect the king, his sailors and soldiers at war, but also [to] endow the king with these powers to give him the abilities to rule over the other noblemen and the people of the islands and to protect them from any foe."[59] The place, hidden or lost, may yet be reclaimed. The site of despair and defeat can be a source of hope and power as well. Again and again Takara returns to the objects and places that have disappeared—not because he is caught up in melancholy repetition, unable to work through loss. Rather, it is that the object is not seen as truly or completely lost: although absent, it may be regained; although defeated, its power may be recovered.

These moments are deeply bound up with feeling—with hope and determination as well as with sadness and disappointment. Takara's project is not simply to convey moments in Okinawan history to his readers or listeners; it is also to communicate this affect, to reawaken it in others. He must draw on the appropriate "rhythms signs and forms" in order to transpose these moments and their related feeling to the materiality of the text, to touch the reader, to convey the emotional charge.[60]

Nancy Munn has written about the logic of transposition in the design of New York's Central Park. Viewers were not intended to simply encounter an expanse of natural space preserved from the depredations of urban construction; the spatiotemporal field of an ideal viewer was mobilized in order to create scenic views. Architects proposed an affect, then set about organizing the landscape so that, when viewed from a given point, the desired feeling would be obtained. In doing so, architects objectified a projection of their own spatial field on the material form of the landscape. This produces what Munn called "a switch point between persons and terrestrial space." Through the sensuous experience of the landscape, successive viewers situated at points designated by the designers could experience the detemporalized spatial field of that original viewer. Takara's poem presumes that the same switch point exists between persons and the representational space that he has so carefully crafted.

in a samurai village

Transposition, if it is to achieve the desired effect, depends on a deeply shared reserve of memory. The economy of the image must resonate with the memory of readers or listeners, articulating with that which they have learned and experienced: not the destruction of any rural village by a colonial regime, but the destruction of a certain yādui in central Okinawa by war and American occupation; not the plight of poor immigrants anywhere, but of the 3,200 Okinawans forced from their homes in Isa and driven across the world to Bolivia; not the need of people everywhere to memorate their ancestors, but the real productive possibility of senkotsu in Okinawa; not the right to creativity and expression, but the determination of one Okinawan woman to dance Chijuyā.

But what of the feelings that are transposed? I have already suggested that Takara's poem is structured like what Adorno—after Benjamin—calls a constellation, a carefully crafted, interrelated formation of images. Following Adorno, the selection and arrangement of these images speaks to their relationship to one another. They are not constructed to explain the consequences of some anterior series of events, they are not a series arranged so that a higher concept can be deduced: "Becoming aware of the constellation in which a thing stands is tantamount to deciphering the constellation which, having come to be, it bears within it. . . . The history locked in the object can only be delivered by an object in its relation to other objects—by the actualization and concentration of something which is already known and is transformed by this knowledge."[61]

What lies before us in the poem are a series of images arranged by the author, images of hope and images of despair: sites of abjection and disarticulation, spatial fields charged with creative power. The poet who has chosen and crafted these scenes of oppression and of possibility is situated outside the resulting construction, and yet the poem bears the material traces of his labor—the conversational, direct style of composition and the references to his wife and daughter and to his own experiences. These are signs of his presence alongside other images, referring back to the whole poem as his creation. There is a kind of homology to the constellation: the poet stands in the same relation to the poem that he has crafted as the dancer to the dance, the old woman to the remains that she roasts, and the author to the image that he cannot depict.

This is the experience that readers are invited to share: to step back from the series of images comprising the poem and to experience the situated position of the author. Beyond sharing, if only for a moment, the affect and the knowledge bound up in its form, the reader is also invited to see the trace of the hand, the voice that has organized the poem, and to stand at the switchpoint and to experience the spatial field that has reached out through space and time, sifting through the horrifying and courageous experiences of countless ancestors, crafting them, distilling them into the text that one still experiences. Responsive readers come to know that the emotions they feel are those that the poet has brought, through his mastery of the craft, to the narrative, and to feel, as the author might feel, that creative action is the appropriate response for a person confronted with the tragedy and pain, the hope and slumbering possibility of these images—to remember, and perhaps to act; or at least act by remembering, taking on the burden and power of the past as the old woman took the remains of her husband with her, inside her.

THE KŌKAI SHINRI: 1997

In the winter of 1997, Okinawa was riven with anger and confusion over Governor Ōta's sudden capitulation to the central government. After months of insistently refusing to act as a proxy, to sign the leases of base land in place of the landowners in protest, Ōta gave in to the government's demands. For many, it was a cynical about-face, a sign of Ōta's final transformation from a social activist and a scholar to a self-serving politician—or confirmation that he was that all along. For others, it was hopeful. Perhaps there was some kind of deep play, perhaps Ōta had been able to exact an unacknowledged compromise or assurance from the central government in exchange for his acquiescence. For some, haunted by decades of similar disappointment, it was a sign of the inevitable defeat that any weak upstart will suffer at the hands of a stronger enemy.

Starting in February 1997, a series of kōkai shinri (public hearings) were held in Ginowan, Kadena, and Okinawa City. Conceived and planned during the fever pitch of resistance, executed in this moment of confusion, the hearings were sponsored by the prefectural government itself, their ostensible purpose to help the prefecture clarify its position on the military land use issue by hearing testimony from all parties involved, ranging from representatives of the Ministry of Defense to individual landowners. In practice, the inquiry became something else entirely. The prefecture appropriated the form of an official fact-finding hearing and its technologies for eliciting testimony. As a consequence, they gave the *hansen jinushi* (antiwar landlords) and other groups committed to the reduction or elimination of the American military bases a public forum for extended presentation of their grievances against the Japanese state. At the same time, inverting the normal relationship between the prefectural and national government, representatives of the Ministry of Defense were called upon to explain everything from national security policy to routine office practices in a public forum. Their positions of authority challenged, representatives of the national government could only repeat prepared statements or simply refuse to respond to questions. Normally, representatives of the state have control of the situation and can dismiss reporters or conclude the hearing at will. However, they did not have control of the agenda at the kōkai shinri, and were kept under public scrutiny throughout the proceedings. With rhetorical flourishes, testimony by the antiwar landlords became indictments of the Japanese state and denunciations of Japanese militarism. The representatives of the Ministry of Defense were forced to listen in frustrated, humiliated silence, paralyzed by their own adherence to bureaucratic procedure. To those present or following the hearings in the media, it was obvious that the performances of the prefecture and the hansen jinushi, had been orchestrated in some way.[62]

The first of these hearings was held on February 21, 1997, at the Okinawa Convention Center in Ginowan. I arrived early, determined to find a spot in the closest parking lot. Spaces around the convention center were already filled by satellite trucks from all of the mainland television channels and news agencies, and I was fortunate to find an opening. As I locked my car, I could see several people peering at me over the top of the hedge that separated the parking lot from the street beyond. Staring back at them, I realized that they were the same plainclothes policemen that I had seen at several recent demonstrations, binoculars and cameras in hand, ballcaps and sunglasses rendering them anonymous but not inconspicuous. As I passed them on the sidewalk, I could see that they had already begun a comprehensive surveillance of the hearing.

Walking to the pavilion at the center of the complex, I was impressed by the severe beauty of the Okinawa Convention Center: huge concrete auditoriums with streaked, green copper roofs clustered together like a group of giant horseshoe crabs. Carefully tended gardens and fields surrounded them. There was a large amphitheater beyond, and finally the sea. Tables and microphones had been set up in front of a fountain in the pavilion, a media center and gathering place for activists. A cordon of Zengakuren[63] students from all over Japan encircled the pavilion, wearing sunglasses, caps, and masks, standing at a kind of parade rest—an unsettling echo of the nearby police lines. A number of hansen jinushi circulated around the tables, talking with reporters. At one point, a group of hitotsubokai members (the owners of the nominal, one-tsubo pieces of land) arrived, with Takara Ben at their center, carrying a green and white banner.

The largest group in evidence was the news media, with video and print seemingly in equal numbers. Camera crews jockeyed for position, setting up in a phalanx along the fountain. Print journalists, more mobile, wandered through the crowd, making their way to key figures as they arrived. Several camera crews and reporters shot stand-ups outside, then hurried into the convention center. I saw the activist Chibana Shōichi, currently at the eye of the storm because of his refusal to renew the lease of land that he owns in the center of the Sobe Communication Site in Yomitan. He was mobbed by reporters, smilingly separating himself from them and joining the other hansen jinushi at the podium in the pavilion.

One by one, activists began what I assumed were some kind of opening remarks. Unfortunately, there was so much shouting from the crowd and feedback from the sound system that it was impossible to understand anything that was being said. Most of the landlords didn't seem to be too concerned, having short one-on-one discussions with reporters while the public address system shrieked.

I was fortunate to get one of the first balcony passes. The prefectural board conducting the hearing was to be seated at a table on the stage; the first floor being reserved for members of the hansen jinushi and their entourages, groups of Zengakuren students, and, of course, the press. I hurried to my seat in the balcony and set out my equipment on the railing in front of me: camera, cassette recorder, spare film, and tapes. As I checked my batteries and equipment settings, a man casually sat down next to me. He was dressed in jeans, a denim jacket over a sweatshirt, sneakers, and sunglasses, despite the comfortable gloom inside the hall. I was somewhat startled as he

in a samurai village

said in a quiet voice, almost to himself: "Can't record anything, I guess. . . ." He turned his ticket over and over, peering at the fine print. "No pictures, no recording, hmm. . . ."

I looked sidelong at him for a moment, then thanked him for bringing this to my attention and put away my gear. I was never quite sure who my friendly neighbor was—someone from Zengakuren? A policeman? Before I could continue our conversation, I was joined in the balcony by several other observers: an American Christian missionary and her assistants, a group of Okinawan university students with their teacher, and several young, well-dressed academics from Tokyo. In the meantime, my helpful neighbor, whatever his affiliation, had dropped off to sleep—he later left during the mid-session intermission. I resigned myself to taking notes and sketching.

Below me, the seven members of the commission leading the inquiry seated themselves at a white-covered table on the stage. Aides hurried back and forth, adjusting and testing microphones, setting out carafes of water, organizing rows of bound references. The media had established themselves on the wings of the stage. I counted at least twenty-five fixed cameras and more than fifty reporters and cameramen. Although the audience faced the committee on stage, media attention was focused, without exception, on the landlords and activists seated in the audience.

At 1:40, the chairman of the committee called the meeting to order. His opening remarks were polite and perfunctory, delivered in formal Japanese. He called for everyone's cooperation in the day's events and introduced Sakamoto Kenichi, the administrative director of the Naha Defense Facilities Administrative Agency.

Sakamoto stepped up to a microphone set in the aisle facing the stage and began a long, flat-toned narration of the history of American bases in Okinawa. He described the ANPO treaty[64] and its importance to the bilateral relations between Japan and the United States, as well as its central importance to the security of the Pacific region. Sakamoto droned on for forty-five minutes, a presentation uncolored by emotion or any kind of dramatic inflection. He moved on to outline the future of the bases, announcing the state's desire to renew each of the leases. He then began a lengthy recitation of each of the bases, the number of landowners, and plots of land within the base, and the uses to which the base land had been put by the American military.

At this point, the Zengakuren students began to heckle Sakamoto with catcalls and shouted anti-ANPO pronouncements. As the students became more disruptive, photographers circulating to capture the action, members of the hansen jinushi approached the students and urged them to be quiet. This tension—whether real or contrived—continued through the rest of the hearing. Undeterred by the interruptions, Sakamoto pressed on.

Kadena Airfield. Located in Okinawa City as well as the villages of Chatan and Kadena. There are 2,301 landowners holding 34 plots, for a total of 39,151.38 square meters of land. The area provided for the armed forces of the United States of America stationed in Okinawa comprises land for schools, family residence, and general use. Included are the streets and roads within the base, barracks, and parking lots, and the security buffer zone that surrounds them. There is land for water reservoirs and storage areas for general construction material. There are runways and the apron, fuel storage facilities and repair sites, warehouses holding supplies for the airfield, and their surrounding security area. Leases will be renewed for a ten-year period starting on May 15, 1997.

As Sakamoto continued to speak, one of the hansen jinushi got up and left his seat, approaching the microphone. The landlord, a middle-aged man in a khaki windbreaker, showed Sakamoto a notebook on which he had written something, then spoke to him quietly. Startled, Sakamoto faltered and interrupted his speech. Two plainclothes policemen in the front row jumped to their feet and escorted the landlord out of the auditorium.

Interruptions continued to plague Sakamoto's speech. Every time that he mentioned the mutual security treaty between Japan and the United States, the Zengakuren students would hold up a row of panels spelling out a slogan denouncing ANPO. Exasperated, several of the hansen jinushi confiscated the cards. Finally, Sakamoto concluded his presentation and sat down. The chairman thanked him politely and introduced the first of the hansen jinushi who would address the committee.

One after another, these elderly Okinawans rose and addressed the audience. Nearly all of the speakers were men, dressed in dark, conservative suits, wearing green armbands identifying them as antiwar landlords. They also wore white headbands and vests inscribed with slogans announcing their commitment to ending the use of Okinawan lands for military purposes, their opposition to war, and their commitment to preserve life.

in a samurai village

Most bore the inscription "Warera no tochi o kaese" (Give us back our land!). This appropriated the reversion-era slogan, "Okinawa o kaese" (Return Okinawa!). Painted on banners and signs, shouted during demonstrations, even used as the title and refrain of a reversion-era protest song, this phrase has problematic associations with the contemporary political situation. While Okinawa is the object of the demand, to whom was it to be returned? In the case of reversion, it was the Japanese state, to whom these demands are now directed. In an effort to rethink the problem, the musician and activist Daiku Tetsuhiro has rewritten the old reversion anthem as *Okinawa ni kaese* rather than *Okinawa o kaese* (Return it [our land] to Okinawa).[65]

"Nuchi dū takara" (Life is a treasure) was also prominently written on the landowners' clothing and banners. A phrase repeated in both verse and song, it has come to be associated with a moment in the immediate aftermath of the war. With the island in ruins, hundreds of thousands dead, the future uncertain, the poet still can say that life is a treasure. Ahagon Shōko, the Okinawan civil rights activist who recently died at the age of 102, published an account of the struggle against the American occupation of Iejima or Ie Island with this as its title. It has become the watchword of the antibase and antiwar movement in Okinawa.

The landowners spoke in standard Japanese, selecting a moderate level of formality—favoring distal-style [-*masu*/*desu*] predicates over more elaborate forms of polite speech or passive locutions that mark much of public speaking. Addressing the audience that now numbered in the thousands, they recounted their experiences during the Pacific War. In painful detail, they told of the loss of their homes, the destruction of their village, and the death of their loved ones. They also forcefully denounced the system that compelled them to lease their land against their will, depriving them of their constitutional rights.

Arime Masao was one of the first landowners to address the hearing. He was a small, trim man with an energetic manner. As he began to speak, his delivery was sharp and clear, the precise diction of a retired schoolteacher. He ridiculed Sakamoto for his long narration. With a dismissive gesture, he said that he rejected the validity of the ANPO treaty and refused to accept the conditions imposed upon them. He would never be convinced by Sakamoto's argument. He referred to the government's treatment of Chibana Shōichi and their continuing, illegal use of his land. Impassioned, he shouted, "Zettai ni yurusaranai desu!" (This will not be endured!)

He countered Sakamoto's historical survey with his own review of the American occupation. He says that the history that Okinawans have experienced is one of repression and destruction. Their native villages, their very way of life, has been destroyed. His voice became hoarse, choked with emotion:

> Even if we just restrict ourselves to Goeku, my *furusato* [native place], there are eight communities completely within the American base: Ukuda, Sēnashi, Kurashiki, Morine, Karakawa, Gotenshiki, Shirakawa, and Dakujaku. Parts of Uechi and Yamauchi are also inside the base. The people from these places have been spread out all over what is now Okinawa City. We live, thinking about our furusato as we go about our daily lives.
>
> Once, those of us from the villages inside the base decided to have a picnic together in order to strengthen the bonds of our friendship. We got permission from the American military, chartered a bus, and drove around inside Kadena Air Base. The older people who had the experience of living there explained life in the villages to the young people, the children and relatives. *That's where the stable was. The school used to be over there. Your house was over on the right. A big river used to flow through here.* The bus was silent as we told them about the villages that still live on in our hearts.
>
> Members of the panel, please have a look at this map that is spread out before you. This is a restored plan of the houses in my furusato, the hamlet of Morine in Goeku village. This is a map that was made by my friend Maesiro Gentoku, a member of the hansen jinushi of Kadena Air Base. With the cooperation of so many of our *senpai* [seniors], we took the vision of the prewar form of our furusato that lives on in our hearts and created this diagram—house by house.[66]

Arime paused to indicate a large, rectangular chart held before the audience by a pair of hansen jinushi. Eschewing traditional forms of representation, Morine was depicted in synoptic overview, a detailed line diagram mapping the streets, houses, market, sugar cane processing site, shrines, and terrain features of a rural Okinawan village. As Arime noted, it was the result of a great deal of coordinated effort: the testimony of survivors of the

Members of the hansen jinushi displaying a map of Morine

old village and their relatives, the labor of scholars and students who conducted interviews and correlated information, and the contributions of local political parties, labor unions, and peace advocacy groups that gave space and support. It depicted, he said bitterly, a place now occupied by rows of homes for American Air Force officers and a monument commemorating the end of the war.

As this reconstruction indicates, there were 160 households in our furusato Morine alone. The whole culture of our daily lives was stolen from us. We are still preoccupied with thoughts of our furusato as we go about our daily routines, living on the periphery of Kadena Air Base. More than fifty-one years has passed since the end of the war but this way of life has only intensified. If we are protected by the Japanese Constitution, why must we endure this kind of prejudice? Although it was stolen from us, Kadena Air Base is still our furusato.

On May 15, 1972, Okinawa returned to her mother country. However, we have yet to escape the effects of the war. We still have to deal with the remains of those who were killed during the battle of Okinawa. We still have to dispose of unexploded bombs. We still endure the ongoing, unfair occupation of the enormous

American bases where the unjust occupation still continues. Even now, twenty-five years after reversion, these unhappy conditions persist! Let me be perfectly clear about it—we citizens who once lived in what is now the American bases are still refugees, fifty-one years after the end of the war.

Later during the testimony, Teruya Shūden, the director of the antiwar landlords' association, spoke to the audience. The alliance that appeared to exist between the prefectural authorities and the antiwar landlords belied the fact that Teruya had run against Ōta Masahide in the most recent gubernatorial election. Arguing that compromise and indecision kept Okinawa from ever overcoming the problem of the American bases, Teruya urged the government to directly confront the issue. A stocky, intense man, Teruya's every movement and expression indicated his anger toward the representatives of the Ministry of Defense and the occupation of his family lands.

This land that I own was bought by my grandfather. Because his family was so poor, he left Okinawa during Meiji and went to Hawaii as a cane cutter. He paid for this land with his sweat, his backbreaking labor. How should I use this precious land? How can I take into account the bitter misery that my grandfather endured? As its owner, that's what I should be free to decide.

He told the audience that no one in his family had ever consented to leasing land to the Americans; they were deceived and coerced. In the aftermath of the war, everyone was told to go to a newly rebuilt community center so that they could help reconstruct the official records that had been destroyed in the war. All families would be required to register their inkan, or family seals. Clerks helped them to stamp their seals on sheets of blank paper, which were then collected. After the residents left, officials wrote the leases above their mark, falsifying their consent, and stripping them of their land.

Teruya paused, then asked the commission to consider why a group of aging sixty- and seventy-year-old Okinawans would create this elaborate representation of their village.

We might be compelled to lease this land, but we want to return to our old villages while we still have our health. We want to let our grandchildren and our great-

in a samurai village

grandchildren hear about our old memories. This is our heartfelt request. This is what we've represented in this map, in this miniature. I don't think that there's a single person who happily leases his land to the bases.

Why did I become a hansen jinush? Throughout the Korean War, the Vietnam War—that was ten years—and the Gulf War, the bombers that have killed our Asian brothers, that trampled their human rights, were launched from our land. The same soldiers who destroyed these lives were also robbing the Okinawan people of their human rights, their lives, their heritage, and their pride.

Another more important reason lies in the war fifty years ago. At the time, I was seven years old, a first-grader at the public school. Japanese soldiers and my schoolteachers had converted part of our family home into military quarters, so I used to listen to their words every night. They used to tell me that if war broke out, I should flee to where the Japanese soldiers were. They told me that they'd protect me. That's what we thought. But is that what happened? Looking back on my own wartime experiences, I realize that soldiers will not protect citizens. That's the only conclusion that I can come to. That is why we will rebuild this rich village [Morine] and restore the land that I inherited from my grandfather to its original bounty, its verdant beauty.

As far as the military bases go, soldiers can't think about democracy. They can't think about human rights. They can't think about peace. Why not? If they were to think about peace or about human rights, they could never go to war. We'd have to have peace. So what do they think about? Discrimination and prejudice. Contempt for human life. That's what they think. And that goes for all soldiers, no matter where they're from. That is why I want this land returned to me without wasting another day. Sometimes I think of myself as a Japanese citizen. But most of the time I don't. Because Okinawa is nothing more than a military colony of Japan and the United States.

Testimony continued in this vein throughout the afternoon. Antiwar landlords, the mayor of Naha (an avowed opponent of the renewal of base leases), members of the hitotsubokai—again and again, the actions of the state were attacked. The representatives of the Ministry of Defense sat in stony silence, enduring furious denunciations and bitter allegations.

At the conclusion of the hearing, the chairman of the commission dispassionately announced that the next hearing would be held on March 12 at the central public hall in Okinawa City. As soon as the hearing ended, the sixteen members of the Ministry of Defense party stalked from the hall to a waiting motorcade. Outside, the landlords were greeted by a wildly cheering crowd —thousands of supporters and reporters, still under the watchful eye of the police. In a month's time, Teruya Shūden and fifteen others were arrested at the Diet in Tokyo, protesting the passage of a law retroactively creating the legal basis for ongoing land expropriation.

There are many important issues to explore in the work of the hansen jinushi.[67] However, at this point I will restrict my discussion to the way in which they deploy the powerful figure of the destroyed yādui. It is particularly compelling that they identify the yādui as their *furusato*, a term that could be translated as hometown or perhaps native place. The trope of the furusato has been the subject of a tremendous amount of critical investigation in Japanese ethnography, and has been engaged by Western scholars as well.

Harry Harootunian has written of the image of furusato invoked by Yanagita Kunio in his critique of the relentless urbanization and modernization of Japan in the early twentieth century, and the ruination of the countryside that it produced. Yanagita's ethnographies poetically objectify the remainder of an earlier everyday world that preceded capitalist modernization, the places and objects that he identified as persisting in the interstices of contemporary networks of production and consumption.[68] Yanagita hoped that his evocation of an earlier way of being would resonate with the subjectively nonsynchronous—the memories and practices, the abruptly foreclosed hopes and ambitions of his readers. The trope of the furusato remained powerfully evocative in the postwar years as Japan once again experienced decades of development and industrialization.[69]

In *Discourses of the Vanishing*, her ethnography of desire and loss, Marilyn Ivy powerfully captures furusato in all its ambiguity: the home that is no longer one's home, the native place from which one is alienated and to which one desires to return. Ivy's citation of the anthropologist Kawashima Jirō is particularly apt: those who are living continuously in the place where they were born do not call that place furusato.[70] How could it be otherwise? Generations after Yanagita first articulated his concern with the destruction of rural lifeways, the vast majority of those who dream of returning to an agrarian village have experienced nothing other than life in the urban, industrial space of contemporary Japan. The countryside offers few alternatives, its landscape relentlessly transformed by industrial capitalism, by construction and demolition, by the ceaseless production of waste. Instead, people endure tiny homes, crowded streets and trains, life dominated by work, saturated by broadcast media, occupied by consumption. Factory workers, store clerks, managers, and bureaucrats dream insistently of their return to a calm and nurturing native place while their daily practices subvert its conditions of possibility.

Still, the fantasy of the rural home and the desire to experience it—to go back to it—seems to have become more intense. The Japanese domestic tourist industry is deeply engaged with this longing, awakening and fueling consumer desire with an endless stream of commodities: television programs and films, brochures and advertisements, package tours and resorts, festivals and pageants. Each offers the possibility of reunion, not with the place of one's own origin, but with what one dreams of as home. Still, satisfaction of this desire is, at best, fleeting; its object an uncanny palliative.

Perhaps it is this longing that brings millions of tourists each year to Okinawa, the desire to find what nativists such as Yanagita and Orikuchi long ago identified as the enduring remnant of archaic Japan. And yet, while tourists and entrepreneurs, folklorists and conservative politicians may dream of Ryūkyū, the hansen jinushi have chosen to live with the painful presence of their furusato. The places that Arime, Teruya, and the other hansen jinushi describe at prefectural hearings are not the furusato of Japanese ethnographic or tourist discourses. They do not testify to the effects of decades of economic development and social transformation, of immigration and separation. The stories that they tell are of the catastrophic destruction of a rural community, of betrayal by Japanese soldiers and the Japanese state, of the appropriation of their homes and their communities by American forces—of life in a military colony of Japan and the United States.

For the jinushi, furusato is most emphatically not the image of the idyllic Okinawan village, with its quaint roofs and tropical gardens, its easy lifestyle. Neither is it the community of opulent villas of Shuri courtiers from which they were sent down. To speak of their furusato enables the hansen jinushi to rip away the manicured lawns and shatter the streets and runways, the barracks and bungalows of Kadena Air Base in order to present the historical actuality of their native place. The Morine that they recall is a place of work and hardship, of pride and accomplishment, a place bought by capital amassed as overseas laborers, cleared or reclaimed through their own struggles. It was space transformed and shaped by their labor.

Profoundly shaped by their experiences, the hansen jinushi are never able to reconcile themselves to one world or the other. They are teachers and writers, farmers and clerks caught up in the details of everyday life; they are rural nobles, the children of courtiers and cane cutters, tormented by memories of a village that is kept just out of their reach. While living in the familiar neighborhoods of Okinawa City, Kadena, or Chatan that surround Kadena Air Base, their lives are unsettled by images of their native place that return to them again and again. Gazing across the fence or standing among the ranch-style homes that line the quiet streets in base housing, they struggle to find remembered landmarks, to recall absent homes and lost pathways. When they watch eisā dancers move through the streets during Obon, when they clear neighborhood tombs during Tanabata, or greet visitors to their home during the New Year festival, they are reminded that the place where their family should meet lies beyond the chain link fence that surrounds Kadena. Morine is lost and always with them.[71]

They have not surrendered their furusato to the demands of Japanese law and American policy, to the tons of asphalt and concrete that overlay it, to the tread of American soldiers, to the erosion of memory. Tours such as the one that Arime described are sometimes possible. A few tombs remain, abruptly rising from a broad expanse of carefully maintained lawn; small yādui shrines remain atop wooded hilltops, unseen by most of the adult Americans whose homes surround them. These sites can be visited with appropriate permits available from Okinawan municipal authorities and clearance from base security. The few landlords who work on base may also regularly drive past old homesteads on their way to and from their shops or offices, perhaps occasionally stopping to furtively place flowers or coins at an obscure shrine. A number of elderly farmers even pass through the gates each day, cultivating vegetables and cutting grasses on the margins of the base.

However, for most, villages such as Morine are recalled through storytelling: anecdotes told after a family gathering or during a late night with friends at the neighborhood center, snatches of an old song heard on an afternoon AM radio broadcast or played by a neighbor in the stillness of a summer afternoon, a conversation inspired by a glimpse of old photographs exhibited at the city hall, an elderly neighbor entertaining children at a neighborhood school. Narration, spoken or sung, and visual representations recall the yādui to both performers and listeners. In this dialogue, memories of the furusato are exchanged and reinscribed; feelings toward the lost villages are experienced, shared, and negotiated.

And yet, these images and sentiments are contested and repressed during the course of daily life. The repetitive practices of work and leisure, its demands and distractions, keep Okinawans elsewhere, occupied with the mundane tasks that dominate their lives. Street maps and road atlases depict the bases in their present detail—how could one travel with a road map that illustrates the manifold of past and present? Images of bases in newspapers and television broadcasts, glimpses caught from passing cars, nearby homes, and sidewalks along the base perimeter represent only the now, to the exclusion of what has gone before.

More to the point, performances such as Sakamoto Kenichi's testimony at the kōkai shinri—the interminable, dispassionate discourse of a bureaucrat, replete with passive locutions and repetition—obscures the traces of a history of conflict, the record of savagery and genocide, of exploitation and dispossession. In its place are platitudes about peace and security, an orderly history of government policies and international cooperation, the numbing detail of leases signed and renewed, of payments disbursed and received. To regulate the future, one must also tame the past.

It is here that the testimony of the hansen jinushi intervenes. It appropriates the juridical apparatuses of the state, enlisting the narratives of the representatives of the Ministry of Defense to make legible the dispositions against which their own testimony will be deployed. It seizes the figure of the furusato from tourist and nativist discourses, rescuing it from narratives that both present it as lost (ushinawareta) to the inexorable forces of capitalist modernity and at the same time available, waiting, a traveler's destination in some eddy protected from the modern world. For the hansen jinushi, their furusato was lost to conflict and complicity—destroyed, confiscated, and bargained away in the negotiations between the Japanese and American states, available to them only if their rights as citizens are respected by the state that should be their guarantor. An object separated from them, the space of their community can no longer be a field of action. They are no longer able to gather in their homes or their fields to perform the meaningful community rituals and everyday practices that produced and maintained relationships with one another, with their ancestral spirits, and with their deities.

However, their furusato remains a basis of action, a material site from which power that enables practical activity to take place, to be effective, derives. The history of Ryūkyū, of Okinawa, demonstrates that a place does not need to be physically occupied in order to serve as a basis of action: Ryūkyūan priestesses were able to draw seji from the hidden space of nirai kanai; to call it forth on behalf of the Ryūkyūan king from the sacred groves of Kudaka Island, across the turbulent channel separating it from the Okinawan mainland. Through their testimony at the kōkai shinri—their oral narratives, their graphic reconstruction of the dispositions of their village—the hansen jinushi were able to reach their lands beyond the fence line at Kadena, and to recreate this furusato, reconstructing a basis of power in the auditorium at the Okinawa convention center.

This is why Arime and his colleagues were committed to representing a site of everyday life, of work and worship, rather than focusing on their experiences of horror and abjection. They were determined to present Morine as a place where they lived and labored, rather than a place of suffering and victimization. Moreover, they created and disseminated these representations through the appropriation of the bureaucratic genres and technologies that facilitated the expropriation of their land: the government-sponsored hearing, the production of official testimony, land surveys and ethnographic interviews, synoptic maps, and print and broadcast media.

Apart from simply demonstrating the historicity of their claims, the hansen jinushi intended to draw on this space as a basis of action in a moment of crisis, using its power and legitimacy to strike when the opportunity was at hand. The jinushi created this opportunity at the hearing at the Okinawa Convention center, playing on Ministry of Defense testimony, bringing together the work of all of their colleagues—historical and ethnographic research projects, stories that had been assembled and rehearsed for years, the tremendous social archive of memory. Through their testimony, their performance, they were able to represent their furusato before a huge number of potential witnesses—witnesses in the sense of those who are attentive and empathetic to the narratives of others who experienced the event itself: witnesses whose personal memories resonated with the stories that they were told; student activists and reporters, policemen and tourists, prefectural bureaucrats, and perhaps even representatives of the Ministry of Defense; families watching reports of the hearings on RBC television or reading accounts in the *Okinawa Times* and the *Ryūkyū Shinpo*; a driver in her car listening to testimony on the radio, or a casual reader leafing through published transcripts in an Okinawan bookstore.

Their testimony was more than a simple transmission of fact—it was grounded in personal experience and suffused with affect: courage and suffering, duty to the community of the living and the dead, hope and anger. In doing so, the hansen jinushi challenged their audience to recognize that they already shared the experience of the destruction of their furusato. That which is a memory of the personal experience of loss for the hansen jinushi also constituted the historical foundation for the exploitation and injustice that all Okinawans experience. The forced appropriation of Morine half a century ago is the necessary condition for the militarization of everyday life in Okinawa today.

What are the consequences of an empathetic reception of the hansen jinushi's testimony? It did not strengthen the governor's resolve to support their claims, nor did it prevent the Diet from brutally rejecting their demands. Still, the narrative of events and experiences that was created in the moment is now shared across a wider community of memory. Perhaps the nostalgia and muted longing that one learns to feel for the commodified furusato will give way to the pain felt for the loss of Morine. Perhaps the calm assurances and glib explanations offered by representatives of the Japanese state will be met with suspicion and anger rather than trust and respect. Perhaps the daily obligation that one feels to ancestral spirits will call for a situated and political response rather than routine offerings of fruit and flowers. Perhaps, gazing across the manicured lawns and wide streets, the barracks and runways of the American bases, one will see intimations of the yādui that once stood in the same place, one might feel that beneath the tarmac lies a village. And perhaps, if the memory of the courage of the hansen jinushi endures, one might be inspired to act in a moment yet to come.

in a samurai village

dances of memory, dances of oblivion

Lift up your hearts, my brothers, high! higher! And do not forget your legs! Lift up your legs too, you fine dancers: and better still, stand on your heads!—FRIEDRICH NIETZSCHE, Thus Spoke Zarathustra

The representation of a form, rediscovered and reinvented on each occasion, exceeds previous conceptions of repetition. And, furthermore, it includes them; because it also involves the return and reintegration at a high level—individual and social—of elements of the past and the surpassed.—HENRI LEFEBVRE, The Sum and the Remainder

NANDAKI BUSHI—THE BALLAD OF THE SOUTHERN GROVE

On a winter evening in 1998, I sat in a darkened theater at the Okinawan Prefectural Archives.[1] Images from the films of the director Moriguchi Katsu flickered across the screen, an exhibition of documentaries that he made in the late 1960s, the final decade of American occupation. Scenes of deprivation—farmers and fishermen struggling on the small drought-wracked island of Kudaka. Scenes also of creative activity—students and workers demonstrating against American rule, the war in Indochina, the storage of chemical weapons on Okinawan soil. And then, *Kataki Tsuchi o Yaburite: Okinawa '71* (Breaking through hard ground: Okinawa '71), the film that I wanted most to see. It was, in part, a chronicle of the Koza Riot—the violent uprising against the American occupation that Fujiki evoked in the performance of *Pōku Tamago*.[2] The scene begins on the evening of December 20, 1970: the streets of Koza—now Okinawa City—the base town crowded up against the massive American Air Force base at Kadena.[3] The camera pans along rows of concrete buildings, sweeping over the seemingly numberless shops, bars, and brothels that cater to American soldiers. The incident that sparked the riot has already taken place off camera. Okinawan men and women crowd the streets, pulling American servicemen from their cars, hurling rocks, debris, and bottles of burning gasoline. Okinawan police and American soldiers struggle ineffectively to restore order. The wreckage of dozens of cars smolders in the streets. Lit from behind by the flames, a woman dances. Dressed in an Okinawan kimono, perhaps she is a musician from one of the minyō[4] pubs in the neighborhood. She steps and turns, her hands describing wavelike patterns in the air as she dances the kachāshī, an exuberant expression of celebration.

Tomiyama Ichirō once told me that reporters who witnessed this moment —or a moment like it—spoke of the odoru shimin gerira, the dancing citizen guerilla. I've often wondered about her decision to dance the kachāshī in that chaotic street. Time after time, people have told me that a celebration is inconceivable without kachāshī. For generations of Okinawans, it has been a physical expression of pleasure and happiness. At the same time, it is an invitation: to dance kachāshī is to call to others to join in, to participate in the creation of the celebration. It also signals the finalization of a performance. Concerts, festivals, plays (even lectures, films, and demonstrations) end with the kachāshī. To see a dancer begin its sweeping gestures is to know that a moment is coming to a close.

I feel a kind of awe as I recall the dancer in Moriguchi's film. How could someone who stood in these streets at a moment of such crisis weigh all of her possibilities and find the courage to dance? Dancing among the burning cars, dancing as rioters stream around her in the street, dancing as soldiers advance toward her in riot formation.

UMIYAKARĀ—THE SEAFARING ROGUE

How can you live in a world in ruins? What can be saved, what is lost? In the aftermath of the war, Okinawans confronted a world in which they had been attacked by the United States, abandoned by Japan, and destroyed by both. Each day was a struggle to recall and to rebuild. Some tried to recreate familiar patterns of daily life in the damp canvas tents and muddy streets of the internment camps. Dressed in fatigues and combat boots, others gathered each morning for work parties. Organized by the soldiers of the American occupation, they would clear away the wreckage of burned buildings and the scorched hulks of tanks and trucks. They looked for traces in the shattered landscape, for intimations of the streets and homes, shops and fields that no longer stood in their familiar sites. They searched for the missing and buried the dead, the sense of loss heavy in the air like an impending storm. The uncertainty of the future was always before them as they waited uneasily for American soldiers to deliver supplies to their temporary shelters. Soldiers who were already building a new world of barracks and runways for themselves in the ravaged fields, a world where Okinawans could work but never dwell.

It was a time to labor and to mourn, but it was also a time to dream. Dreaming of laughter, of an escape from sadness. Onaha Būten and Teruya Rinsuke used these dreams to create the *nuchi nu sūji*, the celebration of life. It was their genius to bring music from the detritus of war: *taiko* (drums) cut from fifty-five-gallon barrels; sanshin crafted from empty cans, parachute cord, and scraps of lumber—happiness from despair, a moment of celebration recovered from days of labor and nights of exhaustion and sorrow. Far away in mainland Japan, Terurin's friend Kohama Shūei dreamed of returning to Okinawa and reuniting with his family. For a year, foraging in the fields and hills around Zushi,[5] he waited and hoped. Could he have survived the jungles of Indochina and the arduous trip back to Japan only to idle away his life like this?

When he finally returned to Okinawa, he found his wife and infant son alive, waiting for him. Slowly, his family came together—his brothers from Palau and Ponape, their families from the camps and from their hiding places in Yanbaru (the mountainous forests of northern Okinawa). They decided to settle in Saundabaru, shuttled by American trucks to the uninhabited wooded hillocks and swampy lowlands to the south of Goya in Goeku.[6] Other refugees from the yādui in Moromisato, Yamauchi, and Yamasato gathered in the same place, living in tents left for them by the Americans, cutting roads and trails, building small houses. Sometimes they returned to the fields around their old villages, building barracks and paving roads and runways under American supervision in the space where they once gathered fodder or cut cane.

Work was difficult and supplies scarce. In 1949, Shūei joined a base construction unit building houses for the occupying soldiers and their families. After two or three years, he moved to the Camp Simon Buckner Officers Club, where he worked for the next two decades. He once told me that when

dances of memory, dances of oblivion

he got the job at Buckner, he knew that he and his family were going to survive.

Still, Shūei was concerned that hard work would not be enough—people needed more than money to rebuild their world. During the war, the Japanese state had policed the pleasures of the people, banning public gatherings and suppressing Okinawan music and dance. After the war, under the indifferent occupation of the Americans, Shūei worried about this absence. Many of the musicians who once performed with him were lost or dead. Theaters were burned to the ground. The fields where revelers once danced had been swallowed by the bases. In this time of hesitant recovery, in the summer evenings after work, Shūei decided to gather the young men of his new neighborhood together in the Quonset hut that served as their community center. There, he taught them the *yakimāji eisā*.[7] Together they worked to master not only the steps and the songs of the eisā, but the style that marked the performances during the festival of the dead in the streets of Nishizato.

When I first met Shūei, he was nearly eighty years old. He carried his age and his experiences well—silver hair swept back from his forehead, a calm, deliberate manner. Although I had heard so much about his voice from my friends, I was amazed at its power when I finally heard him speak. He sounded uncannily like his friend Kadekaru Rinshō.[8] I doubt that anyone listening to their recorded duets could tell them apart.[9] His voice was rich and complex, layered with harmonics. It was not the high, clear tenor of a Roscoe Holcomb, but it carried traces of the same melancholy. He spoke with economy—slowly and softly, drawing people toward him, focusing their attention. And yet, beneath it, I could hear an undercurrent of strength.

Although he had lost most of his hearing and retired from active minyō performance a decade earlier, he remained a powerful presence in the neighborhood: one of the first performers to host a radio broadcast after the war, the brilliant *utasā*[10] who endlessly toured Okinawa with Kadekaru, who built his house with the profits from a single performance, the *jikata*[11] who trained and led the youth group that danced the eisā at Expo '70 in Osaka. His personal history was written in the framed objects that surrounded him in his living room: certificates of achievement in classical Ryūkyūan performing arts, minyō awards, photographs of the youth group in Osaka, and commendations for his diligent service at Camp Buckner.

Since the war, the young men from Shūei's neighborhood have always had

Kohama Shūei and his nephew Morihiko

a reputation for being tough. Even so, his confident, quiet presence—seated on a folding chair watching a rehearsal, standing in the courtyard of his house during Obon—frightened the hardest members of the *seinenkai*, the neighborhood youth organization. Although he could no longer hear the music, he watched the jikatas' fingers moving along the fretless neck of their sanshin, their faces as they sang, the steps of the dancers. Regardless of their stature, he would call a dancer or a musician aside, quietly critique their performance then—with a smile—send them back to the field.

Shūei was the third son of one of the leading families of the yādui Nishizato, a family that traced its origins to the kingdom of Nanzan in Itoman. They took great pride in belonging to a nobility that predated the Shuri court. For several generations, the house of Kohama had been part of the diaspora of impoverished nobility that had been resettled in the mountains of northern Okinawa. As their fortunes improved, successive generations established independent households, first in the Nago area, then to the south in Goeku. This is where Shūei was born.

As the Pacific War began, Nishizato was a yādui of about twenty-four households, wooden farmhouses with thatched roofs. It was located several kilometers to the south of Morine, the community that figured in the hansen jinushi's performance at the kōkai shinri. Along with other small yādui called Gofukuji and Akabira, Nishizato was administratively attached to the long-established farming hamlet of Moromisato: the characters used to express "Nishizato" literally mean "western hamlet," an identity defined by its relationship to Moromisato. The commoner households of Moromisato proper, an area with a population four or five times greater than Nishizato, were tightly clustered together and surrounded by fields, a typical pattern of rural settlement known evocatively in Okinawa as shima, or island. Moromisato was home to local administrative offices as well as the community shrine and the priestesses who maintained it.

In contrast, the houses of the yādui to the west were dispersed throughout the fields. Dirt roads linked the households, radiating out to connect the yādui with the surrounding communities. As dispossessed members of the former court nobility, they had no priestesses; they established only a small sacred grove on a hilltop at the center of their village and maintained a small clearing where people could gather for community rituals, for performances, or simply to play. The residents of the yādui were not attached to the communal landowning practices of the commoners in the rural villages and took advantage of Meiji land reforms to buy parcels of land from either the local villagers or from the central government. Although the impoverished nobles in the yādui might occasionally sell some of the vegetables and livestock that they raised for their own use, most of their money came from the sugar cane that they grew in their fields. There was a small satoya, or sugar press, in the yādui; it was also possible to haul cut cane via a narrow gauge railroad network to Kadena for processing and sale.[12]

Shūei was already a well-known utasā in central Okinawa before the Pacific, often performing with his friend Kadekaru Rinshō. At the same time, Shūei had been one of the men responsible for teaching eisā to the young men of Nishizato. The yādui in the Goeku area came together for many of the annual celebrations: dancers from Nishizato had a reputation for dynamic performances, their jikata for their striking vocal style. In central Okinawa, only young men of noble ancestry[13] were allowed to participate in eisā, and then only with the groups from their natal communities. Until Shūei decided to resume the dance after the war, it was inconceivable that outsiders would be allowed to join. Shūei broke with tradition, disregarding the objections of many of his friends who had lived in Nishizato. Shūei not only allowed but encouraged everyone to dance. If the disparate group that had come together in his neighborhood were to survive the aftermath of the war, he was sure that they would need the eisā.

In the decades after Shūei began to teach the yakimāji eisā to the refugees resettled in Saundabaru, the neighborhood changed dramatically. During the 1950s, they were joined by displaced or unemployed farmers from all over central and northern Okinawa and workers from Kyūshū and Amami Ōshima, as well as laborers from other outlying islands. For more than a decade, the survivors of the yādui continued to hold onto the deictic promise of Nishizato, hoping that they would be able to leave the unproductive land east of Moromisato and return to their ruined farms to the west, land now inside Kadena Air Base. However, by 1958, the survivors of the yādui felt that it was more and more unlikely that they would be able to go back to their old village; together with their new neighbors, they decided to change the name of their community to Sonoda—"Sonda" as it is regularly pronounced. Although "Sonda" sounds very much like "Saundabaru," the original place name of the community, it was written with completely different Chinese characters. The most common interpretation of this combination of characters is "gardens" or "fields." However, I've also been told that "Sonda" can be understood as "the space where events take place—like a niwa or nā." A compelling image for the gritty neighborhood with its crowded streets, small houses, tiny gardens: Sonda as a field, but a field of action as well as of simple agrarian production.

By the late 1950s, American military necessity and city planning had fixed the boundaries of the community, and Sonda had assumed the shape of a wedge pointing north, a shape that it maintains today. The area of the neighborhood is roughly 249,000 square meters, its western limit anchored by the central ridge of the island that runs along a north-south axis, descending to Moromisato Park and a series of fields and marshes and broken by fingers extending from the central highlands. Route 330, an overland highway running southwest to northeast, defines this western boundary. It is Route 330 that links Kadena Air Base with the Marine combat bases to the north and with the military harbor at Naha to the south: its four lanes are almost always choked with the traffic that surges back and forth from the tourist resorts and construction projects in northern Okinawa and the business districts and commercial airport in Naha. To the west of Route 330, the wide streets of Nakanomachi and Sentā form an orderly grid lined with a disorderly collection of bars, nightclubs, clothing stores, souvenir shops, restaurants, and hotels. Beyond the entertainment district lies Kadena Air Base, its fortified complex of magazines and hardened runways stretching almost to the western coast. Chatan, with its tourist boutiques and fashionable apartments, occupies the tiny strip of land left between Kadena and the East China Sea.

Sonda's eastern boundary is formed by a wide street that leads from Route 330 southwest to Kodomo no Kuni,[14] the local amusement park and zoo, separating Sonda from the neighboring community of Goya. The base of the triangle is made up of a street dividing Sonda from Kubota on its southwest border, and Shimabukuro in Kitanakagusuku on the southeast edge of the community. A network of streets and alleys crisscrosses Sonda—some wide enough to allow two cars to pass, others a mere footpath.

Although there is a strip of residences along the southern edge of Sonda, most homes are tightly compressed into a crescent situated in the northern apex of the wedge. At the time of my research, Sonda was made up of 1,164 households and 2,359 residents. A number of businesses such as restaurants, bars, retail stores, and hotels were scattered along the Sonda side of Route 330. Like Shūei, many residents of Sonda spent the years of the American occupation working on-base or in base-related jobs. Some continue to do so, but the number of jobs available on-base has continually declined since reversion. For the most part, they are the footsoldiers of the construction, service, and retail industries that provide the jobs for most Okinawans. They are carpenters and painters, masons and electricians, auto mechanics, policemen, sales clerks, bank tellers, and parking lot attendants. There are still a few fishermen in Sonda, including several who have turned to aquaculture, growing mozuku[15] for the Japanese table. Although municipal statistics show that a number of professional workers also live in Sonda, most residents are working class. Many Sondanchū—as the residents of the community are called—also earn income from base leases, either through direct ownership or payments that they receive from relatives who are the primary landowners. Within the center of the community, in the lowlands to the east of Moromisato Park, a few farmers continue to work their fields, growing a variety of crops from bitter melon and mango to cabbage and potatoes. Goats, chickens, and even some cattle can be found in small pens scattered here and there; one elderly man even continued to maintain a horse-drawn cart that he rode each day to his fields on the edge of town. Household gardens are common, and every bit of open space—between houses, around tombs—seems to be under cultivation.[16]

The uneven stone or concrete walls of residential compounds line the streets of Sonda, broken here and there by gates, driveways, or the sliding windows of a storefront. Rooftops jut above walls covered in flowering bougainvillea and yūna. Instead of the idyllic wooden cottages topped with red tile that appear so often in Okinawan tourist brochures, most of the houses here are squat cubes, built of either cement blocks or poured concrete. While a few dilapidated wooden houses huddle beneath massive roofs of gray concrete tiles, there are many modern homes—flat-roofed or, playing on traditional styles, with red-tiled roofs trimmed in white. Here and there, larger buildings arise among their low-slung neighbors: apartment houses and a few small hotels. The entire community appears to be fortified against a second onslaught of the conflict that ravaged Okinawa half a century ago.

HANA NU KAJIMAYĀ—PINWHEELS IN THE WIND

On a summer evening in 1998, I stood on the stairs of the Sonda Community Center.[17] I was about two kilometers south of the point where the Koza Riot began, only a couple of hundred meters from the club where I once gazed into the darkened streets of Koza. A focal point of neighborhood activity, the community center stood in the midst of a group of turtleback tombs atop a ridge overlooking Moromizato Park. As I had done every night that summer and the summer before, I joined dozens of men and women in the pounded clay courtyard as we prepared to dance eisā.

In fields and parking lots across central Okinawa, thousands of young Okinawan men and women practice eisā throughout the summer, preparing for three nights of dancing during Obon.[18] If the seinenkai is fortunate enough to be invited, the dancers will come together again for the island-wide eisā exhibition that follows. In recent years, many scholars have struggled to understand the politics of remembrance in Okinawa.[19] However, little scholarly attention has been paid to eisā, the most widespread modality

dances of memory, dances of oblivion

of public memorative practice in the islands. As my friends often told me, eisā was necessary so that they could respond to the demands and desires of the ancestral spirits, to the hundreds of thousands who were killed during the war.

It's said that eisā is danced to escort the spirits of the dead from their tombs back to their homes and to entertain them during Obon; to narrate and embody the history of impoverished Okinawan courtiers sent down from the capital; to express and sustain the pride and honor of these neighborhoods, the power and the artistry of the dancers; and to create and share karī, the gift of happiness and belonging produced in performance, necessary for life. Koza—Okinawa City—has emerged as the focal point of eisā performance, and Sonda became the most famous of the groups within the city.

At almost every public performance I've attended, eisā is introduced as an ancient Okinawan performing art described in the *Omorosōshi*,[20] its origins lost in Ryūkyūan antiquity.[21] People have told me that eisā has its roots in the *nenbutsu odori*—the dance to memorate the spirits of the dead—brought to Okinawa by Buddhist missionaries from Kamakura and practiced widely throughout the seventeenth century. I've also heard that eisā bears a strong resemblance to the memorative rituals of the Ryūkyūan court once performed before the royal tombs during the seventh month, and described by emissaries from the Korean peninsula during the fifteenth century.[22] The members of the youth group are interested in these accounts and often discuss them, arguing with visiting anthropologists and folklorists; several members carry out their own research or collaborate with local scholars, conducting interviews, sketching and painting, publishing essays about eisā and its history. However, for the most part, it is not eisā's dimly remembered origins that capture their imagination, that drive their long hours of storytelling and debate. Their concern is with recollecting their own past, with recreating their own dance.

The Sonda *kōminkan*—Sonda's community center—is saturated with traces of this past. Its straight, simple lines evoke the construction of the family tomb, the traditional Okinawan home, and the palace of the Ryūkyūan king at Shuri. Generally rectangular, one long side is open, and several steps lead down to a large rectangular courtyard. Of course, there are obvious differences: squared, institutional poured concrete rather than the ubiquitous

The Sonda Kōminkan

turtleback shape of the tombs or the gleaming red-lacquered timbers of the palace at Shuri; a pounded clay courtyard instead of the tightly fitted paving stones of a nā;[23] and chain link fence rather than an ornamental stone wall.

Nonetheless, the echoes of the tomb are compelling. Before the war, dancers and musicians from Nishizato gathered on summer evenings in courtyards of the crypts that lay on the edge of their hamlet. Night after night, they danced and sang before the spirits of their ancestors, practicing for the day that would bring eisā again to the streets of their villages and the courtyards of their homes. Their practices were both pleasurable and demanding, away from the fields where they labored each day, from the discipline of the home, from the regulation of the state, resisting the pressure and the lure of labor migration to the mainland or the South Pacific. In the company of their friends and the spirits of their ancestors, farmers and laborers became dancers and musicians.

Those tombs and villages are gone. The material presence of the ancestors, so painstakingly ordered and attended by their families, was fragmented and dispersed—destroyed along with many of the lives of those who

dances of memory, dances of oblivion

memorated them. And yet, for those who survived, relationships with the spirits of the ancestors were too precious to lose, obligations to the dead too great to ignore. Rebuilding the tombs and recollecting the ancestors was one of the first priorities of Okinawan households in the postwar reconstruction. However, tombs and household altars are not the only places in which the spatial fields of the ancestors were reinstalled. The kōminkan itself is a site of repeated daily labor to situate and recall the dead. It is a space that is filled with the creative activity of dancers who struggle to express their desire to understand—and to change—the world around them.

Virtually every inch of available wall space is covered with the graphic traces of Sonda's past. Row after row of framed photographs showing generations of dancers; certificates noting the youth group's performances in decades of annual eisā competition in Okinawa City and their appearances throughout Japan; letters of appreciation from prominent Japanese politicians, performers, and admiring fans. There are group pictures for every year of the seinenkai's history: their famous appearance at Expo '70, at festivals throughout Okinawa, at performances across mainland Japan, with Japanese rock stars, television news anchormen, Olympic skaters, and former prime ministers. To the right of the most recent pictures, a full-length mirror is bolted to the wall: aspiring dancers can anticipate and enjoy their own inclusion into the archive of representations. Huge embroidered banners hang from the rafters, commemorating youth group victories in the Zento Eisā Konkuru, the island-wide eisā competitions that have been held since 1958.

The oldest picture, a framed black-and-white group photograph above the door shows a group of men, lean and sunburned, staring gravely at the camera. They are dressed in short, working kimono and wearing farmers' woven conical hats. One or two men hold sanshin and several drums are lined up in the foreground. These are the first dancers to come together to dance eisā after the war.

As I walked around the room, I saw more recent photographs, black-and-white giving over to color. In the late 1950s, women began to join the youth group. The clothing of the dancers also changed. When they were all dé-classé nobles, they proudly wore the modest kimono of the farming village where their families were born. When participation in the seinenkai was opened to everyone, noble or commoner, native or outsider, men began to

Interior of Sonda Kōminkan, showing photos and awards

wear the garb of a stylized Okinawan samurai, while women continued to wear the kimono of rural commoners.

Kohama Shūei told me that he and his friends were inspired to select costumes that would help the young men and women of the neighborhood to create a dramatic impression on the audience and judges at eisā performances, particularly the Zento Eisā Konkuru. One cannot help but notice the powerful representations of gender and class in these images, in contrast to the conditions of Okinawan daily life. Imagine the attraction that representations of strong, handsome Ryūkyūan warriors have for a cook at a base club or a servant in an American household; or the possibilities that a graceful, laughing rural dancer presents to a maid at a cheap hotel or a prostitute in a crowded club. And yet, the gendered assignment of class seems puzzling. In a neighborhood so proud of its samurai heritage, why should the women be consigned to the status of commoners?

Shūei provided the answer. The costumes that they chose were not un-mediated representations of the Okinawan past; rather they were selected

dances of memory, dances of oblivion

from the most popular plays and dances of the Okinawan theater—the Uchinā Shibai.[24] Thus, costumes not only referred to favorite images and idealized qualities of the past; they also suggested the protean expressiveness of theatrical performance. Regardless of the attire that performers wore in the world of labor, on the streets of Koza, they could claim the right to transform themselves in the dance. They were free to choose, regardless of the burden or the privilege of their heritage. However, in doing so, they also opened themselves to the judgment of the audience gathered for performances: an appropriated image could only be maintained if the dancers demonstrated that they were equal to it.

In the photographs, men wore white trousers with a short-sleeved jacket and a blue silk vest trimmed in black and tied at the waist with a golden sash, black-and-white leg armor strapped to their legs, and long sashes of red or violet tied around their heads. Women were dressed in conservative indigo kimono with splashes of white crosshatching on the dark field and violet sashes, their hair pulled back with violet ribbon.

The images displayed in the kōminkan are important elements in mediating the transmission of the varying versions of the seinenkai's past. They provide visual linkages between the interior space of the kōminkan and other people, places, and events distributed over space and time: traces of other moments, graphic reminders that figure practices of recollection. In the quiet hours of the afternoon, during the hurried moments before a rehearsal, in the long hours of talking and drinking after a performance has ended, they are looked at, pointed to, used as a touchstone for the storytelling that is as much a part of eisā as the dance. Young members listen attentively to the stories told by their seniors. One evening finds the OBS[25] talking about Yakimāji and the moashibi, the illicit parties where the young men and women of the surrounding villages gathered while Kohama Shūei and Kadekaru Rinshō entertained them.[26] At the same time, it is not some kind of pristine refuge from the world of work, from the space of the nation. Several old men from the neighborhood sit around a table and talk about their experiences in the Pacific War or during the occupation. On another evening, OBS repeat their older brothers' stories about burning American cars during the Koza Riot, helicopters overhead, tanks in the street. Conversations also often embrace business and politics—negotiating jobs and recruiting supporters. And yet, discussions always seem to return to eisā: this year, last year, the great years of the eisā competition. Eisā is an endlessly interesting, inexhaustible subject: the proper way to hold a drumstick, the meaning of a lyric, the merits of another neighborhood's eisā, a recent performance, a performance yet to come.

Outside, we prepared for rehearsal—just as we did every evening during the three months preceding Obon. Most of the dancers came to the kōmin-kan directly from work. From the dress of the members of the youth group, it was clear that Sonda was a working-class neighborhood. A majority of the young men were in sagyōfuku—the uniform of the construction worker, the painter, the general contractor: baggy, calf-length trousers in vivid pastel colors, white T-shirts, and towels knotted around their heads. High school boys were still in their school uniforms: black trousers and white shirts. The remaining young men were dressed in current hip-hop fashion: shiny sweats—Adidas but not Nike; baggy denim shorts or pants, large, blocky sneakers, oversized jerseys: Fubu, Mecca, the Japanese national soccer team.

Young women came in fashionably tight blouses with wide collars and flared pants. A few were in matching knee-length skirts and vests, the uniforms of local banks and offices. None of the high school girls still wore their school uniforms. Younger girls were in wide-leg jeans, clunky, thick-soled sneakers or sandals, and undersized GI T-shirts (Seabees and Hell-blasters). Style means attention to detail: the right jewelry, a cool G-Shock wristwatch, good haircut (bleached or dyed), and color contacts—green or variegated blue best of all.

Two rows of folding chairs had been set up at the top of the stairs, microphones in front of each. The jikata (sanshin musicians) sat there with the other OBs, tuning their instruments, warming up their voices, running a soundcheck, catching a last smoke before practice. Ten to twenty years older than the younger members, their dress and manner was notably different. They joked with one another in Uchināyamatuguchi, a conversational fusion of Okinawan and Japanese that is far more dependent on Okinawan than the speech of the younger members.[27] These older men sported punch perms, crew cuts, the "all back" pompadour and were dressed in jeans and polo shirts, designer sweats, aloha shirts, and chinos. One saw flashes of gold—gold watches, gold jewelry, gold teeth.

Remnants of cigarettes were stubbed out, and empty water glasses stacked. Cellular phones, pagers, watches, lighters, cigarette packs, and wallets were removed from wrists, belts, and pockets, and lined up along the steps and windowsills. Everyone moved down from the steps or out from the inside of the building and filed down onto the watered clay surface of the courtyard. The lead jikata laughed, shouting to the new dancers: "Unless you decide that you're going to try to do this better than everyone else, your dancing won't ever amount to anything!"

Dancers came to the kōminkan to play, but it is a form of play that has its costs as well as its rewards. The dancers have shrugged off many of the more conventional chances for recreation that contemporary Japanese society offers, even in Okinawa. They have—if only for the moment—refused the distractions of mass culture, of television, bars, games, parks, and films. At the same time, they have refused certain kinds of work: more profitable employment in the dense urban areas of Naha or Urasoe, mainland Japan, or America; labor in the remaining bars, brothels, or nightclubs of nearby Nakanomachi. They cannot meet the demands of employers for overtime, for different hours, or selfless devotion to their jobs. For the most part, they have also turned their backs on the intellectual labors of the juku (cram school) and the university.[28] The dancers have also sacrificed one of the most treasured goals of a worker—sleep. The toll taken on laboring bodies is inescapable, but sleep offers a daily refuge from work, a chance to recover one's strength, to heal. Perhaps even the opportunity to dream. Instead they commit themselves to hours of arduous and demanding activity that, until recently, marked them as hooligans and lowlifes in the popular imagination.[29]

Standing in the courtyard, drummers adjusted the carriage of their instruments and dancers shifted their bodily hexis to that of the dance. Men lowered their hips, turned their knees out, and sank into a wide stance. Head up, shoulders back, hands on hips, a look of quiet confidence on their faces. Women feet together, legs and back straight, hands at their hips, faintly smiling. The men's position is hard; the women's more relaxed. The older members continue to work their way through the formation, physically moving dancers into the appropriate stance.

To the front, the jikata counted out the beat and drove into "Nandaki Bushi" ("The Ballad of the Southern Grove"), the first song of the eleven pieces that make up their eisā. After the first measure, the drums joined in. With the simultaneous sound of fifty drums being struck, the dance began. The song is sung in unison, the lyrics in Okinawan. For twenty minutes or

Eisā practice at the Sonda
Kōminkan

more, the songs continue and the dancers dance. Women work to make the
stately grace of the dance seem effortless. Along with the male dancers, their
performance draws heavily on Okinawan folk and classical genres, creating
the figure that organizes the eisā, elegant and controlled. The drummers
dance a counterpoint to this. Leaping and turning, beating out a rhythm that
is sometimes straight, sometimes syncopated, they struggle to maintain
Sonda's reputation of speed and physicality: dancers whose bodies are already exhausted and injured from long hours of harsh, physical labor; dancers for whom this evening's exertions are a respite before another day of
work. Sweat from the dancers splashes the ground—some people say that if
you scratch away the clay, it's salt all the way down to the roofs of the tombs
at the bottom of the hill.

During their performance—the orchestration of drumming, song and
dance—they conjure the account of a journey, assembled and sung from
narratives of the past. A complex secondary genre, eisā is a cycle of narratives

dances of memory, dances of oblivion

that recount the diaspora of the Ryūkyūan nobility—more than a century of travels encompassing life in the days of the Ryūkyūan kingdom, their impoverishment and exile to the mountainous northern forests, their struggle to return to the capital once more. Each of the songs narrates the experiences of a particular time and place where the former nobles lived along their journey. Some are songs that were composed during the period that they represent; others are later representations of that time and place. With their own particular chronotopes, their own narrative organization of space and time, the songs are bound together by the formal structure and the performative production of the dance. Together they compose the unity of the work, the utterance. All are woven together, harmonized in performance by the powerful rhythm of the drums that opens the dance. Eisā's heartbeat, say the dancers. These songs are also fitted together by the similar stylistics of the dance: stepping and spinning, first clockwise, then counterclockwise. The way that shimedaiko—the small, hand-held drums—are extended at arm's length, then swung in dramatic underhand arcs.

The initial songs are elegiac accounts of the past, narrating what could be called Ryūkyūan mythic time, a powerful fusion of time and space. Even the titles of the songs—"Nandaki Bushi," "Chunjun Nagari," and "Kudaka"[30]— are redolent of the Ryūkyūan past. The past to be sure, but a past that differs significantly from conventional historical representations. There is no more than a glimpse of the everyday world that gives shape to festival and ritual. There is no definite sense of the conditions of agricultural labor, trade, courtly governance, or war. There are no suggestions of hardship or loss; only mastery, pleasure, and plenty. The moment recounted in the song eschews any reference to the expected subjects of Okinawan history: diplomatic relations with China, military expansion into the Amami islands, Satsuma's invasion of Shuri, or Japanese colonialism.

The performance is organized by a chronotope of cycled, not cyclic time.[31] The practical repetition of festivals such as Obon and Tanabata (a Japanese summer festival celebrating the mythic reunion of two lost lovers) is emphasized as if it is entirely natural. These festivals are disconnected from any larger cycles, agrarian or political, with which they were usually associated. What's more, the spaces that are depicted are virtually inseparable from the rituals that they contain: shrines, sacred groves, village clearings. There is a strange compressed immediacy to the performance. As Bakhtin has written, "This is a dense and fragrant time, like honey."[32] The singers' voices are filled with the reported speech of nobles, their gender unspecified, the time indeterminate—singing of eisā today in the words and voices of eisā from the past. In this transposition, the performers sensuously experience the narratives of the past as they create them again in the moment.

Midway through the cycle of songs, the performance changed. Before the Pacific War, the songs that followed continued to advance the sequence of spatial representations of the courtiers' diaspora. Songs like "Nakijin Bushi" and "Goeku Bushi"[33] were markers on a path that led from the wilderness of northern Okinawa, then south to the fields and hamlets surrounding Nishizato. In the aftermath of the war, musicians like Kohama Shūei felt that there was something incomplete about the old cycle of songs. Why should the manifest form of the dance express sentiments—the bitterness of exile, longing for a return to the capital—that the performers no longer shared? They decided to shift the emphasis of this part of the performance to songs that more closely expressed the desires and experiences of neighborhood youths. In the postwar world, courtiers were no longer dependent on the backward glance to Shuri or their lost villages. Instead, they created their place, producing it in their confident, expressive actions.

The movements of the performers also became more dynamic and complex. The pattern of earlier dances was taken and transformed by changes in rhythm and tempo, pauses, dramatic shifts in the level of the dancers. The new songs were exuberant compositions characterized by syncopated rhythms and intricate sanshin fingerwork—a departure from the stately pace and pastoral lyrics of the first section. The anonymous narrators of earlier songs were also replaced with the distinct, individual voices of young men and women. They recounted their experiences of anticipation and hope, of desire that is intensely and explicitly sexual. The feverish need for the return of affection, yearning for the evening's revelries and a passionate embrace:

I'm in love with a seafaring rogue
and I can't even eat.
In the middle of the road I stand, transfixed.
My parents are heartbroken.

Here, in the words of a young Okinawan woman, the singers describe the intensity of their emotions: they are entranced, immobilized by longing. The moment that the narrator describes, that they have created, leaves no room for anything else. They also sing of defiance and transgression—refusing to accept an arranged marriage demanded by Japanese convention,[34] rejecting dutiful labor and the submission to authority in favor of creative performances, drinking, and romantic celebrations. Reality and imagination are woven together in interesting and complex ways. Dancers choose to create narratives of uncommodified sexuality and personal choice in the time that they might otherwise spend in bars and clubs. Who is to say which is more real or more fulfilling? At the same time, the moments recreated in the peformance suggest that their determination has a cost. Autonomy has its bounds, and desire cannot always be fulfilled. A powerful tension emerges in the performance, the tension between hope and loss.

Like the voices heard in these songs, the dancers also face the consequences of their dance—fatigue, disappointment, the sacrifice of opportunities for material advancement. Still, they throw themselves into the moment, struggling to equal—to exceed—the standards set by their predecessors through half a century of performances, and determined to master the most forceful strikes, the most furious arcs of the drums, the most spectacular spins. They dream that they will build on the forms of the past, adding something new, something of their own creation. Hence the lead jikata's comment, "Unless you decide that you're going to try to do this better than everyone else, your dancing will never amount to anything!" Close to exhaustion, their voices hoarse, uniforms dripping with sweat, they conclude the dance with an exultant burst of energy.

Eisā speaks in many voices. Of course, it calls out to the audience present: friends and family, ancestral spirits, tourists. It speaks to others as well—absent parents, companions, and lovers—drawing on the captured speech of singers represented by jikata of long ago. It would also be possible to think of another level of address to the song, what William Hanks has called the covert addressee.[35] The singers speak to themselves in their words and their actions, repeating again and again these narratives of what they can do, of who they are. Through this repetition, the singers bring the world of eisā, the world of the work into themselves, into their everyday lives.

Writing of the existential problem of ethics, Paul Ricoeur has said that to recall the objects of memory opens the possibility of astonishment for the remembering subject. The recognition of the relationship between act and actor can be profoundly disturbing. One is no longer able to dissociate the general idea of a personal history that led to this moment from the memory of a particular event that was performed in the past. How is it that the "I" that I am now was capable of the specific act of the remembered "I?"[36] Can I feel that feeling again in this moment? Eisā compounds this by transposing the words and gestures of others into direct speech and action, into performance. The experience of each moment represented in the work is embodied by the dancers. The past is mobilized in a manifold of experiences in the present. The singers feel the authority of these voices in their own song, the power of the dances in their own bodies. They are challenged by the familiarity and the strangeness of the performance: "Can I feel the experience of others in the performance that I am now creating? Am I also the narrator to whom I give voice?

These questions are important to the members, a sign of their determination to transform themselves from the young men and women who began learning the eisā together into those who are fully capable of the dance. To become those who are able to produce karī.

Karī is often described as a gift of happiness and belonging produced in performance and necessary for life.[37] As Okinawan performing artists such as Teruya Rinsuke have said, the role of a performer is to convey—to attach this portion of happiness to their audience. When I discussed the idea of karī with the jikata and the older members of the youth group, they often explained the importance of karī for the well-being of the community as well as the happiness of the individual. All events unfold according to the relationship between things: karī enables human actors to create and maintain these relationships. It strengthens and renews the bond between the living, the ancestral spirits, and those yet to be born.

In Okinawa, significant effort and artistry is expended to transform the corporal remains of the dead, to craft a place for the ancestral spirits, and to incorporate them into social relations distributed across space and time. Eisā is an important part of this process. Eisā does not simply pass along a portion of happiness to the audience that they would otherwise be without. In eisā, the dancers draw upon their aesthetic, productive powers to recollect and recreate the very relationships that make life worth living, in which the living and the dead can join each other in happiness. *Churaku nashun*, people say—to make beautiful. In the moment of the dance, filled with the complex patterns described by their bodies in movement, their voices raised in song, the rhythm measured out by their drums, they create place and a time, a community of beauty.

Can this beauty obscure as it creates? As Paul Ricoeur has written, there are consequences to representations of the past if they put history at the risk of forgetting.[38] Is this true of the time and space filled by eisā? Certainly, the cycle of songs eschews any direct reference to the abjection, the horror of the eras that they depict—although minyō that take up these themes certainly exist.[39] Nonetheless, as I have suggested, any reference to the past always carries the charged ambiguity of a beauty underwritten by the memory of pain and loss, a joy tempered by sadness and despair. The beauty of the performances begun by Kohama Shūei and his friends was driven by the need to renew life in a shattered world. The dancers who still gather to learn and to perform the eisā know this well. They do not need sympathetic native ethnologists, advertising executives, or popular musicians to explain to them the value of their dance. They do not need to be told of the burden of Okinawan history—of war, colonialism, and oppression. They feel it every day in the ache of their tired limbs, their joints bent and twisted by labor long before the ravages of age take them, their skin burned and dried by long hours in the sun. They feel the shame of occupation in the long detours that the bases impose on their travel to work, in the way an English word like "houseboy" rolls off their grandfather's tongue, in the crops that they can neither plant nor harvest, in the money from base leases that fills their pockets after trickling down through grandparents, uncles, and parents. They know it in the longing for a lover who is away searching for work in Osaka or Kawasaki or is spending the evening pouring drinks for some businessman in Nakanomachi, in the desire for a new car, a comfortable house, a private room that they will never own. They see it in the faces of their mixed-blood siblings, in the tears that streak their grandmother's cheeks as she kneels in prayer at the family tomb. They hear it in the laughter of drunken Marines and affluent Japanese tourists. They taste it in the awamori that they drink through long afternoons and evenings of boredom, frustrated by the lack of work. How can it be completely forgotten in the dance?

dances of memory, dances of oblivion

Instead, they have the courage to put aside memories of horror and abjection, to allow these inescapable fears and anxieties to slip into a kind of oblivion during the performance. In the courtyard of the community center, in the space soaked with the sweat of generations of dancers, they create something of beauty in the shadow of the horrors of the past. This is why today's dancers no longer need to be of noble ancestry. They have learned to do the things in practice that were once the exclusive provenance of those of noble birth. Hour after hour, night after night, they have developed the skill and artistry to dance the eisā, to create karī, to rebuild what has been broken, to make a place for the living and the dead in the world that they have been given.

KŪDĀKĀ—THE BALLAD OF KŪDĀKĀ ISLAND

In 1998, the youth group planned to commemorate the fortieth anniversary of their incorporation as Sonda. The summer would be marked with celebrations (benefit concerts, dances, a reunion) culminating in Sonda's performance to close the 1998 Okinawan Eisā Festival. Early in the summer, several of the older members began to discuss the possibility of returning to perform in Nishizato—in the heart of Kadena Air Base. Although it was possible to enter the base singly or in small groups to care for a shrine or tomb, to consult with a local deity or with ancestral spirits, no one had thought to do so to dance. However, the decision was not as simple as it seemed. Bitter divisions remained among base landowners, and between Okinawans in general after the shocking defeat of the antibase movement during the previous year. Strong undercurrents of hope and anxiety emerged in the discussions that followed—concerns with awakening memories that people thought had been worked through long ago. In the end, after long debate, the visit proved to be quite easy to arrange: a letter, a sympathetic official at Kadena's Public Affairs Office, the American calculus of costs and benefits. After all, it was only a dance.

On an oppressively hot July afternoon in 1998, I walked along the narrow street leading from Route 330 to the community center. Cars were parked tightly along both sides, and I wondered what it was going to take for everyone to get back out again, let alone allow the youth group's small support truck to leave. Groups of older men and women, well dressed, stood

dances of memory, dances of oblivion

along the street, talking and laughing. Kohama Morikatsu waved me over to introduce me to his older sister. Although she also lived on the main island, her husband worked to the north, so they had relocated to the Gushikawa area. Her oldest son had joined the youth group this year and was making his debut as a dancer; still, she said, she would have attended a performance like this in any case. Morikatsu gestured down the hill toward his house and told me to stop by later. His family would be having a party after our performance—his relatives had come home from all over Okinawa.

Although I had arrived at the kōminkan hours before our scheduled departure time, it was already crowded with people. Several of the younger members were stacking drums, checking them for cracks and tightening the bindings. The youth group's flags—long green pennants mounted on heavy bamboo poles—had already been decorated with fresh palm fronds. Too tall to be kept in the kōminkan, they were lashed to a railing outside. A number of OBs wandered around, teasing the younger members and checking their preparations. Most of the young dancers and drummers were already getting dressed, tying the stylized leg armor around their ankles, wrapping sashes around their waists, knotting scarves around their heads. More and more elderly men and women arrived at the community center, sitting at tables reserved for them. I stood with Kiyuna Kō-chan, a former assistant head of the youth group and a self-appointed instructor of the younger dancers as well as a cousin of the Kohama family. He told me that the older people in the neighborhood were extremely excited about the chance to see eisā performed in their old village after more than half a century of exile. Kō-chan and I checked one another to see that our uniforms were in order and left to walk out to Route 330.

There were two buses parked along the highway—one borrowed from Ai no Mura, a senior home owned by a former resident of the neighborhood, and another from the Okinawa City Office of Education. The drivers were two particularly colorful OBs. A column of cars from the neighborhood was already lined up behind our buses—parents, grandmothers, and girlfriends waved excitedly to the dancers. I saw my wife, Atsuko, and our kids in our small car near the end of the formation. Photographers and reporters from the Okinawa Times and Ryūkyū Shinpo joined us, riding along on the bus.

When we reached the gates of Kadena Air Base, Iha Masakazu (or Kajū, as everyone called him) and Kohama Morikatsu, the head of the community organization as well as the Nishizato Kyōyūkai (a league of former residents of Nishizato and their families), got down from the bus, paperwork in hand, and talked to the Air Force and Japanese civilian guards. Several permits had been secured—letters from base administrators allowing the dancers to enter the base and perform in the ruins of Nishizato, and permits from the Okinawa City municipal authorities to allow families and friends to visit Nishizato. After a long discussion between the community leaders and the guards, Kajū and Morikatsu returned to the bus to tell us that there were some problems with the documents authorizing our visit. Although the correct forms had been used, the Japanese paperwork was not completed to the satisfaction of the guards. What's more, several of the cars carrying members of the youth group and their families didn't have child seats that met with base requirements. A quick compromise was reached: several members who worked on base would ride in the personal vehicles and register the passengers as their guests; everyone else could board the bus and ride with the rest of the group. The remaining cars were parked in a lot by the gate, passengers redistributed, and the buses were allowed to enter.

And so it was that I found myself on a bus taking other members of the youth group the three or four kilometers from Sonda to Nishizato. A short trip, but one that could also be measured in decades, in thousands of miles. One of my friends—a former head of the youth group, now a jikata—sat next to me, his six-year-old son on his lap. As we passed the Kadena USO (United Service Organizations) and entered a residential neighborhood, everyone was pressed to the windows of the bus. My friend pointed outside, saying to his son: "Look out there—that's America!" All around us, people talked about the contrast between the straight, wide boulevards, broad lawns, and massive banyan trees of the base and the cramped streets of Okinawa City. Behind me, another veteran member of the youth group in his forties laughed: "Sasuga Amerikā" (After all, it is America).

After some confusion about the route, the buses stopped in the parking lot of a large, self-service gas station. To the southeast, a sloping berm about two meters high led to a large, grassy field. The field was level and roughly square, perhaps fifty meters on a side. To the east, the field rose sharply to a tree-covered knoll. Fifty or sixty members of the Nishizato Kyōyūkai were already there—some had spread blankets at the edge of the knoll and were having a picnic before the performance. The younger members of the youth group pushed a heavy cart carrying the sound system up the berm; others carried extra drums, sanshin cases, and boxes filled with drumsticks and spare equipment.

I could see conflicting emotions in the faces of the members of the kyōyū-kai. Several elderly women led their grandchildren around the crest of the hill, pointing out absent sites in the landscape. Others stood together, holding each other for support, some wiping their eyes as they wept quietly. It is difficult to imagine the riot of memories and emotions that they must have experienced: to stand once again in a place you knew as a site of labor and daily life, to watch eisā in the fields where you once danced, to find yourself again in the place of wartime horror and abjection, to confront the complex and contradictory rush of emotions—the pain of loss returned, the joy and guilt of survival, the gratitude and shame of ownership. To reclaim—if only for a moment—the right to determine the use of a place which you own, from which you have been excluded, which provides the income that sustains you in times of hardship, where perhaps you have labored as a gardener, a maid, a waitress.

My friends were also confused, forced to confront a place that they had heard so much about, that was so central to the reputation of the Sonda eisā, and yet had never been so real, so present. Questions arose quietly, that would be discussed through the next several evenings. "Is this America? Is it our home? Does a place belong to us—do we belong in a place—where we have never been, where we may never return? What will it mean to make ourselves visible—like this, here, now? Can we simply come here to dance and then forget the other stories and struggles into which this place is woven?"

While the crowd and the dancers intermingled, the leaders of the seinen-kai and several of the OBs climbed to the knoll, following a trail around to a small clearing on its north side. At the center of this small area was a small concrete structure shaped like a house, probably no more than a meter high. As I looked to the east, across rooftops of the Banyan Tree Club and the base library and toward Okinawa City, I could see a series of gently rolling hills stretching out to the base perimeter fence. One of my friends, standing next to me, told me that most of them were surmounted by similar structures marking the sites of the original shrines or sacred groves of the yādui in the area.

Mrs. Kohama was laying out sticks of black Okinawan incense, a round

Members of the kyōyūkai and the
seinenkai making offerings at the
shrine at Kadena Air Base

lacquer tray of fruit, and several piles of tissue weighted with fragments of coral—spirit money—as offerings to the shrine. While she and several other ladies arranged these objects to their satisfaction, I noticed that there were other offerings already present, mostly coins placed at the edge of the concrete platform on which the shrine was constructed. When they were finished, they knelt to pray. The youth group leaders spread hand towels on the ground to protect their white trousers from grass stains before joining them in prayer. After a moment, Kajū walked over to the sound system and asked everyone to join the members of the kyōyūkai in wū tū tū, prayer to the ancestral spirits. The newspaper photographers moved around the shrine, snapping pictures, while the reporters hovered at Mrs. Kohama's shoulder, waiting for her to finish with her devotions.

When the prayers were finished, the dancers gathered on the edge of the field, adjusting their clothing, tentatively striking the drums. The jikata had all put on short blue jackets with the characters for Sonda Youth Group

dances of memory, dances of oblivion

emblazoned on the back and collar. They tuned their sanshin and warmed up their voices. The leaders of the youth group walked the field, checking its surface and thinking about the space available. Kajū then had a brief discussion with the leaders of the kyōyūkai before returning to the clustered dancers and drummers.

Because of the restricted space, he announced that we would dance in a box formation similar to the way we practiced at the community center. Drummers were divided in two large groups on the flanks and a single line across the front and rear; the men and women dancers were arranged in alternating columns in the center. The whole formation faced the shrine and the assembled members of the kyōyūkai.

Everyone got into place, made last-minute adjustments, and looked around at their friends. Afterward, people talked about the tremendous excitement and energy that they felt. As the jikata struck the opening notes of "Nandaki Bushi," the dancers erupted in a wild laughter—something that I had never heard before. As we began to dance, my legs felt astonishingly heavy. Perhaps it was the combination of long nights of practice, days of work, the anxiety of performance in this place? I was conscious of every movement, the uneven ground beneath me, the thick grass. Before the kyōyūkai, in this place, I focused intently on the dance, both participating and watching, doing and seeing, conscious of lowering my hips, of raising and positioning my hands and arms, controlling my turns. The faces of the audience were expectant, elated. Kō-chan and Shingo were dancing next to me—anxious, exhilarated—calling out responses and whistling. The pattern produced by the dancers turning in massed formation, the pounding of the drums thundering in my ears—and then, shouting, dancing, I was swept up in the performance—the twenty minutes that followed passing in an instant, an eternity.

Can we speak of a boundary between audience and performers? As much as the performers themselves are working to understand the narratives that they produce, their audience is made up of those who have already mastered it, who understand and anticipate it. As we danced, I saw the elderly women of the kyōyūkai also dancing atop the hill. The faces of children singing, clapping, energetically beating small drums. Everyone whistling, joining in the shouted responses. In the parking lot, Okinawan workers emerged from the kitchen of the Banyan Tree Club, cheering—an old man dancing. Americans joined the Okinawans gathered around the field. Some were friends of the dancers, coworkers from offices and stores on-base. Others like a group of young Marines, were drawn by the sound and cheered enthusiastically. And then, all too soon, the dance was over. Tired dancers greedily gulped down drinks offered to them by workers from the club, others collapsed to the ground in exhaustion. One of the drummers sat on the slope, his head in his hands—sick from the heat.

Kajū took the microphone from the jikata and thanked everyone for coming. This was Iha's second year as the leader of the youth group, and he ran the performances with a quietly commanding presence. Although he was only in his mid-twenties, he had been dancing for more than a decade. The OBs had been impressed by his youthful persistence—he came to watch every practice, every day—and they let him join well ahead of his friends. He had become something of the public face of the Okinawan eisā; his photograph was featured prominently in Okinawan tourist brochures and posters, and even in a number of Japanese popular magazines such as Mono.[40]

Speaking in the formal Japanese commonly used in public address, he detailed all of the people who had contributed to the performance, from the base workers who had signed us in, to the kyōyūkai for providing the buses. Next, he introduced Takamiyagi Jitsuei, the leader of the community organization. Bowing formally, Takamiyagi also spoke in polite Japanese, thanking everyone for attending. After fifty years, he said, it's wonderful to get back and show everyone what Sonda has done. His voice thick with emotion, he said that he was proud to see that what was considered impossible for so long could be done so well.

A number of the other young men and women of the youth group—assistants to the leader—stood and offered their brief greetings to the kyōyūkai and expressed their appreciation for being able to participate in this memorable event. Then Kajū announced that we would dance again. Breaking out of the static formation, we would perform the michijunē or muramawari[41]—encircling the village with our dance. Regardless of fatigue, dancers pulled themselves to their feet, straightened their clothing, took up their drums once again. One of the veteran members of the youth group grabbed the youth group's green and gold banner; led by the drums, the rest of us formed a long double column behind him. Like the dances that wove through the alleys of Sonda during Obon, the dances that once encircled the yādui that stood in this same spot. Here, there were no streets to follow, no

dances of memory, dances of oblivion

buildings to give shape to the dance; instead, it was our dance that gave shape once more to Nishizato. Our column turned and turned, forming a wide circle, filling the cleared space before the knoll. As the ring advanced and reversed itself again and again, we danced and sang, working once more through the eisā.[42]

The anthropologist Marc Augé has written of the interplay of remembrance and forgetting in ritual—what he calls the three figures of oblivion: return, suspense, and beginning (or rebeginning).[43] A lost past is found by forgetting the present; the present is intensified by cutting it off from the past and future; the future is reclaimed by forgetting the past. I find these figures provocative, and yet somehow inadequate to understand the Nishizato eisā that I have just discussed. In the small field at Kadena, in Nishizato, the moment is charged with the memories of the past and the emotions that they invoke—complex, intense, personal, and ambiguous. While the mundane concerns of the present may fade, there is also excitement and anticipation for the dance that is about to begin. With the dance, all of the memories that have flooded the consciousness of the dancers and visitors are brought into a relationship, a constellation, with the embodied memories of the eisā, their alternative images of the past. A melancholy return to the lost yādui arrayed against the memories, the experience of creative, dynamic samurai. And yet, the constellation does not imply resolution—I cannot believe that the pain and ambiguity of remembrance is subsumed in the joyous experience of eisā. Ultimately, these constellations are deeply personal and vary greatly—living with, thinking through the tension, the contradiction fusing communion and dissensus.

At the same time, the dancers and their audience are drawn together, coordinated in the experience, the production of eisā. Dancing under the gaze of the kyōyūkai, another relationship comes into play. Ancestral spirits, so densely present in the neighborhood tombs, the household altars, the community center in Sonda, so weak and unremembered in this place, are called to the dance. The karī produced in the eisā weaves these relationships together once again. Between the dancers and their elders; the Sondanchū and the Americans who watch, wonderingly; the living and the dead. The spatial field of ancestral spirits, engaged at the shrine, in the tentative cycle of the first dance, in the confident michijunee that followed, is renewed. The

Dancing the yakimāji eisā in the fields of Nishizato at Kadena Air Base

divided flame, used by nativists to represent the manifold presence of the spirits of the dead, is rekindled in the space of the ruined village, in the heart of an American air base. To think this through in Henri Lefebvre's terms, the space of Nishizato is only available as a field of action, a space in which rituals take place, for a moment. Renewed in memory, it continues as a basis of action, a reservoir of power from which the strength of the individual, the household, and the community derive and into which they invest their energies.

And the dancers? They remain mechanics and construction workers, farmers and clerks caught up in the details of everyday life; they are rural nobles, the children of courtiers and cane cutters, tormented by memories of a village that is kept just out of their reach. And in the eisā, they are also artists and warriors, powerful and creative. They are all of these, yet never fully any one of them. It is in the tension between these roles, these positions, that holds out possibilities for the dancers and their audience to reconsider their world.

dances of memory, dances of oblivion

CHUNJUN NAGARI—AS FLOWS THE CHUNJUN

Unkē—the return. The first night of Obon.

For too long, eisā had been confined to courtyards and parking lots, danced endlessly, night after night. To bodies in training and at rest. To those who have abandoned the dance altogether but still feel its call in a certain position of the hand, a step made just so. To recordings half-heard on an afternoon AM radio broadcast, muted music in a supermarket, an insistent drumbeat on the edge of sleep. To the reserve of memory, where it waits, a trace sometimes encountered with the pain of regret and loss, with anticipation. "Machikantī!" people say, speaking of eisā, "I can't wait!" Which is to say that they do wait, anxiously, enthusiastically, for the moon to be full once again in the seventh month. For Obon, the festival of the dead.

Then, as the moon rises on the first night of Obon, eisā returns. Not, as it once did, from the tombs, when dancers greeted the spirits of the ancestors as they returned to this world. The ancestral spirits have already found their way back, leaving tombs cleanly swept and decorated with fresh offerings, following the candles set on doorsteps to light their way home. They have already joined their families gathered before the household altar for commensal dinners and celebrations. Eisā leaves the courtyard of the community center where it has circled for months and for hundreds of miles, filling the bodies of the dancers, transforming them, renewing and recreating itself. It runs along the narrow, darkened streets, and alleys of the neighborhood, into doorways and houseyards; it finds itself in the photographs and awards that decorate the living room of Kohama Shūei's house, in the memories of an old woman who draws herself up to join in the dance, in the excitement of a young boy who runs to find his small drum, in the pleasure of the ancestral spirits gathered in their homes. It turns again to the streets, drawing the families in its wake, laughing and dancing.

It leaves the neighborhood, racing now into brightly lit streets lined with bars and restaurants, into the courtyards of the houses of wealthy and powerful men, colliding with other eisās, other dancers. It welcomes the gaze of neighbors, of tourists, of the television cameras that cluster along its path. Finding itself already in these places, remembered and expected, it struggles to show that it more than fulfills its promise in memory. In doing so, it

dances of memory, dances of oblivion

transforms itself again. And yet, in these same places, it also encounters difference: that which it is not, that which it is no longer. In its passage, it no longer skirts the fields and villages that held so much hope for the impoverished nobles of the yādui—its passage to shrines and tombs and to the sea is blocked by chain link fence and razor tape. The voices of rioters in the streets of Koza are silent, replaced by the din of ceaseless traffic along the asphalt highway and the rumble of jets overhead. In the face of this difference, it continues unhesitatingly. The rhythm of the drums, powerful and insistent, the movements of the dancers, synchronized and impeccably executed, fill the time and the space of the streets. The moment is filled with the rhythm of eisā. Accepting the praise, the enthusiasm and the gratitude of the audience, it makes its way through the streets, bringing them karī.

TŌSHINDOI—THE TREASURE SHIP FROM CHINA HAS COME!

On the night of September 4, 1998, I sat on the cracked pavement of a parking garage, my back resting against a concrete pillar, my drum tucked under my arm. A streetlight cast a dim, bluish light across the alley. Drummers sat all around me, alone or in small groups. Talking among themselves, smoking, drinking the ice water brought to them by the first-year dancers. Although it had to be close to midnight, the heat was still oppressive; my clothes were dripping with sweat. The women stood together in the street, tired but unwilling to wrinkle their kimono by sitting. Several OBS were smoking and laughing in front of the open door of a house. Inside, I could hear one of the jikata playing a popular folksong while the rest joined in the family banquet spread out for the departing spirits. More dancers and drummers continued to arrive, as they had all evening. Some were members that I'd seen around or danced with last year, but who were too busy to make it to practices and performances this year. Others came back from other towns in Okinawa where they'd been working, a surprising number from jobs or school in mainland Japan.

It was Ūkui, the third and final night of Obon, and we had already been dancing through the narrow streets and alleys of Sonda for several hours. For the last three nights, we had danced mile after mile, covering what seemed to be every road, every path in the neighborhood. We danced in courtyards, in parking lots, in the middle of the street, accepting the hospitality and the gifts of the households and businesses that we visited.[44] This would be the last rest break before climbing up to the main streets of Koza. I really felt the effect of three nights of dancing. My left hand was stiff from carrying a drum for hours, the heavy calluses lining my fingers had begun to tear away. My right shoulder ached from an old injury that I had aggravated. Too much drinking, too little sleep. It was much the same with everyone else. Around me, dancers and drummers—particularly the veteran performers—favored injured knees and shoulders, struggled with increasingly painful back injuries. The everyday world of labor exacts a price from those who struggle to escape its regulation; or perhaps I should say that those who do so are painfully reminded of the price already paid by all who labor.

All too soon, the leader of the youth group and his assistants were calling for everyone to line up. Gathering up our equipment, adjusting our uniforms, we moved back into the road. By now there were nearly one hundred dancers. With little direction, we formed a double column: ōdaiko (the large red-lacquered drums) and the youth group's standard bearer to the front, shimedaiko to their rear, alternating pairs of male and female dancers behind them. The jikata—five men in blue silk kimono, wearing conical hats decorated with pink and white paper flowers—stepped into a space between the drummers and the dancers.

A dozen or so OBs carried red flashing lights and sacks, in which they placed the envelopes or loose bills given to the youth group. There were chondarā—other OBs dressed in peasant kimono with dangling red fundoshi, or loincloths, their faces painted like clowns, their outfits topped with stiff wigs made of coconut fiber or broken hats discarded by the jikata. Two of them carried empty kerosene cans that they played like shimedaiko, another a mop handle that he deftly spun like a lance. Beyond this, the youth group was joined by hundreds of followers: neighborhood children, anthropologists and folklorists, community officials, mainland students and teachers on holiday, tourists from all over Japan, members of folk dance preservation societies, newspaper photographers and film crews, well-known Okinawan musicians, boyfriends and girlfriends of dancers, and members of other youth groups that have some kind of relationship with Sonda.

Although everyone was clearly exhausted, enthusiasm crackled through the formation. Once we had climbed up to Moromi Hakken Dōri—a business street of tiny bars south of Sonda—it would be time for ōrāsē, a fight.[45]

Older members often spoke of the violent clashes with other youth groups that marked the eisā of earlier years. Rocks and bottles were thrown from the audience; groups might even one attack another with heavy bamboo staffs or lash out with fists.

After climbing a steep, uneven alley, we emerged into the brightly lit arc of the bar district. Moromi Hakken Dōri was a narrow street that intersected Route 330 in Kubota, turning north and east before arching back to join the main road once again. The whole crescent was probably no longer than five hundred meters. By day, it was deserted; by night, luridly flickering signs beckoned potential customers into dozens of tiny bars that seemed to me to be always deserted. Passing their open doors, I felt a sour blast of dank air from the air-conditioned interior, although I could hear nothing from within. I was breathing hard, my chest pounding with fatigue, feeling what I feared was my last surge of adrenaline. Far back in the formation, I could hear a muted call and response from the dancers. One of the men was shouting out something, lost in the pounding of the drums. The women, their voices keen in response. "Give us some sake!" Ahead of us, the youth group's banner bobbed up and down as the standard bearer danced to the rhythm of the drums.

Perhaps I had been too focused on the dance during my first year, but I was completely unprepared for the sight that greeted me. Tonight, thousands of spectators of all ages thronged the streets. As we advanced into the street, they parted before us, pressing up against the walls and storefronts. People were everywhere, sitting on the sills of upper-story windows, on rooftops, lining outside stairs. The spectators laughed and waved, children darting through our formation as we advanced. People came together in these streets—people who would be unlikely to associate under other circumstances: not just locals, but Okinawans and mainland Japanese from across a broad spectrum of classes, American soldiers from the bases, tourists, scholars, performers, broadcasters. At times, the crowd threatened to surge up from the curb, out from the doorways and alleys. However, there always seemed to be OBs close by to gently remind spectators to keep back, or to firmly move aside anyone who ignored their warnings.

The sanshin continued to repeat the same droning figure, and we followed the standard bearer deeper and deeper into the bar district. Then, on a signal from the jikata, the standard was lifted high, and everything stopped.

dances of memory, dances of oblivion

People rushed at us from all sides. Elderly bar owners hurried their hostesses into the street, carrying trays full of glasses of iced oolong tea or awamori to us. Reporters from NHK[46] and local radio stations moved in to question cooperative looking dancers. Cameramen moved up and down the ranks. Tourists asked to join the dancers in photos. Local merchants signaled to the chondarā or the OBs, formally handing them envelopes bearing offerings or asking for dancers to enter their clubs for brief performances. The offerings were accepted; the requests were politely declined. Now was not the time for distractions—ōrāsē was only moments away.

The crowd before us literally seethed. For the past decade or so, eisā has been growing in popularity and tourists throng to performances, not only in Okinawa proper but also in mainland Japan. However, this popularity has also been a source of conflict and critical reflection. In the Okinawan community in Taishō-ku in Osaka, performances have been riven by controversy.[47] Local activists encouraged the young men and women of Taishō-ku to dance eisā in order to develop their pride in being Okinawan. They also hoped that the dance would be a source of pride to older members of the community who have suffered from the prejudice of mainland Japanese throughout their lives. In many ways, their eisā was an enormous success: thousands of people come each year to watch the dancers perform. However, the presence of so many aggressive spectators discourages the older members of the community from attending. After enduring years of discrimination, they were unwilling to publicly participate in performances that identified them as Okinawans before a Japanese audience, regardless of any putatively positive valuation. At the same time, the insistent clamoring of tourists to join the dance has created other problems. For activists such as Kinjō Kaoru, the festival has become another occasion for Japanese tourists to demonstrate their impulsive desire for fashionable products and the colonizer's thoughtless appropriation of the property of the colonized.[48] As he bitterly reflected, any Japanese who honestly respected Okinawan culture should simply stay away.

Sonda has been subjected to the same flood of visitors. Mainland tourists come to Sonda throughout the summer, but their numbers swell during the days of Obon and the island-wide eisā festival that follows. The members of the seinenkai anticipate these visits and are prepared to deal with their nearly overwhelming numbers. During performances, OB volunteers direct traffic and control tourist presence, keeping them out of the way of the dancers and insisting that they don't interfere with local residents. At the same time, they treat them like guests, with kindness and respect. They allow them to beat on the drums after practice, seat them at tables in the kōminkan, offer them food and drink, entertain their questions, include them in conversations, even teach them to dance. Moments such as this are opportunities for the dancers to demonstrate their confidence and their pride in their dance.

Iha Masakazu, the charismatic young leader of the seinenkai, told me that members of the youth group dance for many reasons: to be with their friends, to carry on a family tradition, to show respect for their ancestors. Still, he said that the most important reason is to be seen.[49] Most of the members spend their working hours in garages, buses, technical schools, grocery stores, hotel lobbies, restaurant kitchens, and shop counters. They long to be seen as something else, and in the images of the past and present members of the seinenkai that line the kōminkan, they have an object for their longing. Jacques Ranciere has written: "All my work on workers' emancipation has shown me that the most prominent of the claims put forward by the workers and the poor was precisely the claim to visibility, a will to enter the political realm of appearance, the affirmation of a capacity for appearance."[50] When these young men and women perform in the streets of Sonda, on the field surrounded by thousands of spectators at the Zentō Eisā Matsuri, before a busload of mainland high school students, they know that they will not only be seen, but they will be seen as powerful, dynamic dancers of the Sonda eisā. Time and time again members have told me of the pride, the pleasure, and the sense of duty that they feel when they are seen in this way, seen by their friends and family, their ancestral spirits, Japanese tourists, and American spectators.[51]

This confidence is reflected in the equal treatment that they accord to their visitors. Young tourists and aging schoolteachers, native ethnologists and professional performing artists, well-known athletes and television personalities all seem to be given the same consideration. However, this does not seem to be an attempt to flatten social distinction. The courtesies extended to guests in Sonda acknowledge the importance of these visitors. As Iha himself wrote in a collection of essays about eisā: "We dance the eisā holding in our hearts the idea that each one of our viewers is our judge. What's more, we are committed to show them a performance that will live up to the expectations that they have for the Sonda eisā."[52] Without diminishing themselves, dancers acknowledge that their guests possess the skill and knowledge to make valid aesthetic judgments. This is an important element in the construction of the work: it enables the dancers to appropriate their audience in the same way that Kinjō feared that spectators would appropriate the performance.

Far off at the end of the street, I saw a banner bobbing above people's heads and heard the ragged sounds of drumming. The youth group from neighboring Kubota approached us from Sonda as we approached them from Kubota. The drummers around me casually finished their drinks, handing cups and cans into the crowd, dropping furtively smoked cigarettes. Rolling shoulders, swinging arms, we calmly moved forward, dividing our two columns into four. Two older members pushed forward from the rear, ōdaiko slung from their shoulders—there were now eight drummers carrying the massive red drums. The chondarā worked the crowd along the edge of our formation, pushing the spectators back, warning them to keep out of the way of our swinging drums.

Kubota continued to approach us, pushing through the crowd like an icebreaker. As they moved closer, the rhythm of their drums and the amplified sound of vocals and sanshin filled the silence that we had created. Finally, they halted when they were no more than ten yards to our front. A space opened between us, and the standard bearers of both groups stepped into the opening, lifting and shaking the huge flags as the crowd roared.

Then, without waiting for Kubota to be completely prepared, our jikata played the opening notes of "Chunjun Nagari"—ōrāsē had begun. We all struck our drums in unison—the sound was tremendous. Kubota had also begun, their version of "Chunjun Nagari" echoing seconds behind our own. For a moment, I worried about the distraction of their competing melody, feared being drawn away from our rhythm. But there was no time for that kind of concern—the dance demanded my whole attention. Lifting and swinging the drum, stepping and pivoting, the perfect strike. Every moment had to demonstrate pride, poise, perfection. Shouting in unison: "Eisā, eisā, sa sa sā sa eisā!"

The utterance references no meaning beyond itself; it is the cry itself, passionate and powerful, that is meaningful. The crowd was joining us too—long wailing whistles, shouted responses. I glimpsed an elderly man dancing in a doorway, the eisā of decades ago. The voices of the women

dances of memory, dances of oblivion

Eisā in the streets of Okinawa City

behind me, sharp and strong. The dancers next to me, behind and in front of me, matching me in every move, perfectly synchronized. How can I describe their expressions—rapturous? I could no longer hear Kubota at all, I couldn't see anything beyond the front of our formation. There was no time, no space for anything but the dance. The repetitions of the figures of the dance came effortlessly. I felt as if I was hitting the drum harder than I ever had before, stepping higher, swinging the drum in powerful arcs. We danced through the cycle of songs, then repeated it again.

I was breathing hard, wiping the sweat from my face, shaking it from my arms. Someone shoved a glass of iced oolong tea into my hand and I drank it off, handing back the empty cup. Kubota was still playing, their formation stretching back the street ahead of us. It was an amazing view, watching the massed dancers. Around me, my fellow drummers made a show of disregarding the spectacle. They laughed, adjusted their drums, called for a new drumstick from one of the chondarā. While the jikata retuned their instruments, Iha sprinted to the front of the column and took the standard

dances of memory, dances of oblivion

from the young man who was carrying it. As he began to dance across the front of the formation, we struck the first beats of the final song, "Tōshin-doi" ("The Treasure Ship from China Has Come"). After a moment's hesitation, Kubota followed.

The crowds who had followed us from Sonda—neighbors and tourists—watched expectantly. The eight dancers playing the ōdaiko formed a circle around the standard bearer. As the leader of the youth group pumped the standard up and down, the drummers leaned in toward him, pounding their drums furiously. Then, as the rhythm of the drums built to a crescendo, all of them—the drummers and the standard bearer—leaped high into the air.

We all began to push forward. Our four-column formation collapsed into eight, then we were all standing shoulder to shoulder, beating the drums furiously. Behind us, the men and women dancers moved forward as well, adding their voices and their clapping to the dance. I'd lost all track of Kubota. Their standard bearer and ours circled each other, bobbing and leaping in the space between groups. The tempo increased, the sanshin booming and percussive. We pressed forward, hammering away as if we could physically drive them back with the intensity of our drumming. I was blinded with sweat, my arms ached with the effort. I was beginning to worry that I couldn't go on any further when I noticed Iha whistling and waving us forward as he danced with the standard. Dancers from both groups set their drums on the ground and leaped into the space between the formations. More and more dancers joined—two first-year members rushed past me, one on the other's shoulders.

The two chondarā who had been pounding kerosene cans leaped into the space between the seinenkai. One put his can down and snatched up an ōdaiko from an exhausted drummer. A first-year dancer held the drum for him, as he beat out the syncopated rhythm of a minyō performance. The jikata shifted to a different version of the standard tōshindoi, moving from the driving, percussive rhythms of eisā to a folk style that showcased their speed and agility. And as quickly as the tempo and the style of the performance changed, the feeling of conflict slipped away. Everone from Kubota and Sonda came together, men and women, laughing and dancing. Everyone was shouting "Kachāshī! Kachāshī!" Tourists were being pulled from the crowd into the street. The dancers offered them their drums, demonstrated gestures, drew them into the dance. Many of the tourists hesitated, laugh-

dances of memory, dances of oblivion

ing nervously; others rushed to join in, waving their arms in imitation of kachāshī, the ecstatic dance that ends every performance. Taking up the drumsticks and the drums that dancers handed to them, they tried to strike up a rhythm of their own.

One of the former leaders of the seinenkai told me that he loved ōrāsē, the chance to put Sonda's skill and artistry on the line in front of an audience, to confront a rival group and show them exactly what they could do. However, he said that the violence that once went along with ōrāsē ruined the moment. Everyone in Sonda was proud of being tough, he said, but a lot of other people in Okinawa were tough too. But there was no one else who could dance like Sonda. Violence detracted from the performance, diminished their accomplishments. What's more, it made enemies in the neighboring communities that should have been brought together by the dance. In the current performance of eisā, dancers like Iha have found a way to bring neighbors together while still demonstrating their skill and artistry.

Once, after a long and demanding practice, I asked several of the older dancers why they still performed. Zukeran Masahide—one of the most active OBs and a colorful jikata—answered without hesitation: "We still have to put the world back together." This is what the dancers work together to create. In the streets where Okinawans have labored for decades, running bars and shops that cater to American GIs and Japanese tourists. In streets lined with faltering businesses, with Naha-based banks and mainland convenience stores, where young men and women from the neighborhood are waitresses and clerks, parking lot attendants and idlers. In streets that are the lines of communication for the American bases, where Japanese and American strategic decisions are executed, along which troops and supplies are moved. In the streets where Okinawans once rioted against American oppression, burning vehicles, beating their occupants, storming the gates of the base.

In these streets, the spectators and performers come together, linked in the production of karī. As I have suggested, this is not simply the distribution of good fortune but the creation of a network of relationships that includes the performers, the diverse group of Okinawans and mainland Japanese, the spirits of the dead. In this place, once built by the labor of their ancestors, a moment is created for them once again. Through the beauty of the performance, the pain and sacrifice of the dancers, the artistry and expressiveness of the dance, ancestral spirits are gathered from their homes and entertained once more. They are given the gift of the eisā before leaving again to return to their tombs, to the other world, to the places where they are believed to dwell until they come back again. Memories of every other performance, every other Obon are drawn into the constellation—the ancestral spirits are shown that the dance that they worked so hard to create is still vibrant. Eisā is not just repeated without change from year to year; it is transformed to honor the legacy of the past and to meet the demands of the present. This is why the peaceful resolution of the ōrāsē is so important. In the place where there has been war, suffering and death, a struggle can be resolved peacefully, a victory can be won without loss, a conflict can end in friendship.

This is why the presence of outsiders is so critical to the creation of the work. It cannot be that the painful burden of the past is easier to bear in Okinawa City than it is in Osaka. Eisā is danced in fields where battles once raged and where other ways of life were destroyed, in streets that bear the material signs of colonial subjugation, poverty, and military occupation, before spectators whose class and ethnicity has long dominated the lives of the dancers. And yet, they have found a tremendous resource in other memories, in other formulations of the past. They are able to draw on all of their performances of eisā, on year after year, mile after mile danced in the courtyard of the kōminkan and the streets of Okinawa City, at festivals in Naha and throughout Okinawa, at Expo '70 in Osaka, in schoolyards, stadiums, and television studios across Japan.

All of these memories are brought into a manifold relationship in the present, conjoined to the work that is created by the musicians and dancers. For the duration of the dance, in the moment marked out by the rhythm and artistry of eisā—a hierarchy of relationships is performed as other memories, other histories fade into a moment of oblivion. Building on Ranciere's observations, the performers make themselves visible, appear before their audience as dancers beautiful and strong, confident and kind. The audience is also constituted in the performance, given an opportunity to be a part of the festival, to join in the dance before them. To be treated as discerning and capable guests, to receive the gift of good fortune. And finally, the spirits of the dead are brought together with them, honored for what they have done, assured that their legacy remains important, given the promise of performances yet to come.

dances of memory, dances of oblivion

Inevitably, the moment ends. As the duration of the dance comes to a close, the memories that had been kept at bay fill the space and the time that had been cleared for the performance. The uneasy accommodation that performers maintain between the worker, the samurai, and the dancer cannot be maintained; the same can be said for the tension between the enthralled spectator, the uneasy visitor to the run-down streets of Koza, the tourist returned from the battlefield, the metropolitan traveler who suddenly realizes that Tokyo is very far away.

As the crowd begins to disperse, we fall into formation once again, laughing and exhausted. Dancing through the darkened streets, we make our way back to the community center. Families return to their homes, tourists to their hotels, the spirits of the dead to wherever it is that they dwell—their tombs, the other world, nirai kanai.[53]

What extends beyond the moment? New images have been produced, old images have been reinvigorated. Representations of the performance circulate in tourist campaigns and commercial advertising, in banal television series and experimental film. A massive banner depicting a powerful dancer in Sonda's attire was hung as a backdrop at an antibase rally in Naha. Both the dancers and their audience carry the memories of the performance into their everyday lives; the dancers also bear the physical transformation of their experiences. After years of dancing with the seinenkai, two older men have become members of the Rinken Band, a popular Okinawan musical group that works to fuse traditional and contemporary forms. One of the young women has become part of a well-known vocal duo. Several members have built on their experiences to become local politicians (both progressive and conservative), and some have been selected to become municipal bureaucrats. In every case, they have told me that their experience of eisā played a critical role in their decision. I have also heard of stories of dancers who quit jobs in the mainland and moved back to Okinawa so that they—or their children—could dance; others refused promotions or transfers so that they could remain active in the group. More common, however, are stories of the traces left in memory: the sense that one is more than who one appears to be in the working world, that alternatives exist to a daily life that is relentlessly commodified and stripped of meaning. The memories of eisā are often brought up against daily experience, informing the way that the world is perceived and understood. It is in this space, open to contradiction and question, that other possibilities exist, that new choices are made legible, and the possibilities of transformative action are explored.

At the same time, I do not want to take away from the importance of the moment itself. It seems that practices are too often considered only to expose their reference to other situations, their relationship to other times and places. Eisā is more than a resistance to social pressure, a displacement of concerns that cannot be addressed in any other way. Eisā should also be understood as a subject, created and recreated in the coordinated activity of the dancers, their audiences, and the ancestral spirits: steeped in the forms of the past, yet driven by creative action in the present, an expression of individual and collective artistry, an archive of historical representations, and a source of strength and renewal. When I recall the image of the dancer in Moriguchi's film, I know that I will never understand the meaning of her dance, or what gave her the courage to raise her hands so gracefully in that burning street. And yet, I do understand the courage to ignore the judgment and expectations of others, to put aside the repressiveness of everyday life, the constant pressures of labor, fatigue, and boredom. I understand the courage to create—I have seen it in those very same streets.

"Mono omou kūkan," "a space to think about things." Sakima Michio's deceptively simple hope comes back to me with renewed urgency when I recall my first visit to his museum.[1] It was an overcast day in early January, the gray clouds saturated with a chill glow from the unseen sun—a day of both light and darkness. By the time I arrived at the museum, slanting rays of sunlight were just beginning to pierce the clouds. I had been driving through the back streets of Uehara in Ginowan City, past newly built restaurants, condominiums, and modern concrete homes. A rusted chain link fence cut a straight line to my right, dividing the quiet neighborhood from Marine Corps Air Station Futenma. Between the fence and the street grew a riot of colorful flowers, curling potato vines, and ragged banana trees. I parked my car near a small playground and walked to the museum, making my way past the immense family tomb that anchored the eastern edge of the compound. Rough paving stones led me on to the museum courtyard, a field of small, raked fragments of coral. Each of the pieces was painted with a number, one for each of those who died in the battle of Okinawa. A mound of rocks, an installation left months earlier to the wind and the rain, was now dispersed across the ground, barely noticed, always underfoot, the numbers still visible here and there.

I paused in the courtyard to stare at the beautiful museum that Sakima had built. Its long, concrete and glass façade angular and sharp, modern and severe in comparison with the gentle curves of the tomb nestled in the wooded hillock. For a moment, I was able to enjoy the silence, the grounds around me empty. Then, the stillness of the afternoon was broken as a flight of helicopters roared overhead, racing to the runway at Marine Corps Air Station Futenma. Following their passage across the sky, I became conscious of the strangeness of my surroundings. The museum was inside the base. It had been built in a salient pressed into Futenma's eastern flank, the fence folded inward as if struggling to seal off this incursion. Sakima, one of the major landowners at Futenma, had negotiated with Japanese and American military authorities to have this section of his holdings returned, including his family tomb. Drawing on the revenues that he earned from land leased to the bases, he built the Sakima Art Museum—a space to think about things.

I was immediately struck by ways in which the museum resembled the traditional Okinawan home, the overdetermined space that figures in so many of the narratives in this book. The front gallery is like a veranda, the three side-by-side exhibition spaces like the main rooms of an affluent villa. In place of the kitchen there is a kissaten,[2] the smell of freshly brewed coffee pungent and thick. The nā—the courtyard—is a place of work where the aesthetic labor of performance and exhibition replaces the daily activities of a farming household. However, the house deviates from the expected plan of the Okinawan house in one notable way—it is oriented to the north rather than to the south. It embraces the direction traditionally associated with evil and misfortune, expectantly facing mainland Japan.[3]

I was fortunate to have Sakima himself as a guide during my visit. His calm and thoughtful manner, his great enthusiasm for the possibilities of art and his passion for politics opened the space for me in a way that I could never have experienced otherwise. Although I had come to see the Maruki's famous paintings of wartime Okinawa, he encouraged me to tour the rest of the museum first.[4] We began in the veranda. A line on the floor was traced out by a long, weathered cable as thick as my arm—perhaps a play on "Okinawa" (knotted rope). Fragments of coral were scattered across the area marked off by the rope—drawing the bleached white surface of the nā and its memoration of tragedy into the interior of the museum. We began to follow the rope along the length of the veranda, stopping to examine installations of objects clustered here and there. Many were playful—laughing faces that looked as if they were emerging from the surface of simple earthenware crocks, ceramic images set into a sheet of cobalt blue glass, carved utensils that were both functional and whimsical. Yet there was also a glimpse of darkness. Faces emerged, half formed, from a wall covered in terra-cotta tiles: laughing, weeping, contorted in unspeakable agony, frozen in a soundless scream. At that moment, I became aware of the deep silence of the museum—those faces crying out, yet making no sound. The noises of children in the park, traffic in the neighborhood streets, and the drone of helicopters overhead were lost.

Near the end of the veranda, I turned to the right—excited, uneasy—stepping hesitantly into the first of the interior galleries. The broad open room was lit with diffuse sunlight, displaying a series of prints made before the Second World War by Käthe Kollwitz:[5] Her representations all focused on relationships: mother and child, living and dead, artist and the self. In their stark expressiveness, they were powerful evocations of poverty, pain, and death. Sakima and I continued through the space, occasionally stopping to examine a print. A gesture to point out a compelling detail, a few words in explanation. We walked in the bright stillness from room to room, my feelings of sadness deepening as if another layer was added with each successive image.

After a time, perhaps half an hour, we entered the third and final gallery. Sakima moved aside to let me enter first. I had taken five or six steps into the room when the assemblage of images on display—their silence, their horror, their beauty—struck me like a physical blow to the chest. A roaring in my ears, my throat tightened, my eyes filled with tears. I wanted to cry out, but no sound came. It was as if I had been caught up in those massive canvases.

Before me rose the vast sweep of *Okinawasen no Zu*—a nightmarish montage of death and suffering during the battle of Okinawa.

To my right, *Chibichirigama*—a painting depicting the experiences of the Okinawans and Japanese soldiers who took refuge in caverns during the American invasion.[6] Okinawans in rags, faces contorted in terror. Farmers charging with bamboo spears in their hands. A woman with her throat ripped out by a Japanese soldier. Their eyes, often blank, stared back as if the rush of incomprehensible horror had purged them of all sensibility. Figures emerged from the smoke-gray background in places, obscured as if by a haze in others, crimson torrents of blood everywhere. Like illustrated scrolls depicting Buddhist hells, these paintings gave form to the unspeakable. There was no lineal narrative, no progressive movement of time. The eye scanning the painting rested on distinct and disconnected, yet interrelated scenes. Resolution was impossible within the frame of the image.

To my left, *Shimukugama*—an empty cavern depicted in waves of black and gray and white. Like Chibichirigama, a place where Okinawans had hidden during the fighting.[7] When American soldiers gathered at the mouth of the cave called out to them to surrender, Higa Heizō, a farmer who had cut cane in Hawaii as a young man, translated their words for his friends. At his urging, the Okinawans came out. Everyone who had sheltered in Shimuku-gama survived. In the Maruki's painting, there is no horror to depict. The cavern is empty—except perhaps for the faint promise of hope.

Sakima and I stood there for a few moments in silence, looking from canvas to canvas. Finally, he said softly, "We all have to decide for ourselves."

It is this commitment, this will to memory that I have traced in this book. The Okinawans that I have written about—the performers Teruya Rinsuke and Fujiki Hayato; the artists and activists that make up the hansen jinushi; the young teachers, bureaucrats, and laborers who studied and performed with Fujiki; the musicians and dancers in Sonda—have all struggled to come to grips with the past. In different ways, they have seen the consequences of war and colonization, of occupation and impoverishment. They have experienced incorporation into a Japanese nation that demands their labor and their lives, valorizes their suffering and loss, and constrains their ambition. For generations, they have been asked to sacrifice themselves, then consign the specific memories of that sacrifice to oblivion. Some of them have responded to this call to service at one time or another in their lives, made their sacrifices and awaited the rewards that have been, unfortunately, diminished or deferred. However, they have never surrendered their memories, given the gift of deep forgetting that would grant the amnesty that Prime Minister Hashimoto and others have so often requested.

Instead, like Walter Benjamin's angel of history, they have kept their eyes fixed on the past. And like Benjamin's figure of remembrance, they have felt the forces that drive them away from the objectified moments that continue to accumulate in their wake. Okinawans are no strangers to the cataclysmic winds that sweep through their world, destroying lives and meaning, pressing them forward remorselessly in the service of progress and capitalist modernity. They have felt the strictures of everyday life—the pressures of labor, leisure, and unemployment; the constraints of a division of labor that determines who will work, who will think, and who will create. They have watched—and sometimes worked in—the massive development projects that have brought highways and tourist resorts, Japanese municipal buildings, and American housing complexes to the spaces where farms, villages, and battlefields once stood. They have known the challenges of scholars and journalists, mainland politicians, television and film producers who appropriate their experiences and abilities. They have strained under the burden of memories that have grown in the telling and the repression, encrusted with pain and guilt and sadness. They have heard the voices of deities and ancestral spirits who have demanded their response. They have felt the temptation to surrender to their fears and ambitions—and to forgetfulness.

However, as many Okinawans have told me, the lull that follows a catastrophic storm is often filled with a wind that rises up in the islands and blows back in the opposite direction. It is this—the *kēshi kaji*—that has caught their wings, allowed them to struggle to explore the ruins, sorting through them for moments that can still be recovered. For, as the events that I have written about suggest in different ways, the will to memory is about more than simple remembrance—if any act of memory can be termed simple. It is about the claims that the past makes on the present, and the promise that it holds for action in the now. It is about the courage and determination that I have seen in the struggle to craft constellations from the material at hand. Images of horror and abjection, of hope and possibility thrown into moving and changing relationships with the present. All of these practices are fragile, always in danger of being overcome or undone. And yet, these Okinawans have labored to remember and to forget, clearing a moment in the present to act. Opening, as Sakima said, a space to think about things.

INTRODUCTION

1. The battle of Okinawa exceeded the standard of savagery set throughout the Pacific War. In the three months that followed the April 1, 1945, invasion, more than 12,000 American and 70,000 Japanese soldiers died in fierce fighting. Perhaps one-quarter of the Okinawan population—more than 140,000 people— was killed outright, murdered or forced to take their own lives by the Japanese soldiers who had been ordered to protect them, or, in fear and desperation, committed suicide.

2. Also known as the Indian coral tree or tiger's claw, the deigo blooms in clusters of red, crescent-shaped flowers before the green foliage emerges.

3. LaCapra, "Trauma, Absence and Loss."

4. Caruth, *Unclaimed Experience*; Caruth, *Trauma*; Eng and Kazanjian, *Loss*.

5. Taira, "The Okinawa Charade."

6. Inoue, "We Are Okinawans but of a Different Sort," 85–104; Hook and Siddle, *Japan and Okinawa*, 188–207.

7. In the end, this strategy failed. Nishida Kenjirō, the LDP challenger for a seat in the Upper House, was defeated in the 1998 elections; Hashimoto himself resigned his office as a sign of personal responsibility for the staggering defeat that left the LDP with the smallest number of seats in the Diet in history.

8. All translations are my own unless otherwise noted. The remarks to which Hashimoto refers at the start of this quotation, and which he made in Ginowan, came on the heels of a prefectural plebiscite in which the Okinawan electorate strongly supported a reduction in the American bases and a redefinition of the laws that governed the conduct of American forces. Appearing with Governor Ōta Masahide, Hashimoto delivered a contrite speech in which he pledged greater support and understanding for Okinawa. Ōhama Nobumoto (1891– 1976), who is mentioned here by the prime minister, was born on Ishigaki

Island in southern Okinawa; he was president of Waseda University in Tokyo from 1954 to 1966.

9. The Yasukuni Shrine is a controversial institution associated with state Shinto, commemoration of the war dead, and the legacies of Japanese fascism.

10. Harootunian, "Memory, Mourning, and National Morality," 144–160; Koschmann, "National Subjectivity."

11. "Ryūkyū" identifies both the archipelago and the kingdom that stretched from Kyūshū to Taiwan until conquered and colonized by Japan in 1867. Japanese authorities disposed of the name, creating Okinawa prefecture; American authorities resurrected the term during the occupation. After reversion to Japanese rule in 1972, the region became Okinawa prefecture once again.

12. Despite its shortcomings, the most comprehensive text on Okinawan history in English remains Kerr, *Okinawa*. See also Christy, "The Making of Imperial Subjects in Okinawa"; Molasky, *The American Occupation of Japan and Okinawa*; Smits, *Visions of Ryūkyū*; and Tomiyama, "The Critical Limits of the National Community." In Japanese, see Hiyane, *Kindai Okinawa no Seishinshi*; Kano, *Sengo Okinawa no Shisōzō*; and Tomiyama, *Kindai Nihon Shakai to "Okinawajin."*

13. *Uchinā* is the Okinawan word used to reference the place Okinawa. It is often used by Okinawans to construct an implicit comparison to Japan or explicitly paired with *Yamatu*, shifting the terms of discussion to Okinawa.

14. Ishihara, "Memories of War and Okinawa," 87–89.

15. Hashimoto, *Seiken Dakkai Ron*, cited in Steven T. Benfell, "Why Can't Japan Apologize? Institutions and War Memory since 1945," *Harvard Asia Quarterly* 6, no. 2.

16. Adorno, "What Does Coming to Terms with the Past Mean?" 115.

17. Ricoeur, *Memory, History, Forgetting*, 460.

18. Harootunian, "Shadowing History," 189.

19. Bloch, "Nonsynchronism and the Obligation to Its Dialectics," 22–38.

20. Ivy, *Discourses of the Vanishing*, 9.

21. The valorization of Okinawan culture is a long-standing conservative tactic. See Hein's and Selden's introduction and the essay by Molasky, "Medoruma Shun," in Hein and Selden, *Islands of Discontent*, 1–35, 161–91.

22. Rancière, *The Nights of Labor*.

23. Ishihara Masaie, "Memories of War and Okinawa," 89.

24. Here I am following the work of scholars such as Dori Laub and Dominick LaCapra, who have suggested that witnessing encompasses the active under-

standing of those who were not the primary victims, a dialogic encounter with representations of the experience of others. Of course, this engagement must be done reflexively and respectfully, with an awareness that this interaction must not be an opportunity for the secondary witness to appropriate the suffering and victimization of others. See Laub, "An Event without a Witness"; LaCapra, "Trauma, Absence, Loss," 696.

25. Ishihara Masaie, *Daimitsu Bōeki no Jidai*; Ishihara Zemināru, *Sengo Koza ni Okeru Minshū Seikatsu to Ongaku Bunka*.

26. Norma Field's harrowing account of the struggle to understand and publicly narrate the wartime suicides and murders in the caverns of Chibichirigama in Yomitan speaks to the will to memory (as Pierre Nora describes it) that animates ordinary people to take action on their own behalf as well as the complex problems that derive from it. Field, *In the Realm of the Dying Emperor*, 33–105. Other scholars such as Gerald Figal, Matt Allen, and Julia Yonetani have taken up these concerns. See Hein and Selden, *Islands of Discontent*, 65–98; Allen, *Identity and Resistance in Okinawa*; Hook and Siddle, *Japan and Okinawa*, 188–207.

27. Rancière, "The Thinking of Dissensus."

28. Lefebvre, "The Inventory," 174.

29. Bloch, *The Principle of Hope*, 12.

30. Eldridge, "The 1996 Okinawa Referendum on U.S. Base Reductions," 879–904.

31. Chibana is the central figure in Norma Field's essay about Okinawa, in Field, *In the Realm of the Dying Emperor*.

32. In 1996, the United States and Japan Special Action Committee on Okinawa (SACO) accords included provisions to close the facility at Sobe; after a decade of delays, the land was returned to Chibana and other landowners on December 7, 2006.

33. Field, *In the Realm of the Dying Emperor*.

34. The phrase I use in the title of this section, "drawing a circle," is the term used by the dancers to describe creating the pattern on the ground that organizes eisā performances.

1. FUJIKI HAYATO

1. Ishihara, *Sengo Koza ni Okeru Minshū Seikatsu to Ongaku Bunka*, 31–80.

2. My thanks to Gakiya Yoshimitsu for this anecdote.

3. Hein and Selden, *Islands of Discontent*, 134–157.

4. Ōyama, *Okinawa Dokuritsu Sengen*; Yasuda and Shingawa, *Okinawa Dokuristu no Kanōsei*; Arasaki, "Okinawa Dokuritsuron no Kyojitsu."

5. Hook and Siddle, *Japan and Okinawa*, 122–123.

6. Miyazato, "Ryūkyūko o Kaku Ongaku," 18–24.

7. Inoue, "We Are Okinawans, but of a Different Kind," 85–104.

8. Two seminal musicians and humorists in postwar Okinawa.

9. My analysis of these performances is based on recordings and transcriptions that I made during my fieldwork in Okinawa from 1996 to 1998, and again in 1999. Versions of some of Fujiki's performances also appear in print. See Fujiki, *Uchinā Mōsō Kenbunroku*.

10. Adorno, *Aesthetic Theory*, 41.

11. Taira, "Dialectics," 167–186.

12. Johnson, *Okinawa*, 261–282.

13. Harootunian, *History's Disquiet*, 33–35.

14. Although I will focus specifically on shusse as deployed in the Okinawan context, the best discussion in English of the concept in Japanese history remains Kinmonth, *The Self-Made Man*.

15. "One-Man Dialogue" would be an apt translation of this section's head, "Hitori Yuntaku Shibai."

16. Created from the prewar villages of Goeku and Misato, Koza was the primary urban area associated with the massive complex of American bases in central Okinawa. After Okinawa's reversion to Japanese sovereignty in 1972, Koza became officially known as Okinawa City. See Molasky, *The American Occupation*, 53–56.

17. Hotels that provide discreet space for short-term assignations. Love hotels are often architecturally fanciful, evoking riverboats, rocket ships or Aladdin's palace. Also known in Japan as fashion hotels.

18. Fujiki's audience varies in number from as few as 50 at small venues such as the Terurinkan, to as many as 180 at larger sites such as Ryubo Hall in Naha.

19. The lord of Nakagusuku Castle during the fifteenth century. When unjustly accused of treason, he committed suicide rather than take up arms against the king. Gosamaru is often depicted as a paragon of loyalty and virtue in Okinawan drama and song. Kerr, *Okinawa*, 98–99.

20. This stream gives its name to the most popular of the melodies performed during Obon, and is a metaphor for the ceaseless flow of good fortune to the faithful.

21. The festival of the dead. See Smith, *Ancestor Worship*, 15–22.

22. A general introduction to the spatial organization of the Okinawan household is provided in Mabuchi, "Space and Time in Ryukyuan Cosmology," 1–19. Further consideration of the situation of household deities can be found in Akamine, *Shima no Miru Yume*. For a critique of Mabuchi's work, see Ota, "Ritual as Narrative." An interesting study of the postwar reconstruction of household space can be found in Ogura, "Gaijin Jutaku no Kensetu to Sono Naiyō." An analysis of the symbolic construction of urban space can be found in both Teruya, "Kindai Ryūkyū no Toshi Keikaku," and Yoshikawa, *Naha No Kūkan Kōzo*.

23. Lefebvre, *The Production of Space*, 1–67.

24. Higa, *Okinawa Minzokugaku no Hōhō*, 27–103.

25. Harootunian, *Overcome by Modernity*, 293–357; Yanagita, *Meiji-Taishōshi*; Yanagita, *Nenjū Gyōji Oboegaki*. For incisive critiques of Yanagita and nativist ethnology, see Figal, *Civilization and Monsters*; Ivy, *Discourses of the Vanishing*; and Koschmann, Ōiwa, and Yamashita, *International Perspectives*.

26. Benjamin, "The Storyteller," in *Illuminations*. See also Peter Osborne's discussion of Benjamin's schema of a fourfold transformation of literary forms and its relationship to the crises of modern society. Osborne, *The Politics of Time*, 134–138.

27. Terurin made these comments to me as we were preparing for a *zadankai* (round table discussion) concerning Okinawan culture and politics at the Koza Café in Okinawa City in the winter of 1997. The panel consisted of the humorists Tamaki Mitsuru, Fujiki Hayato, and Teruya Rinsuke; the musician Miyanaga Eiichi (Chibi); and myself. Terurin told me that there were two points about traditional Okinawan culture that he thought were absolutely imperative to emphasize to contemporary audiences. The first was the power of words, or *kotodama*. The second was the spirit of things, a concept that he chose to express by the term *animizumu*, the Japanese pronunciation of "animism." There are a number of other terms, such as *mononoke*, that could be selected to express this concept. The use of *animizumu*, however, is common among anthropologists and folklorists. It seems to me that Terurin's selection of these two concepts for emphasis, as well as the terms that he chose to represent them, is indicative of his deep involvement with nativist ethnology, a point that I will take up in chapter 2.

28. Terurin himself is more than a casual reader of Japanese folklore and nativist thought. In addition to his work as a musician, comedian, and actor, he also

studied both anthropology and psychology at the now disestablished Kokusai Daigaku in Koza. See chapter 3 for a detailed discussion of Terurin's career.

29. Harootunian, *Things Seen and Unseen*, 60.

30. Harootunian, *Overcome by Modernity*, 293–357.

31. Christy, "The Making of Imperial Subjects."

32. Nihon Hōsō Kyōkai, or the Japanese Broadcasting Association.

33. He now also announces his performances on his website.

34. A popular writer and performer, Tamaki is the former lead singer of the Rinken Band and current leader of the comedic group Shōchiku Kagekidan, as well as the director of Asibinā, a small theater operated by the Okinawa City government.

35. There are a number of performative genres in Okinawa and Japan that have influnced Fujiki. Rakugo, a formalized style of Japanese storytelling, has been popular in Okinawa since the early years of the twentieth century. Workers in the Okinawan ghettos in Osaka and Tokyo were exposed to rakugo and discussion and citation of rakugo performances were common in prewar Okinawa. (See Morioka and Sasaki, *Rakugo*). Likewise, manzai and the sketch comedy of performers from Yoshimoto Kōgyō have a tremendous audience in Okinawa, as it does throughout the main islands. Western comedy is also influential, disseminated through cinemas throughout Okinawa, programs carried on Japanese television, as well as on the English-language armed forces channel, the Far East Network, which is broadcast in the open in central Okinawa. For a discussion of Fujiki's work with Tamaki Mitsuru, see Ota, "Appropriating Media, Resisting Power," 145–170.

36. Former lead vocalist of the Rinken Band and member of Shōchiku Kagekidan. Now a radio host and actor in local theater. Commonly referred to with the diminutive "Yoshibō."

37. A *pō pō* is an Okinawan crepe. The title could be translated as "A Confection of Laughter."

38. The intellectual historian Gregory Smits discusses the work of the eighteenth-century Ryūkyūan writer Heshikiya Chōbin, who viewed the night as the authentic site for counterhegemonic practices: "Hesikiya . . . stress[es] the oppressive nature of the day's dawning. At night, out of society's gaze, the aji and the prostitute enjoy themselves as nature intended. In the oppressive light of day, however, the aji must sneak back to his residence." See Smits, *Visions of Ryūkyū*, 121.

39. Nishioka, "Kari & Karijusji."

40. Ikemiya, *Okinawa no Yūkōgei*, 13–20.

41. Chondarā is the Okinawan reading of the term *ōkyōtaro*, which refers to a young man from the capital. In practice, *chondarā* indicates a number of different kinds of performers and performances, including itinerant practitioners who use handheld puppets to perform household purification rituals, local groups whose dances depict mounted noblemen from the capital, and the clowns dressed in peasant garb that accompany eisā dancers. Local histories trace the origin of chondarā performance to Buddhist missionaries from Japan, who arrived in Okinawa during the Muromati era. The role of chondarā remains in eisā performances, and the coastal community of Awase continues to present chondarā dances; the household purification rituals seem to have fallen out of practice after the end of the Pacific War. See Ikemiya, *Okinawa no Yūkōgei*, 13–20. For a discussion of itinerant performers in the context of the Japanese main islands, see Jane Marie Law's work on *kadozuke* or courtyard performance. Law, *Puppets of Nostalgia*, 49–88.

42. Community dances during Obon to welcome, entertain and send off the spirits of the dead. Hori, *Folk Religion in Japan*, 83–139.

43. Teruya Rinsuke, *Terurin Jiden*, 3–16.

44. Benjamin, "The Storyteller," 85.

45. Teruya Rinsuke, *Terurin Jiden*.

46. Often referred by the rather unwieldly term *Uchināyamatuguchi*, or a creole of Japanese and Okinawan.

47. I recorded extremely similar greetings in performances by the rakugo artists Tatekawa Shinnosuke (in 1998) and Katsura Sanshi. See also Masuyama, "Towards an Understanding of Rakugo"; Morioka and Sasaki, *Rakugo*.

48. Medvedev and Bakhtin, *The Formal Method in Literary Scholarship*, 130.

49. Fujiki also occasionally presents formal rakugo performances.

50. Bakhtin, "The Problem of Speech Genres," 74.

51. Discussion of these can be found in Lebra, *Okinawan Religion*, 54–57.

52. Okinawashi Heiwa Bunka Shinkōka, *Misato Kara Ikusayo Shōgen*.

53. *Tennōsei* is the prewar imperial system, marked by unreflexive devotion to the emperor.

54. This most powerful ideological term was introduced into everyday speech in the aftermath of the Japanese defense of Attu in the Aleutians in May 1943. A Japa-

nese garrison of about 2,500 soldiers fought to virtually the last man against an invading American force that outnumbered them nearly five to one. John Dower explains the term thus: "*gyokusai* [is] a word composed of two ideographs that literally meant 'jewel smashed.' The expression derived from a line in the sixth-century Chinese history *Chronicles of the Northern Chi'i*, where it was stated that on matters of principle, the man of moral superiority would break his precious jade rather than compromise to save the roof tiles of his home. The term came to mean choosing to die heroically in battle rather than surrender—choosing death before dishonor." See Dower, *War without Mercy*, 231–233.

55. For a discussion of the murder of Okinawans accused of spying, see Tomiyama, " 'Spy' "; Allen, *Identity and Resistance in Okinawa*, 27–51.

56. A Japanese-American soldier.

57. Tomiyama, *Senjō no Kioku*.

58. Tomiyama quotes this excerpt from a letter written by an Okinawan soldier in the Japanese army at Bouganville to his son, originally published in Kinjō, "Dochaku no Bunka wa Kaihō no Buki Tariuru ka." Tomiyama, *Senjō no Kioku*, 8.

59. Performed as a series of blackouts, often with Fujiki paired with Gakiya Yoshi-mitsu, these sketches have become classics of contemporary Okinawan comedy. They have recently become available in Japan on a DVD of highlights of ōshō-chiku performances.

60. This joke and its variations are staples of rakugo performance as well. I have heard the famous rakugoka Katsura Sanshi tell a variant of it, substituting a numbed leg for the injured arm.

61. "Shattered jewels."

62. "One man must kill ten."

63. "I can't imagine that when everyone fights for this island, for Japan, with no thought of sparing their lives, that I would be the only one to be left alive."

64. The Kerama Islands occupy a strategic position to the southern flank of the American invasion. Japanese defense planning called for these swift torpedo boats to be launched from concealed positions in the Keramas and to infiltrate the American fleet, detonating when they could inflict the maximum damage to American shipping—and killing the pilot. Feifer, *Tennōzan*.

65. "The Strong Japanese" and "No Going Barefoot!"

66. Sakima, "Ryūkyū no Tonsai [Butamatsuri] no Fūshū ni Tsuite," 475–484.

67. I recorded a more detailed version of this myth during a visit to Kudaka in March 1997. Slightly different accounts can be found in Higa, "Ina No Denrai," 15.

2. THE HERITAGE OF HIS TIMES

1. Also the name of the entertainment district in Edo (Tokyo), much romanticized in Japanese popular culture.

2. See Okinawashi Heiwa Bunka Shinkōka, Koza, 28–140, esp. 83, 94–99. See also Molasky, *The American Occupation of Japan and Okinawa*, as well as Yoshida, "Love Suicide at Kamaara."

3. The Silver Shopping District.

4. Statistics published by the Bank of the Ryūkyūs (Ryūgin) show that 30 percent of the American bases in Japan are located in Okinawa, or 75 percent if those used jointly with the Japanese Self-Defense Forces are excluded. Gavin McCormack lists a flat 75 percent, but notes that this accounts for 20 percent of the land on the main island of Okinawa. While there are military facilities in the forested northern region of Okinawa, most arable land in central Okinawa lies within the boundaries of the bases. At the time of my research, there were more that 27,000 American military personnel stationed in Okinawa; the number of Americans associated with the bases exceeded 50,000 when dependent families and civilian employees are also taken into account. Tamanori and James, *A Minute Guide to Okinawa*; Johnson, *Okinawa: Cold War Island*, 261–282.

5. Bechtel Group, *Economic Development for Okinawa: A Program for Success*. For a critical perspective, see Taira, "Okinawa's Dilemma."

6. Yonetani, "Playing Base Politics."

7. I find it interesting that the literature of the Nakasone administration refers to this project in the context of "the dream expands." If the island were to be constructed off the east coast of Okinawa, it would indeed take its place with other sacred islands such as Kudaka (see the discussion of Kudaka in chapter 1), islands often associated with dreams and dreaming in the Okinawan imaginary. However, if it is a dream island, it has its nightmarish counterpart in the planned construction of the floating heliport in Nago, or the recently scrapped "City of the Future" built in the ocean at the site of the failed 1975 Marine Expo, also in Nago. It might be productive to examine the depiction of the Dream Island, resembling nothing so much as an aerial view of an American base, to elicit the symbolic vocabulary of the dreams of conservative Okinawan politicians.

8. Transcripts of these programs can be found in Tamaki, *Okinawa no Machizukuri, Chiki Okoshi*, 136.

9. Although I have opted to represent this Okinawan word as chanpuru in my

discussion of Terurin's work, FM Champla used this idiosyncratic romanization in advertising copy.

10. The nickname "Terurin" is a contraction of the first syllables of his family and personal names. Thus, *Teruya Rinsuke* becomes Terurin.

11. The Terurinkan or Terurin House is Terurin's home on Ippē Street, behind Park Avenue in the Chūō district of Okinawa City. At present, it houses Terurin's sanshin store, a small theater that accommodates perhaps fifty, and Terurin's residence. In the past, it has also been the site of a pension, the studios of Maruteru Records, and a short-lived printing company that Terurin operated. Along the exterior wall, black block letters identify the building as the embassy of the Independent Republic of Koza, an entity presided over by Terurin in his incarnation as the president of Koza.

12. The word *sanshin* literally means "three-stringed," and yet it has become so routinized that people rarely consider this meaning. When he refers to his own instrument as a "yonshin" (four-stringed), it seems to strike listeners as comical.

13. Vertically striped leg armor worn by warriors of the Ryūkyū kingdom and by contemporary dancers and actors in costume dramas or festivals.

14. Onaha Zenkō, a dentist, humorist, and performer. He was known as Būten or Būten Sensee (Dr. Būten), and popularly referred to as the Chaplin of Okinawa. Būten died in 1969 at the age of seventy-two. "Warai no Mabui: Mirai e," 22. Terurin makes the interesting observation that many dentists in prewar Okinawa were also performers.

15. Teruya Rinsuke, *Terurin Jiden*, 176–192.

16. As noted earlier, Tamaki is a comedian, actor, writer, and director of an Okinawan theatrical troupe known as Shōchiku Kagekidan. Their name is a homophone of the title of the famous film and theatrical company in mainland Japan, written with characters to suggest that their work is comedic. For a discussion of their performances, see Ota, "Appropriating Media, Resisting Power."

17. It has since been relocated to Nishihara, and Shuri Castle has been reconstructed.

18. Kokusai Daigaku was a private university founded in 1962. In 1972, it was incorporated into Okinawa Kokusai Daigaku (Okinawa International University) and relocated to Ginowan. See Teruya Rinsuke, *Terurin Jiden*, 273, for more on Terurin's experience, and Kozashi, *Kozashishi*, 600–607, for a discussion of the founding of the university.

19. Tomiyama, "The Critical Limits of the National Community," 165–179.

20. I should note that Murai Osamu has suggested that Yanagita's project may have more in common with that of scholars such as Torii Ryuzo than has been previously thought. By locating the remainder of archaic Japan in Okinawa, Yanagita was able to direct scholarly attention to the South Seas and dismiss the possibility of continental Asian—particularly Korean—origins of the Japanese people. See Murai, *Nantō Ideorogī no Hassei*.

21. Harootunian, *Overcome by Modernity*, 293–328.

22. Figal, *Civilization and Monsters*, 105–152.

23. Harootunian, *Overcome by Modernity*, 324–325.

24. Christy, "A Fantasy of Ancient Japan," 61–90.

25. Figal, *Civilization and Monsters*, 129–130.

26. Storytellers primarily associated with the narration of silent film.

27. The exchange of karī is dealt with in detail in chapters 1 and 5; Terurin also marked his transition from Japanese to Ryūkyūan with a joke. He asked for mainland Japanese members of the audience to raise their hands—a dozen or so men and women did as he asked. He then asked them to keep their hands up if they could understand Uchināguchi (Okinawan)—everyone lowered their hands. With a smile, he plunged into his recitation in classical Ryūkyūan.

28. Harootunian, *Overcome by Modernity*, 300–303.

29. Žižek, "How Did Marx Invent the Symptom?" 29.

30. Bauman, *Story, Performance and Event*, 32.

31. For more on the notion of cunning, see Detienne and Vernant, *Cunning Intelligence*. See also de Certeau, *The Practice of Everyday Life*.

32. Tenku Kikaku Inc., *Uchinā Poppu*.

33. Chikushi and Teruya, *Okinawa ga Subete*.

34. Connerton, *How Societies Remember*. While Connerton's argument is provocative, it clearly requires revision on a number of points. He is too willing to accept that discussion of World War I is not enjoined by powerful prohibitions; nor does he consider how the discussion of the war of the brigands may in some way be related to silence concerning World War I. Still, his general observations about social memory are worth considering.

35. For more on the Okinawan diaspora and the place of Okinawan labor in Osaka, see Tomiyama, *Kindai Nihon Shakai to "Okinawajin."*

36. This return migration was arrested by the outbreak of the Pacific War. For example, during the battle of Okinawa, most of the yādui in the Goeku and Misato area were destroyed. Survivors were interned in camps after the war, and

most resettled elsewhere throughout central Okinawa when their land was confiscated for the construction of the massive complex of American bases. This pattern of spatiotemporal movement is memorated during shīmī, the spring festival during which families gather for celebrations in the courtyards of their ancestral tombs. Shīmī observances begin with the tombs in which the most recently deceased members of their family are interred, and proceed to those more distant in historical time. The shīmī of many families in central Okinawa who claim noble descent begin at the local crypts, then proceed north to the urban Nago area, then small villages in rural Yanbaru, before turning south to sites surrounding the capital such as Shuri, Naha, or Urasoe, or even Itoman to the south. In this way, they recreate in reverse chronological order the pattern in movement from the capital to the south (or even from Itoman, former site of the kingdom of Nanzan).

37. Kano, Sengo Okinawa no Shisōzō, 17.

38. Statistics from the 1883 census show that there were already 402 households in Goeku area that were identified as shizoku or noble, accounting for 36.2 percent of the households in the region. By 1915, the number of noble households had grown to 731, or 46.6 percent of the households surveyed. Other impoverished nobles moved further north, settling for the most part in similar marginal communities. Okinawashi Heiwa Bunka Shinkōka, Kindai Tōkeisho ni Miru Rekishi, 127–134.

39. Also known at the Kuroshio, or the Japanese Current. It flows north from the tropical regions of the Pacific, sweeping past Okinawa and the main Japanese islands. It is strongly associated with Ryūkyūan and Japanese maritime trade and the cosmopolitan possibilities that this trade created. See Yanagita, Kaijō no Michi.

40. Yanagita, "Minkan Denshōron," 333–339.

41. Rimer, Culture and Identity, 99–127.

42. Ishihara Masaie, "Memories of War and Okinawa."

43. Teruya Rinsuke, Terurin Jiden, 176–192.

44. In his discussion, Terurin gives no account of the venue; neither does he describe the composition of the audience or prove his assertions about Okinawan linguistic proficiency in comparison to the Japanese. Terurin has little interest in producing a historically accurate account. Instead, I would paraphrase de Certeau's reading of the work of Marcel Detienne: he uses his reporting of anecdotes in order to recite his own tale.

45. Teruya Rinsuke, *Terurin Jiden*, 249–266.

46. Kishaba Eijun (1885–1972), a noted Okinawan author, ethnomusicologist, and authority on the culture of the Yaeyama region. Through his work with Columbia Records of Japan, a great deal of Okinawan folk music was recorded and released nationally, including the now famous *Asatoya Yunta*.

47. Although, to be fair, the works of native ethnologists such as Yanagita are widely read in Japan.

48. While the term *amakudari* is used to indicate the descent of the gods from the heavens, it has taken on a more popular meaning of the profitable reemployment of retired government bureaucrats in the industries that they were once charged with overseeing or regulating.

49. In his study of the Macartney embassy to Qing China, the historian James Hevia elaborates on this process: "Lesser lords are said to come to court and make offerings. That is, they present petitions and local products, things unique or special to their domains. This latter notion is particularly intriguing; it implies that local products are a means for differentiating one domain from another. Moreover, the same term is used to define 'tribute' presented to the court from within the Qing imperium." The Qing emperor entered into tributary relationships with these lords in order to recognize their existence and to engage in a benevolent process of instructing and guiding their development. As Hevia explains, court ritual produces an elaborate and highly calibrated system that encouraged compliance and punished deviance, the object being the integration of foreign peoples into the pattern of imperial civilization. Hevia, *Cherishing Men from Afar*, 121.

50. The theme of the discussion is a playful appropriation of Yanagita's history of Ryūkyū in *Kaijō no Michi*.

51. It is not my intention to present an exhaustive analysis of the Qing tribute-trade system, or even to elicit the nuances of Ryūkyūan participation. I am simply concerned with explaining Terurin's use of the idea of amazing or unusual local products. For a general discussion of the tribute-trade system, see Arrighi, Hamashita, and Selden, *The Rise of East Asia in World Historical Perspective*, 1–43.

52. Propp, *Morphology of the Folktale*.

53. *Mazekoze kongō bunka* is the term that Terurin employs.

54. A stir-fried dish with tofu as the primary ingredient.

55. A stir-fried dish with reconstituted dried wheat gluten soaked in eggs as the primary ingredient.

56. A chanpuru variant made of stir-fried soybean sprouts.

57. Goya is bitter melon. The dish includes sliced goya, tofu, and scrambled eggs, and perhaps leftover pork, canned pork luncheon meat or corned beef, and green onions or carrots.

58. Ota, "Appropriating Media, Resisting Power," 162–163.

59. Pratt, *Imperial Eyes*; Bhabha, *The Location of Culture*.

60. De Certeau, *The Practice of Everyday Life*, 3–43.

3. THE CLASSROOM OF THE EVERYDAY

1. The name Tāchī Māchū is the Okinawan reading of *futatsu no tsumuji*, or two crowns (the whorl of hair surrounding the highest points on one's skull). In Okinawan popular discourse, this is both an explanation of and excuse for wild behavior, particularly in a young boy or man. Interestingly, Fujiki claims that he himself has only one.

2. Minyō pubs are venues for the presentation of Okinawan popular folk music. Prominent musicians such as Ganeko Yoriko and Yohen Aiko operate pubs in the Okinawa City area.

3. A famous Okinawan singer, sanshin player, and songwriter, as well as the founder and producer of Nēnēsu, one of the first Okinawan groups to become popular in the World Music scene. Nēnēsu has recorded with musicians such as Sakamoto Ryūichi, Ry Cooder, and David Hidalgo of Los Lobos.

4. It is also commonly used to refer to awamori, the Okinawan distilled rice liquor.

5. Okuno, *Okinawa Koninshi*, 93–144.

6. Terurin specifically refers to Huizinga, *Homo Ludens*.

7. Teruya Rinsuke, *Terurin Jiden*, 307–309.

8. A massive ceramic figure of a mythical lion, the guardian of not only temples but also private homes in Okinawa.

9. During the fall and winter of 1996–1997, the Okinawa Prefectural Government sponsored a series of public hearings (*kōkai shinri*) in Ginowan, Okinawa City, and Kadena, during which prefectural officials, landowners, and citizens in general were able to question representatives of the Japanese Ministry of Defense concerning the forceful reappropriation of land for U.S. military use. See chapter 4 for further discussion of the kōkai shinri.

10. Fujiki, *Uchinā Mōsō Kenbunroku: Fujiki Hayato no Rabirinsu Wārudo*.

11. The Japanese interior or home islands. This colonial-era term deictically high-

lights the sense that Okinawa is somewhere other than part of Japan proper. However, there is a strong sense of ambivalence to the terms used to locate Okinawa. I have never heard Okinawans refer to their islands as *Gaichi* or any of the other possible locutions that would index Okinawa as a colonial site.

12. For a discussion of the notion of *doxic* regularity, see Bourdieu, *Outline of a Theory of Practice*, 164–165.

13. This discussion resonates in interesting ways with Heidegger's consideration of the distinction between *Vorhanden* (things ready to hand) and *Zuhanden* (things under control) in *Being and Time* (56).

14. Lion dances, practiced throughout Okinawa and Japan but originating in China. One of the Okinawan newspapers had an ongoing series featuring the elements of the shishimai of one particular region of Okinawa each week.

15. Sacred groves.

16. Takara Kurayoshi is a historian of Ryūkyū and the former director of the Urasoe Public Library, making him also a successor of Iha Fuyū. He is the author of influential histories such as *Ryūkyū no Jidai* and *Ryūkyū Ōkoku no Kōzō*, one of the editors of the Ryūkyū Shinpō's historical series *Shin Ryūkyūshi*, an organizer of the movement to rebuild Shuri Castle, and an influential figure in movements to consider local history and reevaluate popular culture in Okinawa City. An iconoclastic figure and an outspoken critic of the excesses of Okinawan politics, he has recently emerged as a public intellectual of the conservative Right.

17. See chapter 1 for an extended discussion of *Remembrance of White Sands*, the performance that is based on this account.

18. One of the main manga or comic book publishing houses in Japan.

19. Kaneshiro, Kanigusuku, and Kanigushiku are all possible alternative readings of this family name.

20. It also seemed to resonate with the conventions of classical Western tragedy: it is the young man's own flaw that leads him to disaster. In this case, he is ruined by his inability to recognize or respect the capabilities of the old man. The distinction from Attic tragedy would be that while the individual is capable of reflection and action, his autonomy is constrained by a social order that he does not fully comprehend rather than the capricious will of the gods. Vernant and Vidal-Naquet, "The Historical Moment of Tragedy in Greece," 23–28.

21. I later learned that Shimabukuro was a very knowledgeable collector of Okinawan pottery.

22. Yamanoguchi Baku's *Kaiwa* is a moving and exhaustive list of these images.

23. A leader of the prewar folk art movement in Japan and president of the Japan Folk Art Association. See Christy, "The Making of Imperial Subjects in Okinawa," 157–162.

24. Hiyane, *Kindai Okinawa no Seishinshi*.

25. See Ishihara Masaie, *Daimitsu Bōeki no Jidai*, for a comprehensive account of the postwar black market economy in Okinawa; see also Yoshikawa, *Naha no Kūkan Kōzō*, 51–78, for a discussion of merchant spaces in Naha.

26. Field, *In the Realm of the Dying Emperor*; Chibana, *Burning the Rising Sun*.

27. Johnson, *Blowback*.

28. Resembling as it does the Japanese national flag, with its image of the rising sun (Hi no Maru), this meal is commonly referred to as a Rising Sun lunch, or Hi no Maru bentō.

29. Hanks, *Language and Communicative Practices*, 207.

30. A neighborhood in Okinawa City. See chapter 5 for a detailed discussion of the community.

31. *Gairaigo* are foreign words represented in a phonetic Japanese syllabary (the syllabary katakana is normally reserved for foreign words) for ease of pronunciation and less marked deployment in speech by native speakers of Japanese. The term *Gairaigo* is constructed of the characters for *words that have come from outside*. Comprehensive guides to Gairaigo are available to Japanese speakers in collections such as the *Kadokawa Gairaigo Jiten* (Kadokawa Gairaigo dictionary).

32. While there are a variety of Japanese terms for tuna, the Gairaigo word *tsuna* is also used, particularly for canned tuna.

33. Was it yesterday?

34. Is it tomorrow?

35. Boas, "On Alternating Sounds."

36. However, his choice of words such as *tuna* and, later, *stew*, do in fact focus on English sounds that have analogs in Okinawan but not in Japanese.

37. Okinawa soba is the theme of a sketch involving the same characters that Fujiki often pairs with *Pōku Tamago*.

38. The idea of "Okinawa time" is a complicated and ambiguous concept. It was originally used as a pejorative characterization of the pace of life in Okinawa, indicating that Okinawans were lazy, unreliable, and lacked the time-consciousness of the modern Japanese. In recent years it has been revalued in some discourses, indicating a slower, more human pace of life, free from the manic intensity of everyday life in the metropolitan centers of Japan.

39. Literally "Forget the [past] Year" parties.

40. In popular discourse in both Okinawa and Japan, it is commonly asserted that Okinawans have the greatest longevity in Japan. While it is true that there is an unusual number of centenarians in Okinawa, statistics about the average Okinawan lifespan are the subject of considerable controversy. See Willcox and Willcox, *The Okinawa Program*.

41. In the end, most of this material was included in the introduction to a collection of translated, recently declassified American documents pertaining to the Koza Riot. Okinawashi Heiwa Bunka Shinkōka, *Beikoku ga Mita Koza Bōdō*.

42. Arakawa Akira, cited in Nakachi, "Ryukyu-U.S.-Japan Relations," 148.

43. Christopher Aldous notes that there was a meeting earlier that evening in neighboring Misato to organize demonstrations against the upcoming removal of chemical ordnance from stockpiles in Okinawa; he suggests that these organizers might have been present. See Hook and Siddle, *Japan and Okinawa*, 148–166.

44. In his writing about Okinawa, Chalmers Johnson focuses on this question of American extraterritoriality in his argument against American imperialism. He describes fifty years of vehicular homicide, rape, kidnapping, and theft in which American servicemen escaped with nominal punishments, highlighting their exceptional status in Okinawa and the inability of Okinawans to equitably pursue claims against these Americans. See Johnson, *Blowback* and *Okinawa*.

45. Tomiyama, "Okuni Wa?" 7–20.

46. This is not to say that there have not been attempts made to establish the causes of the incident: Aldous surveys them in his essay "Mob Rule." A couple of weeks after my meeting with Fujiki and Onga, I found myself at a New Year's party in the company of a number of Okinawan and mainland Japanese activists, representatives from indigenous rights groups throughout East Asia, a prominent member of the American Indian Movement, and a former leader of Sekigun, the Japanese Red Army. While a group on stage sang "The Internationale" in Uchināguchi to sanshin accompaniment, several long-time Okinawan activists told me about their experience of the uprising. They said that members of an organization known as the Ryūkyū Liberation Front happened to be in Koza for an end-of-the-year party. When the riot erupted, they took to the streets and incited the crowds to attack American cars and invade the bases.

47. Nelson, "The Moai."

48. Students for the "Shima Masu Juku" are selected from a broad field of candi-

dates and membership is quite prestigious in the Okinawa City area. Graduates include a number of active young government officials, as well as the director of the local radio station and tourist bureau. The objects of the seminar are to understand local history and culture, and to advance these ideas through community development projects.

49. A ritualized battle between neighboring youth groups dancing through the streets during Obon, the festival of the dead.

50. Tōshindoi is a celebration of the return of treasure ships from China during the age of the kingdom of Ryūkyū.

51. At the time of the Pacific War, Yomitan was a small coastal village. On April 1, 1945, the American invasion force landed on the beaches at Yomitan. More than three thousand Okinawans living in the Yomitan area were killed in the intense naval bombardment that preceded the invasion and the savage fighting that followed. Virtually every house and every structure was destroyed.

52. The performance that I describe here is grounded in a kind of Bakhtinian heteroglossia in which a performer selects one of the possible voices in her world to reflexively create a critical and embodied account of the past. At the same time, it bears certain similarities to the constructive melancholia that Judith Butler describes in her essay "Melancholy Gender/Refused Identification." Although Butler emphasizes the internalization of primary homosocial affect as constitutive—even in its prohibition—of the performance of a heterosexual gender, she also suggests that this internalized object can be recalled (remembered) in practices that challenge the oppressive constraints of a unified subjectivity. See Butler, *The Psychic Life of Power*, 132–150.

4. IN A SAMURAI VILLAGE

1. I am speaking here of the Chinese zodiac, in which each year of a twelve-year cycle is assigned an animal, which is presumed to be iconic of the character of those born in that year. Extremely popular throughout Japan, the cycle is observed with some difference in Okinawa.

2. The poet Yamanoguchi Baku was born in Naha in 1903. As a young man, he left Okinawa and settled in Tokyo. His work explored the life of the impoverished working class, leavening a clear and critical view of contemporary society with a self-deprecating sense of humor. Although he returned to Okinawa only briefly,

he continued to engage the problem of Okinawan identity, the legacies of the Japanese colonial era and the Pacific War, and the American occupation.

3. Takara, "Yādui," 110–115. The poem had been originally published several years earlier in the journal *Kairyū*.

4. Here Takara writes, "Hichui chui chui"—an onomatopoeic representation of the cry of the plover. In Okinawan, this is also a homophone for the word indicating a single person (*hitori* in standard Japanese). Together, it conveys a sense of loneliness and isolation.

5. The *Hibiscus tiliaceus*, or sea hibiscus, known for its vivid yellow blossoms. While in full bloom, blossoms will sometimes drop from the tree suddenly, intact. As such, it is sometimes used as a metaphor for sudden death or abrupt endings. The Japanese journalist Chikushi Tetsuya has said that he and his wife named their daughter Yūna because of the beautiful flowers borne by the tree; his Okinawan acquaintances all reacted in horror at the inauspicious connotations of Yūna as a child's name.

6. Amulets promoting such everyday desires as success in school, an easy pregnancy, or traffic safety are available for sale in Japanese temples and shrines. However, earlier amulets were made in the form of a pouch. Wearers would fill it with a small amount of soil from their native village so that a small piece of home would be with them always. In her essay about the activist Chibana Shōichi, Norma Field vividly recounts the inverse image: Okinawan baseball players at the Kōshien or annual high school baseball tournament in mainland Japan, before the reversion to Japanese sovereignty, filling pouches with soil from the playing field. Although it is commonplace for players to take the black sand of the Kōshien Stadium as a souvenir, Field powerfully evokes the pathos of the image: young Okinawans whose islands were brutally colonized by the Japanese state, devastated in the Pacific War, and abandoned to decades of American occupation, scrambling to gather the soil of their conqueror, under the sign of their homeland. See Field, "A Supermarket Owner," in *In the Realm of the Dying Emperor*.

7. The Land of the Sun likely refers to contemporary Japan, often represented by the figure of a red sun on white field—the Hi no Maru flag, so famously burned by Chibana Shōichi. However, this introduces some temporal ambiguity: the old woman's passage could be during the colonial period, the prewar era of ultra-nationalism, or the postwar reversion era.

8. Without fixing the identity of the narrator as Ben himself, his wife is indeed a distinguished performer of classical Ryūkyūan dance.

9. Along with Noborikawa Seijin, Kadekaru Rinshō is probably the best known male minyō performer in postwar Okinawa.

10. Yanagita writes about the Black Current (Kuroshio, or Japanese Current) in *Kaijō no Michi*.

11. Watson, *Cold Mountain*.

12. Watson and Hiroaki, *From the Country of Eight Islands*.

13. Hiyane, "Ōta Chōfu no Dōkaron," in *Kindai Okinawa no Seshinshi*.

14. Christy, "The Making of Imperial Subjects in Okinawa"; Tomiyama, *Gendai Nihon Shakai to "Okinawajin."*

15. Mabuchi, "Space and Time in Ryūkyūan Cosmology"; Ota, "Ritual as Narrative."

16. Tomiyama, "Okinawa Sabetsu to Puroretariaka."

17. Mukai, "Sotetsu Sigoku"; Christy, "The Making of Imperial Subjects in Okinawa."

18. In *The Production of Space*, 38–46, Lefebvre introduces a tripartite formulation of social space, composed of spatial practices, representations of space, and representational spaces.

19. Christy, "A Fantasy of Ancient Japan"; Yanagita, *Kainan Shōki.*

20. Inoue, "The Identity and Politics of Locality." The absence of any discussion of the American bases or the heterogeneous communities that surround the bases stands out clearly in Lebra's otherwise compelling ethnography: Lebra, *Okinawan Religion.*

21. Many other representations of rural village life are complex and ambiguous, representing varying degrees of these extremes. For example, Okinawa Rengo Jimukyoku, an Okinawan production team, released a film entitled *Kichi ga Nakatta Koro: Showa no Hajimegoro Ginowan e no Tabi* (When there were no bases: a trip to Ginowan in the early years of the Showa era) in 2004. It represented daily life before the Pacific War in the Ginowan area, focusing on the Ginowan *machigwa* (*ichiba*, or public market) and Aragusuku village, a rural community that was fragmented and partially destroyed by the construction of the Marine Corps Air Station at Futenma. Computer-generated animation provides uncanny images of quotidian practices in the households, fields, and market of the prewar community. While the film itself eschews juxtaposing contemporary images of the site, its release at the height of the struggle to close the base and return it to the community cannot be ignored. An equally complex example would be the work of the Japanese filmmaker Nakae Yuji. In films such as *Nabbii*

no Koi (Nabbie's love) and *Hoteru Haibisukasu* (Hotel Hibiscus), he strives for a realistic visual depiction of the unevenness of everyday life in rural Okinawa, of poverty and American occupation. However, this insight is soon squandered as he inexplicably invests these representations with the same longed-for organic totality that regularly characterizes nativist discourse, evacuating the film of any progressive political content.

22. Although this happened throughout central Okinawa, detailed, moving accounts exist of the American destruction of Isa for the construction of Futenma Marine Corps Air Station and of the confiscation of a considerable portion of Ie Jima (Ie Island), off the northwestern coast of Okinawa. See Molasky, *The American Occupation of Japan and Okinawa*; Ahagon, *Beigun to Nōmin*.

23. For a general discussion of the antibase and antireversion movements in Okinawa, see Arasaki and Nakano, *Okinawa Sengoshi*; and Nakachi, "Ryūkyū–U.S.–Japan Relations." For a more detailed study of antibase activism among landowners, see Arasaki, *Okinawa-Hansenjinushi*. The circumstances surrounding the antibase movement in the mid-1990s are dealt with in Arime, *Kusatī*. In particular, *Kusatī* includes the transcript of a moving public presentation about the objectives of the hitotsubo movement. See also Okinawa Mondai Ronshū Iinkai, *Dairi Shōmei Kyohi*.

24. These activists derived their name from their strategy of convincing sympathetic base landowners to sell a tract of land (the market for military property in Okinawa is quite active, considered by many—cynically or realistically—to be a stable source of income for years to come) which they would then subdivide into small parcels of a single *tsubo* (about two square meters) and distribute among individual activists. This strategy served to give the activists both a legitimate voice in issues concerning base lands and a vote as to their dispositon, even if the vote could be, as I have described, overridden by municipal or prefectural authorities. It also complicated the efforts of the Ministry of Defense to manage military land, adding hundreds of landowners to the list of those who need to be contacted, consulted, and paid in the routine process of maintaining the leases.

25. Augé, *Oblivion*.

26. Smith, "The Living and the Dead."

27. Yanagita, *About Our Ancestors*.

28. Harootunian, *Overcome by Modernity*; Ohnuki-Tierney, *Kamikaze, Cherry Blossoms and Nationalism*, 77–79, 97–101.

29. Kerr, *Okinawa*, 31–32, 110–111; Lebra, *Okinawan Religion*, 95–121.

30. The term for this intervention—the Ryūkyū *shobun*—loses much of its force when translated, as it has often been, by an innocuous locution such as "the Ryūkyū measures." In fact, a much more accurate rendering would be "liquidation."

31. See Angst, "The Rape of a Schoolgirl"; and Sturdevant and Stolzfus, *Let the Good Times Roll*.

32. In many ways, Okinawa's conflicted colonial history is manifested at Naminoue. Shinto shrine construction at indigenous sacred sites and the installation of the spirit of a member of the imperial family was a predictable aspect of the production of space throughout the Japanese colonial empire. Similar construction and enshrinement characterized colonial planning and development in Harbin, Taipei, and Seoul. Okinawa is perhaps unique in not simply maintaining this site after the Japanese defeat in World War II, but in actually reconstructing the shrine.

33. Scholars generally refer to yuta as shaman; yuta themselves often adopt this same characterization. Yuta have the ability to mediate human relationships with Okinawan deities and the spirits of the dead. Sato, "Globalization and Identity in Okinawan Shamanism," 27–49.

34. Household rites are mediated by the use of the *ihai* (*ihē* in Okinawan), a tablet on which the posthumous Buddhist name awarded to the deceased has been placed. The ihai is inserted into a frame known as the *tōtōmē*, with a row of tablets representing deceased male relatives on top and female relatives on the bottom. The tōtōmē is placed on a shelf at the top of the altar; offerings are presented upon the lower shelves. Other memorative objects are sometimes used. A photo may be placed in or near the altar, one ihai left freestanding for special emphasis; certificates awarded to the deceased or copies of the household register may also be placed near the altar or in a drawer located in its base. Occasionally, photographs of the imperial family or prominent figures such as wartime military officers may also be displayed—even in Okinawa.

35. An increasingly popular Okinawan notion of paradise, the spiritual homeland beyond the sea, often described as an ethereal island somewhere in the nearby waters where the ancestral spirits live in happiness. Lebra's research suggested that few Okinawans during the 1950s understood the concept of *nirai kanai*. However, the term has gained currency in popular discourse, and I found that most people understood what was meant by it even if they did not believe nirai kanai to be the destination of the spirits of the dead.

36. Munn, "Excluded Spaces," 451.

37. Although all are quite large by mainland Japanese standards, Okinawan tombs are of varying sizes. At the same time, the kin groups that maintain them vary in size and composition: from large corporate associations in Itoman, Shuri, and Naha that share a single, massive tomb, to single household tombs in the community where I worked in Okinawa City.

38. See Munn, "Excluded Spaces," 446–465; Lefebvre, *The Production of Space*, 190–191.

39. Hubert, *Essay on Time*, 51.

40. The twenty-four calendrical rituals were performed twice monthly throughout the lunar year.

41. Tanaka, *New Times in Modern Japan*.

42. Dana, "Haka—Rekishi Genten kara Mita Shosō," 281–308.

43. Ibid.

44. See Oshiro Tetsuhiro's stunning novella, "Turtleback Tombs."

45. Kozy K. Amemiya has carried out groundbreaking research on the American resettlement of thousands of Okinawans in the pestilential Bolivian jungle. See Johnson, *Okinawa*, 53–69.

46. Graeber, "Dancing with Corpses Reconsidered," 262.

47. The relationship between households is a subject of enormous interest, regularly discussed and the popular subject of storytelling and debate. Most families keep elaborate genealogies: some were safeguarded along with other household treasures during the war, others carefully (if imaginatively) reconstructed. In most bookstores, guides are readily available for the amateur genealogist; many families have even commissioned and published detailed studies of their family history. A close friend of mine has a record of his descent from the southern dynasty (Nanzan), showing the seventeen generations that precede his family, and the broad horizontal relationships that have been produced over the years. In addition to their surname, households also have a *yagō* or "house" name that relates their family to a spatial site of remembered or imagined importance: "beneath the pine tree" or "deep in the mountain fields" are names of the main house and a branch household of two of my neighbors in Okinawa City. Informal yago also narrate amusing or memorable characteristics of households, coupled with their surnames: "fat cheeks" Kinjō, with obvious connotations; "tile roof" Kyan, denoting either an ambitious person who remodeled his home when the rest of the homes in the community had thatched roofs, or of a poor neighbor who continues to live in the same simple farmhouse. Among those claiming descent

from the Ryūkyūan nobility, male children within the family are assigned a *nanogashira*—the first character of their personal name, shared by male siblings, that indicates the branch of the royal family from which they are descended. With few notable exceptions, surnames are ambiguous markers of relationship while the nanogashira are clear and intentional. The historian Takara Kurayoshi has told me that this practice has been largely abandoned by those of noble descent remaining in the Shuri-Naha area; it remains a regular and accepted practice among the rural former nobility in the areas where I worked.

48. Margaret Lock points out that, while nearly 99 percent of the dead are cremated in contemporary Japan, this is a fairly recent development. During the late Tokugawa era, the high population density in expanding urban areas made cremation an attractive alternative to burial; Buddhist temples began building crematoria to meet this need. These facilities were later moved to the edge of the urban areas because of concerns with pollution. As a consequence of a re-surgence of nativist sentiment, cremation was outlawed in 1873; in 1887, this position was reversed by a law requiring the cremation of those who died of infectious diseases. Although the practice became quite popular in urban areas, as late as 1925, only 43 percent of the dead were buried. In John Embree's 1939 monograph *Suye Mura*, there is no mention of even the possibility of cremation in his discussion of mortuary practice in rural Kyushu. See Lock, *Twice Dead*, 66–67; Embree, *Suye Mura*, 215–220.

49. Lebra, *Okinawan Religion*, 200–201.

50. I have observed two general types of urns, known as *zushigame* or *jūshigāmi*, in Okinawa. One style is simple and unglazed with a small lid; the other is elab-orately decorated and glazed, shaped generally like an Okinawan castle—the remains of both husband and wife can be placed in this urn together. It is generally held that the simple urns were used by those descended from com-moner families, the ornate reserved for nobles. According to Lebra, a set order is followed in placing the bones in the urn: "feet, legs and pelvis are entered first, followed by the backbones, arms and lastly the skull." In the more ornate urns, the skulls of husband and wife are placed side by side in the lid, which is provided with windows so that the spirits can observe the outside world. Exam-ples of urns used by the Ryūkyūan nobility acquired by Basil Hall Chamberlain can be seen on display at the Pitt-Rivers Museum at Oxford: this particular urn is the subject of a documentary film by the director Minato Chihiro, *Chamberlain's Zushigame*. See *Okinawan Religion*, 200–201.

51. Kawahashi, "Kaminchu."

52. Hertz, *Death and the Right Hand*.

53. Benjamin, *The Arcades Project*, 471.

54. De Certeau, "Oppositional Practice," 3–43; quotation from 41.

55. Ferguson, "Global Disconnect," 234–254. The difference would be that Ferguson's intention is to demonstrate that these sites of disconnection are necessary elements in the disciplinary construction of a global socioeconomic order. My concern is to contrast their disarticulation and abasement with the characteristics of other kinds of spatial formations.

56. Defeated in a civil war in the late twelfth century by the victorious Minamoto, this conflict is narrated in the *Heike Monogatari* and provides material for a host of novels, ghost stories, and films.

57. Yanagita, *Legends of Tono*.

58. Yanagita, *Kaijō no Michi*.

59. Wacker, *Onarigami*.

60. Ibid.

61. Adorno, *Negative Dialectics*, 163.

62. The role of Arasaki Moriteru, the Okinawa University professor, Marxist intellectual, and theoretician of the antibase movement, deserves further investigation. Likewise, the relationship between planning cells in the prefectural government, various Okinawan antibase organizations, unions as well as mainland radical activists such as Zengakuren (the leftist student union), should be explored more deeply.

63. Zengakuren—a contraction of *Zennihon gakusei jichikai sōrengō* or All-Japan Federation of Students' Self-Governing Associations—is the overarching organization of radical student unions.

64. The Treaty of Mutual Cooperation and Security between Japan and the United States; first ratified in 1952, it was revised despite considerable popular protest in 1960.

65. Tomiyama Ichirō has written of the problematic ambiguity of this locution in "Okuni Wa?" 7–20.

66. The hansen jinushi testimony is based on my notes, and my translation of material reproduced in Arime, *Kusatī*.

67. For example, it would be productive to consider the genres within which they recount their experiences of the war. Saul Friedlander and Dominick LaCapra have studied the possibilities of representation in the narration of trauma and

genocide. In the Japanese context, Lisa Yoneyama has written about survivors of Hiroshima and their efforts to narrate their experiences. Yoneyama examines the complex articulation of their projects with peace and antinuclear movements, as well as discourses in which Japanese suffering is conflated with the misery of the victims of Japanese wartime aggression. She also perceptively discusses the constraints imposed by narrators' choices of genres, and the prejudice that storytellers endure as a consequence of identifying themselves with the subject position of Hiroshima survivors. In the case of Okinawa, the Akutagawa Prize–winning novel *Suiteki* by the Okinawan author Medoruma Syun presents a relentless critique of the self-serving narration of war experience in contemporary Okinawa. See Friedlander, "Introduction"; LaCapra, *Representing the Holocaust*; Yoneyama, *Hiroshima Traces*; Medoruma, "Suiteki."

68. Harootunian, *Things Seen and Unseen*, 407–439.

69. Jennifer Robertson has written perceptively of the ambivalent place of furusato in contemporary discourses, and contention over the experience and representation of native place in domestic development projects and in life within newly constituted suburban communities. Robertson, *Native and Newcomer*, 14, 25–37, 182.

70. Ivy, *Discourses of the Vanishing*, 103–108.

71. The verbal *shinobu* is used repeatedly in the testimony. For example: "Furusato o shinobinagara seikatsu o shite imasu" (I live my life longing for my native place). *Shinobu* has the connotation of longing for an absent object, often an object that is irretrievably lost.

5. DANCES OF MEMORY

1. The titles of each section in this chapter are taken from songs in the Sonda eisā cycle.

2. See chapter 3.

3. For a fascinating account of the history of Koza and its place in Okinawan literature, see Molasky, *The American Occupation of Japan and Okinawa*, 53–69.

4. Popular folk music.

5. A rural community near Kamakura. Repatriated Okinawan soldiers and laborers were quartered in an internment camp near Uraga; Shūei left and lived by his wits in the Zushi area until he could arrange return passage to Okinawa.

6. As part of the postwar administrative reorganization of central Okinawa, the

two villages of Goeku and Misato would be joined together in 1950 to become Koza City. Koza would, in turn, be renamed Okinawa City with reversion to Japanese sovereignty in 1972.

7. *Yakimāji* is an Okinawan expression meaning "burned all around." It describes a fire that occurred before the war in the Nishizato yādui, in which all of the fields surrounding one of the residents' stable were burned but the stable itself survived. Even now, it is occasionally used to denote the Sonda eisā. One could understand it as a metaphor for the providential survival of something important when all around it is destroyed.

8. The late Kadekaru Rinshō was famous for his expressive vocal style as well as his sanshin artistry. A prolific recording artist, he was well known throughout Japan and his recordings are popular among roots music aficionados outside Japan as well.

9. One recording of their duets is still available; Shūei told me that the Ryūkyū Broadcasting Company sometimes plays recordings of his old radio show in the early morning hours.

10. A minyō artist, a singer, and sanshin performer.

11. Musicians who provide the vocal and sanshin accompaniment for eisā. They are usually the most experienced members of the seinenkai, directing the dance through the tempo, duration, and intensity of their performance.

12. Okinawashi Heiwa Bunka Shinkōka, *Kindai Tōkeisho Ni Miru Rekishi*, 51–52. Onga Takashi, a historian with the Okinawan municipal government, also gave me a copy of a sketch map that he and his fellow researchers had created for an unpublished history of Okinawa City area yādui based on interviews with former residents.

13. That is to say, those who could trace their patrilineal ancestry to the Ryūkyū nobility. In prewar Okinawa, most of the young men of the yādui married women of other yādui, so it would be unusual for a child not to be of bilateral noble descent. The question of allowing those of commoner ancestry to dance—to say nothing of mainland Japanese—was unlikely to have arisen before the war.

14. Kids' Country.

15. An edible seaweed extremely popular in the Japanese health food market.

16. Although the Okinawan diet shares many elements of mainland Japanese cuisine, small household gardens seem to be devoted to produce that is explicitly associated—by both mainland Japanese and Okinawans—with Okinawa.

Mango, papaya, banana, bitter melon, winter melon, loofah, small red peppers, and purple potatoes are common.

17. Although Okinawa returned to Japanese sovereignty nearly thirty years ago, there remain some distinctions between the administrative designation of Okinawan and mainland Japanese communities. In the urban administrative structure of mainland Japan, Sonda would likely be a *ku*, or ward, or perhaps only a subdivision of a neighboring ward. In fact, this system of designation has been used in the past in Okinawa City. However, communities such as Sonda are now referred to as *aza*, a rather archaic-sounding designation for a section of a village.

18. See Okinawa Zentō Eisā Jikō Iinkai, Eisā 360°, 24–35; Gibo, Eisā.

19. In addition to Michael Molasky's work, Norma Field has written of the conflict that emerged in Yomitan surrounding local efforts to recall and narrate experiences of the Pacific War. Gerald Figal has examined the public production of peace memorials and the articulation of tourism and the peace movement in Okinawa. Field, *In the Realm of the Dying Emperor*; Figal, "Waging Peace in Okinawa."

20. The general name given to a collection of sixteenth-century Ryukyuan poetry, sometimes called the Okinawan Manyōshū.

21. China Sadahiro, a well-known historian of religion—and younger brother of the famous utasā and producer China Sadao—once told me that this popular account of eisā's origin is, at best, ambiguous. *Yesa* (as *eisā* is often pronounced in Okinawa) does appear in the *Omorososhi*, but there is no indication of what the term might mean.

22. Ikemiya, "Eisā no Rekishi," in Okinawa Zentō Eisā Jikō Iinkai, Eisā 360°.

23. In Ryūkyūan architecture, the nā is the courtyard of a home. It is a mediational zone between the interior space of the home and the space of the community beyond the household wall.

24. For thoughtful reflections on the Okinawan stage, see the work of activist and photographer Ishikawa Mao, especially Ishikawa, *Okinawa Shibai*.

25. "Old Boys." Older members or former members of the seinenkai. Most no longer perform, or no longer do so as dancers or drummers.

26. Kohama Shūei and Kadekaru Rinshō were close friends, performing together before the Pacific War and reuniting to form a trio with Teruya Rinsuke after the war ended.

27. Heinrich, "Language Planning and Language Ideology," 153–179.

28. This is not universally true. One former leader of the youth group became a local

high school teacher after graduating from Ryūkyū Daigaku or the University of the Ryukyus. Two of my friends also graduated from Ryūdai: one is working for a high-tech company in Sapporo, another is an apprentice with an Okinawan independent filmmaker.

29. In the 1980s, the Japanese tourist industry turned its attention to Okinawa, valorizing the possibilities of Okinawan culture. Since then, many Okinawan popular and folk performers have risen to national prominence and mainland tourists throng to Okinawan festivals. Still, until recently local teachers groups encouraged young men and women to focus on their studies and to work to become both politically aware and socially mobile. For many of these teachers, hanging around at the kōminkan exposed students to the drunken troublemakers and apprentice criminals that they believed populated the hardscrabble neighborhoods of Okinawa City.

30. "The Ballad of the Southern Grove," "The Chunjun River Flows," and "Kudaka Island" respectively.

31. Bakhtin, "Forms of Time," 103.

32. Ibid.

33. Nakijin is a rural region near Nago; Goeku was a central Okinawan village now integrated into Okinawa City.

34. Okuno, *Okinawa Koninshi*.

35. Hanks, *Intertexts*.

36. Ricoeur, *Memory, History*, 124–132, 461–462.

37. Teruya Rinsuke, *Terurin Jiden*. When Kohama Shūei wrote the characters for karī in the margin of my notebook, he chose a pair that means "a portion of happiness." Karī is often paired with the verb *tsukeru*—to attach. When I've discussed the idea of kari with the jikata and the older members of the youth group, they often explain that karī, while specific to Okinawan performances, is equivalent in meaning to the Japanese *engi*. Engi is conventionally understood to mean good luck or good fortune. Realized in the same action as tsukeru, engi can be distributed to bring good fortune to its recipient. However, engi has more complex, historical meanings as well. Grounded in Buddhist philosophy, engi is defined as destiny or relatedness—a concept clearly related to notions of karma.

38. Ricoeur, *Memory, History*, 456.

39. Hein and Selden, *Islands of Discontent*, 192–227.

40. *Stuff*, a glossy men's magazine about style and the consumption of fashionable objects such as vintage watches, designer furniture, and hi-tech electronic

equipment. In addition to material goods, the magazine also details desirable experiences, from dining in an exceptional restaurant to observing the most meaningful folk festivals. It was in this context that Iha appeared.

41. The term *shimamūi* is also used occasionally.

42. I am reminded of Terence Turner's account of Kayapo performances in Brazilian relocation camps. Despite the rectilineal organization of the camps, Kayapo performers danced in a circular path that recalled the form of their abandoned villages. In the case of Sonda, the remembered form is resuscitated in the space that gave it shape more than fifty years earlier. See Turner, "Representing, Resisting, Rethinking," 285–313 (esp. 289–291).

43. Augé, *Oblivion*.

44. Virtually every household that we visited made a gift to the seinenkai. It seemed to be the consensus that households should offer about 10,000 yen, although many gave less and a few gave more. In 1998, over the course of the three days of Obon, the seinenkai received cash contributions totalling 1.5 million yen. Visitors would also arrive at the kōminkan throughout the day during Obon, leaving bottles of awamori or sake and cases of beer or soda as presents.

45. *Ōrāsē* (or *gāē*) has a real sense of conflict. Okinawan bullfighting (*tōgyū*) is also sometimes referred to as *ōrāsē*.

46. The Japanese national radio and television system.

47. Kinjō Kaoru, cited in Nomura, *Muishiki no Shokuminchishugi*, 175–177 n. 128.

48. This is precisely the point that Nomura makes in citation of Kinjō.

49. For an interesting discussion of the desire to be seen among Japanese youth, see Sato, *Kamikaze Biker*.

50. Rancière and Hallward, "Politics and Aesthetics," 202.

51. Sato, *Kamikaze Biker*.

52. Okinawa Zentō Eisā Matsuri Jikō Iinkai, *Eisā 360°*, 306.

53. The spiritual homeland beyond the sea.

CONCLUSION

1. The website for the Sakima Art Museum can be found at http://sakima.art.museum/.

2. Coffee shop.

3. Another exception would be Shuri Castle, which faces toward the west, toward China.

4. The Marukis—Iri and Toshi—are famous for their collection of paintings depicting the horrors of the bombing of Hiroshima. At Sakima's request, they painted a series of canvases representing the battle of Okinawa. At the time, Maruki Toshi was losing his sight and was concerned that he would not be able to complete his work. In addition to serving as curator of his museum, Sakima is trained in acupuncture and moxibustion. He treated Maruki Toshi throughout the creative process: it was, Sakima explains, a collaborative effort to represent the war.

5. An Austrian artist (1867–1945), inspired by expressionism, whose work focused on the human consequences of war.

6. The suffix -gama indicates that the site is a cavern.

7. Perhaps the space that Shimajiri Yoshiko described during her performance in Fujiki's seminar.

Adorno, Theodor. *Aesthetic Theory*. London: Routledge and Kegan Paul, 1984.

——. *Negative Dialectics*. London: Routledge and Kegan Paul, 1990.

——. "What Does Coming to Terms with the Past Mean?" In *Bitburg in Moral and Political Perspective*, edited by Geoffrey H. Hartman. Bloomington: Indiana University Press, 1986.

Ahagon Shōkō. *Beigun to Nōmin*. Tokyo: Iwanami Shoten, 1973.

——. *Inochi Koso Takara*. Tokyo: Iwanami Shoten, 1992.

Akamine Masanobu. *Shima no Miru Yume—Okinawa Minzokugaku Sanpo*. Naha: Bōda Inku, 1998.

Allen, Matthew. *Identity and Resistance in Okinawa*. Lanham, Md.: Rowman and Littlefield, 2003.

Arasaki Moriteru. "Okinawa Dokuritsuron no Kyojitsu." *Okinawa Times*, May 30, 1997.

——. *Okinawa-Hansenjinushi*. Tokyo: Kōbunken, 1996.

Arasaki Moriteru and Nakano Yoshio. *Okinawa Sengoshi*. Tokyo: Iwanami Shoten, 1976.

Arime Masao. *Hansen Jinushi no Genryū o Tazunete*. Haebaru: Akebono Shuppan, 1997.

——, ed. *Kusatī: Kōkai Shinri Tōsō no Kiroku*. Gushikawa: Yūna Insatu Kōgei, 1998.

Arrighi, Giovanni, Hamashita Takeshi, and Mark Selden. *The Rise of East Asia in World Historical Perspective*. Binghamton, N.Y.: Fernand Braudel Center, 1997.

Asato Eiko. "Okinawan Identity and Resistance to Militarization and Maldevelopment." In *Islands of Discontent: Okinawan Responses to Japanese and American Power*, edited by Laura Hein and Mark Selden. Lanham, Md.: Rowman and Littlefield, 2003.

Augé, Marc. *Oblivion*. Minneapolis: University of Minnesota Press, 2004.

Bakhtin, M. M. "Forms of Time and of the Chronotope in the Novel," and "Discourse in the Novel." In *The Dialogic Imagination: Four Essays*, edited by Michael Holquist and Caryl Emerson. Austin: University of Texas Press, 1981.

——. "The Problem of Speech Genres." In *Speech Genres and Other Late Essays*, edited by Caryl Emerson and Michael Holquist. Austin: University of Texas Press, 1996.

Bauman, Richard. *Story, Performance and Event: Contextual Studies of Oral Narrative*. Cambridge: Cambridge University Press, 1986.

Bechtel Group. *Economic Development for Okinawa: A Program for Success*. New York: Bechtel Group, 1988.

Benjamin, Walter. *The Arcades Project*. Translated by Howard Eiland and Kevin McLaughlin. Cambridge, Mass.: Harvard University Press, 2002.

——. "The Storyteller: Reflections on the Works of Nikolai Leskov." In *Illuminations: Essays and Reflections*, edited by Hanna Arendt. New York: Random House, 1988.

Bhabha, Homi K. *The Location of Culture*. London: Routledge, 1994.

Bloch, Ernst. "Nonsynchronism and the Obligation to Its Dialectics." *New German Critique*, no. 11 (spring 1977).

——. *The Principle of Hope*. Volume 1. Cambridge, Mass.: MIT Press, 1995.

Boas, Franz. "On Alternating Sounds." In *A Franz Boas Reader: The Shaping of American Anthropology, 1883–1911*, edited by George Stocking. Chicago: University of Chicago Press, 1982.

Bourdieu, Pierre. *Outline of a Theory of Practice*. Cambridge: Cambridge University Press, 1991.

Butler, Judith. *The Psychic Life of Power: Theories in Subjection*. Stanford: Stanford University Press, 1997.

Caruth, Cathy, ed. *Trauma: Explorations in Memory*. Baltimore: Johns Hopkins University Press, 1995.

——. *Unclaimed Experience: Trauma, Theory and History*. Baltimore: Johns Hopkins University Press, 1996.

Chibana Shōichi. *Burning the Rising Sun: From Yomitan Village, Okinawa—Islands of U.S. Bases*. Kyoto: South Wind, 1992.

Chikushi Tetsuya and Teruya Rinsuke. *Okinawa ga Subete*. Tokyo: Kade Shobō Shinsha, 1997.

Christy, Alan. "A Fantasy of Ancient Japan: The Assimilation of Okinawa in Yanagita Kunio's Kainan Shoki." In *Productions of Culture in Japan*. Chicago: University of Chicago, Center for East Asian Studies, 1995.

——. "The Making of Imperial Subjects in Okinawa." In *Formations of Colonial Modernity in East Asia*, edited by Tani Barlow. Durham: Duke University Press, 1997.

Connerton, Paul. *How Societies Remember*. Cambridge: Cambridge University Press, 1999.

Dana Masayuki. "Rekishi Genten Kara Mita Shosō." In *Shinryūkyūshi (Kindaihen)*. Naha: Ryūkyū Shinpōsha, 1993.

De Certeau, Michel. "On the Oppositional Practice of Everyday Life." *Social Text*, no. 3 (autumn 1980).

Detienne, Marcel, and Jean-Pierre Vernant. *Cunning Intelligence in Greek Culture and Society*. Chicago: University of Chicago Press, 1991.

Dower, John. *War without Mercy*. New York: Pantheon Books, 1986.

Eldridge, Robert D. "The 1996 Okinawa Referendum on U.S. Base Reductions: One Question, Several Answers." *Asian Survey* 37, no. 10.

Embree, John. *Suye Mura: A Japanese Village*. Chicago: University of Chicago Press, 1972.

Eng, David, and David Kazanjian, eds. *Loss: The Politics of Mourning*. Berkeley: University of California Press, 2002.

Fanon, Frantz. *The Wretched of the Earth*. New York: Grove Press, 1986.

Feifer, George. *Tennozan: The Battle of Okinawa and the Atomic Bomb*. New York: Ticknor and Fields, 1992.

Ferguson, James. *Expectations of Modernity: Myths and Meanings of Urban Life on the Zambian Copperbelt*. Berkeley: University of California Press, 1999.

Field, Norma. *In the Realm of the Dying Emperor*. New York: Vintage Books, 1993.

Figal, Gerald. *Civilization and Monsters: Spirits of Modernity in Meiji Japan*. Durham: Duke University Press, 1999.

Friedlander, Saul. "Introduction" to *Probing the Limits of Representation: Nazism and the "Final Solution,"* edited by Saul Friedlander. Cambridge, Mass.: Harvard University Press, 1992.

Fujiki Hayato. *Uchinā Mōsō Kenbunroku: Fujiki Hayato no Rabirinsu Wārudo*. Urasoe: Okinawa Shuppan, 1996.

Gibo Eijirō. *Eisā: Okinawa no Bon Odori*. Haebaru: Naha Shuppansha, 1997.

Graeber, David. "Dancing with Corpses Reconsidered: An Interpretation of "famadihana" (In Arivonimamo, Madagascar)." *American Ethnologist* 22, no. 2 (May 1995).

Gramsci, Antonio. *Prison Notebooks*. New York: International Publishers, 1992.

Granet, Marcel. *Chinese Civilization*. New York: Meridian Books, 1960.

Hanks, William F. *Intertexts: Writings on Language, Utterance and Context*. Oxford: Rowan and Littlefield, 2000.

——. *Language and Communicative Practices*. New York: Westview Press, 1996.

Harootunian, H. D. *History's Disquiet: Modernity, Cultural Practice, and the Question of Everyday Life*. New York: Columbia University Press, 2000.

———. "Memory, Mourning and National Morality: Yaskuni Shrine and the Reunion of State and Religion in Postwar Japan." In *Nation and Religion: Perspectives on Europe and Asia*, edited by Peter van der Veer and Hartmut Lehmann. Princeton: Princeton University Press, 1999.

———. *Overcome by Modernity: History, Culture and Community in Interwar Japan*. Princeton: Princeton University Press, 2000.

———. "Shadowing History." *Cultural Studies* 18, nos. 2–3 (March/May 2004).

———. *Things Seen and Unseen: Discourse and Ideology in Tokugawa Nativism*. Chicago: University of Chicago Press, 1988.

Hashimoto Ryūtarō, *Seiken Dakkai Ron*. Tokyo: Kodansha, 1994.

Heidegger, Martin. *Being and Time: A Translation of* Sein und Zeit. Translated by Joan Stambaugh. Binghamton: State University of New York Press.

Hein, Laura, and Mark Selden, eds. *Islands of Discontent: Okinawan Responses to Japanese and American Power*. Lanham, Md.: Rowman and Littlefield, 2003.

Heinrich, Patrick. "Language Planning and Language Ideology in the Ryukyu Islands." *Language Policy* 3 (2003).

Hertz, Robert. *Death and the Right Hand*. Glencoe, Ill.: Free Press, 1960.

Hevia, James L. *Cherishing Men from Afar: Qing Guest Ritual and the Macartney Embassy of 1793*. Durham: Duke University Press, 1995.

Higa Masao. *Okinawa Minzokugaku no Hōhō*. Tokyo: Sinbōsha, 1982.

Higa Shunchō. "Ina no Denrai: Nōgyō Seikatsu no Hajimari." In *Higa Shunchō Zenshū*. Naha: Okinawa Taimususha, 1971.

Hiyane Teruo. *Kindai Okinawa no Seishinshi*. Tokyo: Shakaihyōronsha, 1996.

Hook, Glenn D., and Richard Siddle, eds. *Structure and Subjectivity: Japan and Okinawa*. London: Routledge Curzon, 2003.

Hori Ichirō. *Folk Religion in Japan: Continuity and Change*. Edited by Joseph Kitagawa and A. L. Miller. Chicago: University of Chicago Press, 1983.

Horiba Kiyoko. *Inaguya Nanabachi—Okinawa Joseishi o Saguru*. Tokyo: Domesu Shuppan, 1991.

Hubert, Henri. *Essay on Time: A Brief History of the Representations of Time in Religion and Magic*. London: Berghahn Books, 2001.

Huizinga, Johan. *Homo Ludens: A Study of the Play-Element in Culture*. Boston: Beacon Press, 1955.

Ikemiya Masaharu. *Okinawa no Yūkōgei: Chondarā to Ninbuchā*. Naha: Hirugisha, 1990.

Inoue, Masamichi Sebastian. "The Identity and Politics of Locality: Henoko, the Heleport Controversy and the Predicament of a Social Movement in Okinawa."

Paper presented at the annual meeting of the Association for Asian Studies, San Diego, Calif., 2000.

——. "We Are Okinawans but of a Different Kind: New/Old Social Movements and the U.S. Military in Okinawa." *Current Anthropology* 45, no. 1 (February 2004).

Ishihara Masaie. *Daimitsu Bōeki no Jidai*. Tokyo: Banshōsha, 1982.

——. "Memories of War and Okinawa." In *Perilous Memories: The Asia-Pacific War(s)*, edited by T. Fujitani, Geoffrey M. White, and Lisa Yoneyama. Durham: Duke University Press, 2001.

Ishihara Zemināru. *Sengo Koza ni Okeru Minshū Seikastu to Ongaku Bunka* ('92 Ishihara-Seminar Fieldwork Report). Edited by Ishihara Masaie and Aragaki Naoko. Ginowan: Yōjusha (Gajumarusha), 1994.

Ishikawa Mao, *Okinawa Shibai: Nakada Sachiko no Ichigyō Monogatari*. Privately published, 1999.

Ivy, Marilyn. *Discourses of the Vanishing: Modernity, Phantasm, Japan*. Chicago: University of Chicago Press, 1995.

Johnson, Chalmers. *Blowback: The Costs and Consequences of American Empire*. New York: Metropolitan Books, 2000.

——, ed. *Okinawa: Cold War Island*. Albuquerque: Japan Policy Research Institute, 1999.

Kadokawa Gairaigo Jiten. Tokyo: Kadokawa Shoten, 1977.

Kano Masanao. *Sengo Okinawa no Shisōzō*. Tokyo: Asahi Shinbunsha, 1987.

Kawahashi Noriko. "Kaminchu: Divine Women of Okinawa." Ph.D. dissertation, Princeton University, 1992.

Kerr, George. *Okinawa: The History of an Island People*. Rutland, Vt.: Charles F. Tuttle, 1958.

Kinmonth, Earl. *The Self-Made Man in Meiji Japanese Thought: From Samurai to Salaryman*. Berkeley: University of California Press, 1981.

Koschmann, J. Victor. "National Subjectivity and the Uses of Atonement in the Age of Recession." *South Atlantic Quarterly* 99, no. 4 (2000).

Koschmann, J. Victor, Ōiwa Keibo, and Yamashita Shinji, eds. *International Perspectives on Yanagita Kunio and Japanese Folklore Studies*. Cornell University East Asia Papers. Ithaca: Cornell University, 1985.

Kozashi. *Kozashishi*. Tokyo: Teikoku Chihō Kōsei Gakkai, 1973.

LaCapra, Dominick. *Representing the Holocaust: History, Theory, Trauma*. Ithaca: Cornell University Press, 1994.

——. "Trauma, Absence and Loss." *Critical Inquiry* 25, no. 4 (1999).

Laub, Dori. "An Event without a Witness: Truth, Testimony and Survival." In *Testi-*

mony: *Crises of Witnessing in Literature, Psychoanalysis and History*, edited by Shoshana Felman and Dori Laub. New York: Routledge, 1991.

Law, Jane Marie. *Puppets of Nostalgia: The Life, Death and Rebirth of the Japanese Awaji Ningyō Tradition*. Princeton: Princeton University Press, 1997.

Lebra, William P. *Okinawan Religion: Belief, Ritual and Social Structure*. Honolulu: University of Hawaii Press, 1966.

Lefebvre, Henri. "The Inventory." In *Key Writings*, edited by Stuart Elden, Elizabeth Lebas, and Elonore Kofman. London: Continuum, 2003.

——. *The Production of Space*. Oxford: Blackwell, 1991.

Lock, Margaret. *Twice Dead: Organ Transplants and the Reinvention of Death*. Berkeley: University of California Press, 2001.

Mabuchi, Tōichi. "Space and Time in Ryukyuan Cosmology." *Asian Folklore Studies* 39 (1980).

Masuyama, Eiichi Erick. "Towards an Understanding of Rakugo as a Communicative Event: A Performance Analysis of Traditional Professional Storytelling in Japan." Ph.D. dissertation, University of Oregon, 1997.

Medoruma Shun. "Suiteki." In *Southern Exposure: Modern Japanese Literature from Okinawa*, edited by Michael Molasky and Steve Rabson. Honolulu: University of Hawaii Press, 2000.

Medvedev, P. N., and M. M. Bakhtin. *The Formal Method in Literary Scholarship: A Critical Introduction to Sociological Poetics*. Translated by Albert J. Wehrle. Goucher College Series. Baltimore: Johns Hopkins University Press, 1978.

Miyazato Chisato. "Ryūkyūko o Kaku Ongaku." *Kēshi Kaji*, no. 15 (June 1997).

Molasky, Michael S. *The American Occupation of Japan and Okinawa*. London: Routledge, 1999.

Morioka, Heinz, and Miyoko Sasaki. *Rakugo: The Popular Narrative Art of Japan*. Cambridge, Mass.: Harvard University, Council on East Asian Studies, 1990.

Mukai Kiyoshi. "Sotetsu Jigoku." In *Shinryūkyūshi (Kindai-Gendaihen)*. Naha: Ryūkyū Shinposha. 1992.

Munn, Nancy. "Excluded Spaces: The Figure in the Australian Aboriginal Landscape." *Critical Inquiry* (Spring 1996).

Murai Osamu. *Nantō Ideorogī no Hassei*. Tokyo: Oita Shuppan, 1995.

Nakachi Kiyoshi. "Ryukyu–U.S.–Japan Relations: The Reversion Movement, Political, Economic and Strategic Issues, 1945–1972." Ph.D. dissertation, Northern Arizona University, 1986.

Nelson, Christopher T. "The Moai: Capitalism, Culture and Okinawan Rotating Credit Associations." *Journal of Pacific Asia*, July 2001.

Nishioka, S. "Kari & Karijusji." Essay posted to *Okinawa Bunka Kenkyū Mairingu Risuto* [OBK-ML], April 22, 1998.

Nomura Kōya. *Muishiki no Shokumicshishugi: Nihonjin no Beigun Kichi to Okinawajin.* Tokyo: Ochanomizu Shobo, 2005.

Ogura Nobuo. "Gaijin Jutaku no Kensetsu to Sono Naiyō." In *Sengo Okinawa to Amerika: Ibunka Sesshoku No Gojūnen*, edited by Yamazato Katsumi and Teruya Yoshihiko. Naha: Okinawa Taimususha, 1995.

Ohnuki-Tierney, Emiko. *Kamikaze, Cherry Blossoms and Nationalism: The Militarization of Aesthetics in Japanese History.* Chicago: University of Chicago Press, 2002.

Okinawa Mondai Ronshū Iinkai. *Dairi Shomei Kyohi: Okinawa Beigun Yōchi Kyōsei Shiyō No! Jidai o Yomu Bukkuretto no. 3.* Naha: Okinawa Taimususha, 1996.

Okinawashi Heiwa Bunka Shinkōka. *Beikoku ga Mita Koza Bōdō.* Gushikawa: Yui Shuppan, 1999.

———. *Kindai Tōkeisho ni Miru Rekishi.* Haebaru: Kindai Bijutsu, 1997.

———. *Koza: Hito, Machi, Koto.* Haebaru: Naha Shuppansha, 1997.

———. *Misato kara Ikusayo Shōgen.* Haebaru: Naha Shuppansha, 1998.

Okinawa Zentō Eisā Matsuri Jikō Iinkai, ed. *Eisā 360°: Rekishi to Genzai.* Haebaru: Naha Shuppansha, 1998.

Okuno Hikorokuro. *Okinawa Koninshi.* Tokyo: Kokushō Kankōkai, 1978.

Osborne, Peter. *The Politics of Time.* New York: Verso, 1995.

Oshiro Tatsuhiro. "Turtleback Tombs." In *Southern Exposure*, edited by Michael Molasky and Steve Rabson. Honolulu: University of Hawaii Press, 2000.

Ōta Masahide. *Dairi Shomei Kyohi no Riyū. Hitonaru Bukkuretto no. 2.* Tokyo: Hitonaru Shobō, 1996.

———. *Okinawa no Minshū Ishiki.* Tokyo: Shinensha, 1976.

Ota Yoshinobu. "Appropriating Media, Resisting Power: Representations of Hybrid Identities in Okinawan Popular Culture." In *Between Resistance and Revolution: Cultural Politics and Social Protest*, edited by Richard G. Fox and Owen Starn. New Brunswick: Rutgers University Press, 1997.

———. "Ritual as Narrative: Folk Religious Experience in the Southern Ryukyus." Ph.D. dissertation, University of Michigan, 1987.

Ōyama Chōjō. *Okinawa Dokuritsu Sengen.* Okinawa: Gendai Shoin, 1997.

Pratt, Mary Louise. *Imperial Eyes.* London: Routledge, 1992.

Propp, V. *Morphology of the Folktale*. Austin: University of Texas Press, 1984.

Rancière, Jacques. *The Nights of Labor: The Workers' Dream in Nineteenth-Century France*. Philadelphia: Temple University Press, 1989.

———. "The Thinking of Dissensus: Politics and Aesthetics," Paper presented at the conference "Fidelity to the Disagreement: Jacques Rancière and the Political," organized by the Post-Structuralism and Radical Politics and Marxism specialist groups of the Political Studies Association of the U.K., Goldsmiths College, London, September 16–17, 2003.

Rancière, Jacques, and Peter Hallward. "Politics and Aesthetics: An Interview." *Angelaki* 8, no. 2 (2003).

Ricoeur, Paul. *Memory, History, Forgetting*. Chicago: University of Chicago Press, 2004.

Rimer, J. Thomas. *Culture and Identity: Japanese Intellectuals during the Interwar Years*. Princeton: Princeton University Press, 1990.

Robertson, Jennifer. *Native and Newcomer*. Berkeley: University of California Press, 1992.

Sakima Kōei. "Ryūkyū no Tonsai [Butamatsuri] no Fūshū in Tsuite." In *Nyoin Seijikō: Rei no Shimajima (Sakima Kōei Zenshū)*, edited by Higa Masao and Gibo Masao. Tokyo: Shinsensha, 1982.

Sato, Hiroaki, and Burton Watson. *From the Country of Eight Islands*. New York: Columbia University Press, 1981.

Sato, Ikuya. *Kamikaze Biker: Parody and Anomy in Affluent Japan*. Chicago: University of Chicago Press, 1991.

Sato Takehiro. "Globalization and Identity in Okinawan Shamanism." *Journal of Pacific Asia* 7 (2001).

Smith, Robert J. *Ancestor Worship in Contemporary Japan*. Stanford: Stanford University Press, 1974.

———. "The Living and the Dead in Japanese Popular Religion." In *Lives in Motion: Composing Circles of Self and Community in Japan*, edited by Susan Orpett Long. Ithaca: Cornell University East Asia Program, 1999.

Smits, Gregory. *Visions of Ryūkyū: Identity and Ideology in Early-Modern Thought and Politics*. Honolulu: University of Hawaii Press, 1999.

Sturdevant, Saundra Pollack, and Brenda Stolzfus. *Let the Good Times Roll: Prostitution and U.S. Military in Asia*. New York: New Press, 1993.

Taira Koji. "Dialectics of Economic Growth, National Power and Distributive Struggles." In *Postwar Japan as History*, edited by Andrew Gordon. Berkeley: University of California Press, 1993.

——. "The Okinawa Charade: The United States, Japan and Okinawa: Conflict and Compromise, 1995–96." Japan Policy Research Institute. JPRI Working Paper no. 28, January 1997. Available at http://www.jpri.org/.

Takara Ben. "Yādui." In Hanazumiyō. Fukuoka: Ashi Shobō, 1985.

Tamaki Tomohiko. Okinawa no Machizukuri, Chiki Okoshi: Tāku and Repōto. Naha: Bōda Inku, 1996.

Tamanori, Terunobu, and John C. James. A Minute Guide to Okinawa: Society and Economy. Naha: Bank of the Ryūkyūs International Foundation, 1996.

Tanaka, Stefan. New Times in Modern Japan. Princeton: Princeton University Press, 2004.

Tasato Yūtetsu. Ronshū Okinawa Shūraku Kenkyū. Naha: Riutsusha, 1983.

Tenku Kikaku, Inc., ed. Uchinā Poppu: Okinawa Karutyā Bukku. Tokyo: Tokyo Shoseki, 1992.

Teruya Rinsuke. Terurin Jiden. Tokyo: Misuzu Shōbō, 1998.

Teruya Seiken. "Kindai Ryūkyū no Toshi Keikaku." In Okinawa no Fūsui, edited by Noritada Kubo. Tokyo: Heiga Shuppansha, 1990.

Thompson, E. P. "Customs and Culture," and "The Moral Economy of the English Crowd in the Eighteenth Century." In Customs in Common. New York: New Press, 1993.

Tomiyama Ichirō. "Colonialism and the Sciences of the Tropical Zone: The Academic Analysis of Difference in 'the Island Peoples,'" In Formations of Colonial Modernity in East Asia, edited by Tani Barlow. Durham: Duke University Press, 1997.

——. "The Critical Limits of the National Community: The Ryūkyūan Subject." Social Science Japan Journal 1 (1998).

——. Kindai Nihon Shakai to "Okinawajin." Tokyo: Nihon Keizai Hyōronsha, 1990.

——. "Okinawa Sabetsu to Puroretariaka." In Shinryūkyūshi (Kindai-Gendaihen). Naha: Ryūkyū Shinposha, 1992.

——. "Okuni Wa?" In Oto no Chikara: Okinawa—Koza Futtōhen, edited by DeMusik Inter. Tokyo: Inpakuto Shuppankai, 1998.

——. Senjō no Kioku. Tokyo: Nihon Keizai Hyōronsha, 1995.

——. "'Spy': Mobilization and Identity in Wartime Okinawa." Senri Ethnological Studies 51. Osaka: National Museum of Ethnology, 2000.

Turner, Terence. "Representing, Resisting, Rethinking: Historical Transformations of Kayapo Culture and Anthropological Consciousness." In Colonial Situations: Essays on the Contextualization of Ethnographic Knowledge, edited by George Stocking. Madison: University of Wisconsin Press, 1991.

Vernant, Jean-Pierre, and Pierre Vidal-Naquet. "The Historical Moment of Tragedy in Greece: Some of the Social and Psychological Conditions." In *Myth and Tragedy in Ancient Greece*. New York: Zone Books, 1988.

Wacker, Monika. "Onarigami: Holy Women in the 20th Century." *Journal of Japanese Religious Studies* 30 (2003).

"Warai no Mabui: Mirai e." *Okinawa Taimusu*, October 4, 2000.

Watson, Burton. *Cold Mountain: 100 Poems*. New York: Columbia University Press, 1970.

Willcox, Bradley J., and Craig Willcox. *The Okinawa Program*. New York: Random House, 2001.

Yanagita Kunio. *About Our Ancestors: The Japanese Family System*. Translated by Fanny Hagin Mayer and Ishiwara Yasuyo. Tokyo: Japan Society for the Promotion of Science, 1970.

——. *Kaijō no Michi*. Tokyo: Iwanami Shōten, 1978.

——. *The Legends of Tono*. Tokyo: Japan Foundation, 1975.

——. *Meiji-Taishōshi [Seisōhen]*. Tokyo: Kodansha, 1993.

——. "Minkan Denshōron." In *Teihon Yanagita Kunio Zenshū*. Tokyo: Chikuma Shobō, 1962–1971.

——. *Nenjū Gyōji Oboegaki*. Tokyo: Kodansha, 1977.

Yasuda Yoshiyuki and Shingawa Keiko. *Okinawa Dokuritsu no Kanōsei*. Tokyo: Shisuikai Shuppan, 1997.

Yonetani, Julia. "Playing Base Politics in a Global Strategic Theater: Futenma Relocation, the G-8 Summit, and Okinawa." *Critical Asian Studies* 33 (March 2001).

Yoneyama, Lisa. *Hiroshima Traces: Time, Space and the Dialectics of Memory*. Berkeley, University of California Press, 1999.

Yoshida Sueko. "Love Suicide at Kamaara." In *Southern Exposure: Modern Japanese Literature from Okinawa*, edited by Michael Molasky and Steve Rabson. Honolulu: University of Hawaii Press, 2000.

Yoshikawa Hiroya. *Naha no Kūkan Kōzō*. Naha: Okinawa Taimususha, 1989.

Žižek, Slavoj. *The Sublime Object of Ideology*. London: Verso, 1991.

CHRISTOPHER T. NELSON is an assistant professor of anthropology at the
University of North Carolina, Chapel Hill.

Library of Congress Cataloging-in-Publication Data

Nelson, Christopher T.
Dancing with the dead: memory, performance, and everyday life
in postwar Okinawa / Christopher T. Nelson.
p. cm. — (Asia-Pacific)
Includes bibliographical references and index.
ISBN 978-0-8223-4349-3 (cloth : alk. paper)—ISBN 978-0-8223-4371-4 (pbk. : alk. paper)
1. Performing arts—Japan—Okinawa-ken. 2. Okinawa-ken (Japan)—History—20th century.
3. Arts and history—Japan—Okinawa-ken. 4. Ethnology—Japan—Okinawa-ken. I. Title.
PN2925.04N45 2008
790.20952—dc22   2008032020